THE INDIAN CITY
Poverty, Ecology and Urban Development

THE INDIAN CITY
Poverty, Ecology and Urban Development

Edited by
Alfred de Souza

© Alfred de Souza 1978

First Published 1978

Published in the United States of America by

South Asia Books

Box 502

Columbia, Mo 65201

by arrangements with

Manohar Publications

2 Ansari Road, Darya Ganj,

New Delhi-11002

ISBN   0—8364—0196—4

Printed at

Dhawan Printing Works

26-A, Mayapuri Industrial Area, New Delhi-110064

for
Henry, Joe, Papa Thiel, Pepe, Stan, Walter

Acknowledgements

It is my great pleasure to acknowledge my indebtedness to the contributors whose papers attain that rare combination of scholarly analysis and social concern. I have to thank Stan D'Souza, Director, and my other colleagues at the Indian Social Institute for their warm encouragement and support. I would like to express a word of special thanks to Andrea Menefee Singh and J. Troisi who helped me in so many ways. Finally, I am grateful to Aleyamma Mathews and S. Gurumurthy for efficient and cheerful secretarial help.

Indian Social Institute   Alfred de Souza
New Delhi

Contributors

M. VAN DEN BOGAERT is Director, Xavier Institute of Social Service, Ranchi, and author of *Trade Unionism in Indian Ports* (Shri Ram Centre, 1970).

W.J. COUSINS is Urban Adviser, UNICEF, New Delhi.

ALFRED DE SOUZA is Director, Department of Research and Publication, Indian Social Institute, and Editor of *Social Action*. He has written and edited several books, the most recent being, *The Politics of Change and Leadership Development: The New Leaders in India and Africa* (Manohar, 1978).

JUDIT KATONA-APTE is Research Associate in the Department of Nutrition, School of Public Health, University of North Carolina.

HAROLD LUBELL is in the Technology and Employment Branch, Department of Employment and Development, International Labour Office, Geneva. He is the author of *Urban Development and Employment: The Prospects of Calcutta* (ILO, 1974).

TAPAN K. MAJUMDAR is Specialist (Sociology) in the Department of Science and Technology, Technology Bhavan, New Delhi. He directed the TCPO survey of squatter settlements in Delhi.

S.V. SETHURAMAN is in the Technology and Employment, Branch, Department of Employment and Development International Labour Office, Geneva. He is the author of *Jakarta: Urban Development and Employment* (ILO, 1976).

KIRTEE SHAH is Director of Ahmedabad Study Action Group (ASAG) and Consultant to the UN.He participated in the Habitat Conference at Vancouver.

ANDREA MENEFEE SINGH was in the Department of Research, Indian Social Institute, and has been a Consultant to the Social Development Branch of the United Nations. She is the author of *Neighbourhood and Social Networks in Urban India* (Marwah, 1976).

K.C. SIVARAMAKRISHNAN was Secretary, Calcutta Metropolitan Development Authority, 1970-76, and Consultant to the World Bank and the UN Conference on Human Settlements.

K.R. UNNI is Professor of Sociology at the School of Planning and Architecture, New Delhi.

PAUL D. WIEBE is in Department of Sociology at the Osmania University, Hyderabad. He is the author of *Social Life in an Indian Slum* (Vikas, 1975).

Contents

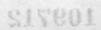

The Challenge of Urban Poverty: An Introduction

Alfred de Souza

India has nearly 80 per cent of the population in the rural areas, yet it has some of the largest cities in the world. No less than nine cities—Calcutta, Bombay, Ahmedabad, Kanpur, Delhi, Poona, Bangalore, Hyderabad and Madras have populations of over one million. The urban population has grown rapidly, recording a growth rate of 38 per cent during 1961-71. Yet, the urbanisation rate was unremarkable since the urban population as a proportion of the total population increased from 18 to 20 per cent. The most rapid growth of population was in cities with a population of 1,00,000 and above in which over 50 per cent of the total urban population is concentrated. Thus, for example, in the decade 1961-71, the population of Calcutta Metropolitan District registered a growth rate of 22 per cent, Madras Metropolitan Area a growth rate of 43 per cent, Ahmedabad Urban Area a growth rate of 38 per cent; Ahmedabad Urban Area increased by 44 per cent and Ranchi by 83 per cent.

The growth of Metropolitan cities in India has been largely unplanned and haphazard and this can be seen from the fact that one-fifth of the total urban population (22 million) lives in slums or squatter settlements. The slum population of most of the cities in India is estimated at 20-30 per cent of the total urban population. This is true of Delhi, Calcutta and Madras, while in Ahmedabad it is estimated that 45 per cent of the total population lives in slums or squatter settlements. In Calcutta, Sivaramakrishnan estimates that 2.5 million people are living in *bustees* or slums—i.e., one out of every 3 or 4 persons in Calcutta. Not only is the urban population unevenly distributed between towns and cities but, even within the city, there are considerable imbalances in population density. In Ahmedabad 25 per cent of the population is concentrated in 400 *Pols* in the walled city where densities can be as high as 1,000 persons per acre. In Old Delhi the population density can rise to 600-700 persons per acre, while in Calcutta the average density is 45,000 people per sq.km.

This profile of the urban population outlines the great urban challenge facing India and also other less developed countries of Asia. This paper seeks to discuss squatter or spontaneous settlements in the metropolitan cities of India not as specific and isolated phenomena but as integrated aspects of prevailing models of urban planning and development.* It is only within such a comprehensive analytical framework which takes into account the assumptions, value systems and development ideology that influence decisions regarding urban planning and land use that one can understand the structural nature of urban poverty, the problems of the Indian city and formulate guidelines that may lead to their solution.

MIGRATION

As Ashish Bose has pointed out, the process of urbanisation has been essentially a process of migration to the city.[1] The largest cities have attracted the largest numbers of migrants from the rural areas because, unlike the small towns, they offer a wide range of employment opportunities which require various degrees of skill and, what is more important, the big cities can provide employment to rural migrants who are largely unskilled and illiterate. As Majumdar, Menefee Singh, Van

*The references given in the footnotes are to sources other than the papers of this volume.
[1]Ashish Bose, 'India: The Urban Context', in S.C. Dube (ed.) *India Since Independence*, Vikas, New Delhi, 1977, p. 106.

den Bogaert, Sethuraman and others are agreed, the primary
reason for rural-urban migration is economic, and the rural
poor migrate to the cities in search of employment rather than
better employment opportunities.[2] There are various types of
migrants who come to the big cities in search of employment
and one can distinguish between the seasonal and recurrent
unaccompanied male migrants who come to Calcutta from
Bihar and Uttar Pradesh from the permanent family migrants
who come from Tamil Nadu. As several studies have shown,
rural poverty is carried over to the city by the mechanism of
rural-urban migration[3] and is most visible in slums and squatter
settlements, environmental deterioration, sub-standard housing
and low levels of health and nutrition. Not much is known
regarding the socio-economic and cultural factors motivating
the decision to migrate from the rural areas to the city and
there is certainly a need of more anthropological studies like
those by Majumdar and Menefee Singh[4] to understand the contextual aspects of migration and the socio-economic consequences
of rural-urban migration both for urban planning and the
migrants themselves.

When migrants reach the city they invariably find themselves pushed into the slums or squatter settlements. One of
the more important reasons why the migrants find themselves
in the squatter settlements is that they depend upon kinship,
caste and regional networks not only for decisions regarding
the choice of destination but also for their adjustment to the
harsh conditions of urban living. As Majumdar notes,

> the spontaneous settlements of the urban poor are not
> merely aggregations of shacks and huts but communities of
> fellow migrants. Each is based on a network of primary

[2]See P. Ramachandran, *Pavement Dwellers in Bombay City*, Tata
Institute of Social Sciences, Bombay, 1972, p. 18; M.S. Gore, *Immigrants
and Neighbourhoods*, Tata Institute of Social Sciences, Bombay, 1970,
p. 38; Subhash Chandra, *Social Participation in Urban Neighbourhoods*,
National, New Delhi, 1977, p. 72.

[3]V.M. Dandekar and N. Rath, *Poverty in India*, Indian School of
Political Economy, Bombay, 1971.

[4]For a fine discussion of this topic see Andrea Menefee Singh,
'Rural-Urban Migration of Women Among the Urban Poor in India',
Social Action 28, October-December 1978, pp. 326-256.

affinities of language, region, village, caste or kin. It enables the rural migrants coming from small village communities to become socialised and acculturated in the complex and diversified environment of a metropolitan city.

The social networks activated by rural migrants also function as mechanisms of recruitment to the urban labour force and financial assistance to cope with the conditions of urban living. Studies undertaken in Bombay, Kanpur as well as in Delhi (Majumdar, Menefee Singh) and Calcutta (Lubell) show kinship networks or, more generally, a 'resource person' to be of crucial importance in the decision to migrate to the city.[5] Though the family structure in Delhi, Calcutta as well as other metropolitan cities is predominantly nuclear, the linkages with the family in rural areas are maintained by the migrants and, as an earlier study of Delhi (1956) concluded, 'the joint family concept still continues to form part of the thinking of Delhi immigrants households'.[6] In a more recent study of migrants in Delhi (1976), Menefee Singh found that 90 per cent of the *basti* families were nuclear, yet 'more than half of the women interviewed said that they considered the joint family the ideal, viewing it as a source of togetherness, protection, help in time of crisis, and economic and social security'. The residents of squatter settlements of Delhi and Calcutta Metropolitan District maintained close ties with kin-groups outside Delhi and Calcutta by visits and remittances. In an earlier study of Calcutta, Asok Mitra[7] estimated that, in spite of their poverty, remittances of immigrant households in Calcutta attained the remarkably high volume of Rs. 276 million.

But to understand the magnitude of urban poverty one has to understand the conditions of life in the urban slums and squatter settlements with regard to basic services (water, health care, nutrition, housing, sanitation, drainage) and occupation and income. Largely because of the elitist metropolitan model of development adopted by the Five Year Plans in India, with

[5]Gore *op. cit.*, p. 50; Chandra, *op. cit.*, p. 75.

[6]V.K.R.V. Rao and P.B. Desai, *Greater Delhi: A Study in Urbanisation 1940-1957*, Asia Publishing House, Bombay, 1965.

[7]Asok Mitra, *Calcutta: India's City*, Manager of Publications, Government of India, New Delhi, 1954, p. 22.

the concentration of investment and resources in the industrial or modern sector, there is a dual economy with dichotomous relationships between the urban and rural sectors and, within the city, between the formal and informal urban sectors. This dual relationship may be conceptualised, as Wiebe does, in terms of a model of dominance and dependency but modified by certain patterns of reciprocity that function to the advantage of the urban poor within the overall framework of inequality and subordination.

EMPLOYMENT AND INCOME

The magnitude of urban poverty can be best understood from the data on employment patterns and income levels of studies conducted in Delhi, Calcutta, Madras and Ranchi by Majumdar, Menefee Singh, Wiebe, Van den Bogaert, Lubell and others.[8] When the urban poor are compared to the rural poor, the former are at a greater disadvantage with the respect to income and also education and employment. In an earlier study[9] it was estimated that 82 per cent of the households in Delhi had incomes of less than Rs. 250 per month. In Calcutta, according to Sivaramakrishnan, 63 per cent of the people living in Calcutta Metropolitan District had incomes of less than Rs. 300, 46 per cent of them having incomes of less than Rs. 200. In Madras, Wiebe found that 80 per cent of the people living in a slum he studied were below the poverty line, while in the squatter settlements of Delhi, Majumdar found that 71 per cent of the households had monthly incomes of Rs. 250 or below, the average income of the households being Rs. 237 although there were 1.6 earners in each household. In another study of squatter settlements in Delhi, Menefee Singh found that the average monthly income of employed women was only Rs. 76 compared to Rs. 192 for men. Over 90 per cent of these women stated that they were working to provide for the minimal needs of their families. With respect to Madras, Katona-Apte states that though in the 1960s a minimum income

[8] See National Council of Applied Economic Research, *Techno Economic Survey of Delhi*, NCAER, New Delhi, 1973.
[9] V.K.R.V. Rao and P.B. Desai, op. cit.

of Rs. 400 per month was required for a balanced diet, only 2.8 per cent of the population of the state had an income of more than Rs. 200 per month.

In spite of this dismal picture of the magnitude of urban poverty, it was found that migrants in the squatter settlements of metropolitan cities were of the view that their standard of living had improved when compared to their situation in the rural areas. Thus, for example, Sethuraman states that 'even the lowest paid worker in the informal sector in Jakarta was better of in relation to has earlier income in the rural areas'. His study of workers in the informal urban sector of Jakarta is also valid for the informal sector in the metropolitan cities of India. In his study of slums in Delhi, Majumdar states that 'though their wages were low in the city, their average earnings over the year were two and a half times more than what they could earn in the rural areas'.

The employment patterns of the urban poor in the slums and squatter settlements are to a great extent influenced by caste, religion and regional factors, and this is especially true of the limited range of employment opportunities open to women. An earlier study[10] of Delhi found that rural migrants to the city tended to be integrated into the economy of the city mainly though their recruitment in the service sector, transport and construction. A more recent study of Delhi squatter settlements by the TCPO (Town and Country Planning Organisation) found that over 80 per cent of the heads of households were involved in unskilled jobs in construction, manual and industrial labour.

According to Lubell the geographic origin of migrants determines their dominance in specific industries or occupations. For example, rickshaw-pullers in Calcutta are mostly Biharis and Oryias while taxi drivers are primarily Punjabis. The jute industry is dominated by migrants from Bihar and Uttar Pradesh; on the other hand, construction workers in Delhi are largely from Rajasthan and in Bombay migrants from its rural hinterland were mostly employed as labourers in textile mills.[11]

[10] *Techno-Economic Survey of Delhi*, op. cit., p. 12.

[11] Harold Lubell, *Urban Development and Employment: The Prospects for Calcutta*, International Labour Office, Geneva, 1974; K.C. Zachariah, *Migrants in Greater Bombay*, Asia Publishing House, Bombay, 1968, 247.

Because both men and women migrants in the squatter settlements are primarily employed in occupations which are held in low esteem and are poorly paid, they perform a wide range of services on which the urban economy depends. Though the occupation roles performed by men and women in the informal urban sector require little or no skills they are, as Majumdar points out, 'essential for the efficient functioning of the urban economy at its present stage of development and the use of technology. They can only be replaced at enormous additional cost to the city's economy'.

The tendency of rural migrants is to continue in the urban environment their caste-specific occupations and, as several studies have shown, there is a marked tendency to shift from wage employment to self-employment. Sivaramakrishnan reports that the *bustees* of Calcutta provide both residential and employment facilities in petty madufacturing, handicrafts and trade.

Though there is scope for occupational change even for Scheduled Caste groups in the urban situation, the choice of occupations is severely limited by low levels of education and skill. From his study of Delhi *bastis*, Majumdar concludes that 'horizontal mobility within the same occupational status is becoming increasingly possible for low caste groups, though vertical mobility as a movement from one stratum to another is still very limited'. The major constraints on the ability of the urban poor to function as entrepreneurs in the informal sector are, as Lubell, Van den Bogaert and Sethuraman point out, little or no access to credit, poor quality materials and lack of markets. Lubell points out that the informal sector in Metropolitan Calcutta functions as 'the labour market of last resort', thus providing the city with 'an enormous reservoir of productive skills'. To make these skills available for the development of the city he stresses the need of market organisation, provision of credit and training.

ENVIRONMENTAL CONDITIONS

The occupational structure and income of the urban poor reflect the extremely difficult conditions under which they have to survive in the slums and squatter settlements of the city.

Squatter families are deprived of such basic services as water, nutrition, health care, housing, education and environmental sanitation. The conditions of life in the squatter settlements of Delhi, Calcutta, Madras and Ahmedabad are graphically portrayed by Majumdar, Menefee Singh, Sivaramakrishnan, Wiebe, Kirtee Shah and Sethuraman. Menefee Singh reports that 'the physical environment of the (Delhi) *basti* is harsh and presents many obstacles to growth and development if compared to the planned areas of the city'. In the *bastis* she studied there were open drains and poorly maintained public latrines that posed serious health hazards, inadequate water supply and no street lighting. In Calcutta, Sivaramakrishnan found that open drains, service latrines, inadequate water taps and street lighting, few paved lanes and *katcha* housing were typical of the deteriorating environment of the *bustees*.

The ecological characteristics of the slums are highly visible and have therefore received wide publicity and attracted hostile reaction from town planners, government officials and administrators. But, as Wiebe points out, 'poverty is their problem; it cannot be related to supposed personal or social deficiencies'. Nevertheless, though the urban poor are denied access to urban political and economic institutions, public utilities and infrastructural services, there is a tendency of the upper income groups and urban planners to consider residents of slums and squatter settlements as 'cancerous growths' that are a hinderance to the development of a healthy environment in the city. As Sethuraman has noted, the attitude of governments towards the informal sector has not been 'exclusively a negative one; rather it ranges from an absolutely negative to a neutral or mildly positive attitude depending on their understanding and concern for the informal sector'. The undiscerning attitude of urban planners, government officials and administrators to the urban poor is perhaps best exemplified in their approaches to the two basic questions of low cost housing and urban renewal.

HOUSING FOR THE URBAN POOR

The decaying tenements of the slum dwellers and the hutments of squatters are the most pervasive symbols of urban poverty. According to the 1971 Census 66 per cent of the households in cities with a population of more than 1,00,000 live in one room tenements. According to the estimates of the National Building Organisation, the shortage of housing units increased from 14.5 million in 1971 to 16.7 million in 1977. The danger of these statistical data is that they tend to make housing for the urban poor a question of the raising of resources rather than a structural problem. Neither State nor the Central Governments can raise the necessary finance to provide housing that conforms to the conventional building code for all the urban poor. It is a fact that the allocation of funds for housing in the Five Year Plans were minimal yet, more important than allocation of funds, is the failure of urban planners to encourage self-help housing by reforming existing housing standards so as to make them flexible and within the reach of the urban poor. The tendency of Slum Clearance Boards and other building agencies has been to construct houses at a cost of Rs. 8,000-15,000 and to charge rents that are beyond the capacity of the urban poor—for whom these houses are meant—to pay. Thus we have what Turner has called 'mismatches between personal priorities' of the poor and 'housing conditions' imposed by urban planners and governmental legislation. It is significant that in the schemes of HUDCO (Housing and Urban Development Corporation) and LIC (Life Insurance Corporation of India), so called "low cost" housing does not take into consideration the incomes of the urban poor. As we saw earlier, 85 per cent of the urban families have monthly incomes of Rs 350 and below. At this level of income the urban poor cannot afford housing that costs more than Rs 3,000-5,000. As Kirtee Shah explains it, in his experiment with low cost housing for the urban poor in Ahmedabad, the cost of the completed house was only Rs 2,860, thus requiring the people to pay a monthly rent of only Rs 20. In an another housing programme at Hyderabad discussed by Cousins, the cost of a house built with assistance from commercial banks was around Rs 5,000. According to Sivaramakrishnan, the cheapest *pakka* house in Calcutta would cost not less than Rs 7,000 with a monthly rental of Rs 45-50 which most of the urban poor having montly incomes of Rs 300 would be unable to pay.

While financial assistance for housing is important, its

influence on urban housing for the poor can only be marginal. A housing strategy to be effective requires a radical change in the building standards currently enforced which have led to the polarisation of urban society through housing patterns that foster the segregation of social groups by income levels. For the poor what is necessary is a minimum standards approach that will reflect not elite and professional preferences but rather an acceptance of self-help housing which involves what Turner and Roberts[12] call a policy of 'incremental building out of current incomes', so that 'small scale building develops in response to family circumstances rather than planning imperatives and provides a social flexibility which may be as important to poor families as any economic benefits'.[13]

Because urban building standards are insensitive to the needs and priorities of the urban poor, the invaluable resource of self-help incremental housing has not been utilised. The consequences of prevailing government housing policies are succinctly outlined by the World Bank in a sector policy paper on housing.[14] It states:

> Many governments have insisted on maintaining high standards which raise the cost of housing and prohibit self-help construction by low-income households. Prohibitive building codes, costly land acquisition procedures and other barriers prevent the poor from building permanent legal houses where they can earn a living. The sentiment "construct big, beautiful and forever", is not unusual. The poor, who are frequently described as "marginal" by those who resent slum and squatter areas, are thus "marginalised" by policy failure.

However, in addition to the unrealistic elitist approach of housing standards and Municipal norms, there is the important question of land values and spatial organisation. At present

[12]John F.C. Turner and Bryan Roberts, 'The Self Help Society', in Peter Wilsher and Rosemary Righter, *The Exploding Cities*, Indian Book Company, New Delhi, 1975, p. 130.
[13]Ibid., p. 131
[14]*Housing*, World Bank Sector Policy Paper, Washington, 1975, p. 15.

land values in the metropolitan cities are artificially manipulated by speculators, and as a result the urban poor have to travel considerable distances to the place of work, or, as Sethuraman notes, 'they are far removed from the market place where they must sell their goods and services'. One can only agree with Ashish Bose[15] when he states that 'poor people must live near their place of work regardless of land values'. It is artificially enhanced land values which make it impossible for the urban poor and even the lower middle class to buy their own land on which to build over time the kind of house that is within their income. As Turner and Roberts[16] rightly note, the housing problem can be solved to some extent if the urban poor are recognised not only as passive consumers but also active participants in the building of their shelters.

A major reason why the urban poor are reluctant to invest in the improvement of their hutments is the lack of security of land tenure which acts as a severe disincentive. Unlike Calcutta where *bustees* are built on privately owned land, the squatter settlements in Delhi, Bombay, Ahmedabad and elsewhere are illegal structures on public land. In a study of squatter settlements in Delhi, Majumdar notes that an important function of slum associations is to provide the urban poor with collective security against eviction or the demolition of the hutments or illegal structures. In a slum development project in Hyderabad, described by Cousins, great importance was attached to providing the slum dwellers with security of tenure to the land on which they were living. As Unni points out in his discussion of the social concerns that should influence slum relocation and urban planning,

> ownership of the plot or a share in the plot which gives the householder sufficient security of tenure, is a basic factor. . . . This element of ownership in a housing policy can develop identity of homelife with the habitat and bring about housing satisfaction.

[15]Ashish Bose, *Studies in India's Urbanisation 1901-1971*, Tata-McGraw-Hill, New Delhi, 1974, p. 237.

[16]John F.C. Turner and Bryan Roberts, op. cit., p. 131.

Housing has to be seen not simply as the provision of houses but as a developmental process in which housing is an integrated response to the socio-economic and cultural preferences of the urban poor. Thus in Hyderabad, a housing project for slum dwellers was viewed in the framework 'urban community development', while the housing scheme for relocated slum dwellers in Ahmedabad was influenced by the values and norms of 'integrated urban development'. In Hyderabad the provision of housing, as a part of the process of community development, was illustrated in terms of three basic linkages: (1) the integration of physical improvement such as drainage, water supply and improved housing within the community development process; (2) the systematic linking of voluntary organisations with the slum community; (3) the linkages between the slums and the informal urban sector with financial institutions and markets in the formal sector of the urban economy. In Ahmedabad, the housing project undertaken by the Ahmedabad Study Action Group (ASAG) for the slum relocation programme was expressed in the profound insight that 'slums are people not places'. According to ASAG,

The slum is more a reflection of attitudes towards life than of physical or environmental conditions. The slum was not simply a housing problem but a complex socio-economic, cultural and political problem. A comprehensive approach incorporating social, economic, educational and motivational inputs, along with housing, would lead to the emergence of an alternative value system and bring about far reaching attitudinal and behavioural changes.

It is necessary to design housing within the framework of the socio-economic and cultural preferences of the urban poor because middle-class conceptions of housing, privacy and over-crowding are quite different from theirs. As Majumdar points out, the tendency of rural migrants to the squatter settlements in the city is to reproduce the same organisation of space and housing patterns which they had in their village of origin. It is because of this that Shah and Unni note that the tendency in the slums and squatter settlements is for family life and activities to spill over into open spaces around and in front of the house. Because the housing scheme in Ahmedabad was informed by great sensitivity to the social and cultural dimensions of housing, great care was taken to get the people to participate in the spatial organisation of the resettlement colony and the design of the houses. In fact, as Shah points out, the reactions of the people to the housing models proposed to them resulted in important changes in the design of the houses.

URBAN RENEWAL

Urban renewal is often identified with optimal utilisation of the ecological resources of the city for the creation of a healthy environment by the demolition of slums and squatter settlements and their relocation on the periphery of the city. We may distinguish two broad approaches to urban renewal: slum improvement by the provision of improved housing, services and social infrastructure; (2) relocation of slums and *basti* dwellers on the fringe of the city. Both these approaches to urban development are costly and entail varying degrees of dislocation for the urban poor.

An interesting example of a massive programme of slum improvement is provided by Sivaramakrishnan. The slum improvement scheme in Calcutta, sponsored by the Calcutta Metropolitan Agency (CMDA), was designed to provide basic services to one million slum dwellers at an average cost of Rs. 100 per head. However, this estimate was later raised to Rs. 146 per head thus involving a total outlay of Rs. 150 crores. Since the *bustees* in Calcutta are built on privately own- ed land, slum clearance, rehousing and improvement, and com- pensation for registered slums was estimated at about Rs. 50 crores. However, it was not the cost of compensation for land so much as the cost of rehousing that prevented large scale slum improvement. The improvement programme under- taken by the CMDA has involved considerable public invest- ment but there is also the problem of the maintenance of public services such as water supply, drainage, sewer networks, sanita- tion and street lighting because of the low level of resources that can be generated by the *bustee* population. It is estimated that the current expenditure on the operation and maintenance of the slum investment facilities in Calcutta will be Rs. 20 million for 1975-76 and this will increase to Rs. 40 million in 1980-81.

Slum improvement, however, has the advantage of improving the physical invironment and the quality of life of the urban poor without disturbing their social organisation and style of life which are related to caste, kinship and ethnic factors. On the other hand, relocation of the urban poor from slum and squatter settlements within the city to sites on the periphery entails high costs both for the city and the urban poor. First, there is the costly extension of basic services and their maintenance. Second, the cost to the relocated urban poor. In the view of Turner and Roberts[17] 'massive and forced transfers of the poor from inner city slums and shanty towns to greatly improved dwellings on the urban periphery generally impoverish the poor'.

The cost of the recent demolition of *bastis* in Delhi and their relocation on the urban fringe is not known, but it is thought that some of these relocation sites involved an expenditure of Rs. 40 crores. The relocation of squatter settlements tends to impoverish the poor because they lose the investment made in the demolished hutments and have to bear additional transportation costs to the place of work; it is also probable that relocation leads to unemployment, especially in the case of women who become unemployed because of the distance from the place of their traditional work. As several studies point out, relocation of slum dwellers has disruptive effects on the employment patterns and style of life of the urban poor because the location of housing near the place of work is much more important than the quality of the shelter. As the World Bank[18] points out,

Refusal to accept existing low-quality housing as at least an intermediate solution to the urban housing problem is common. The consequence is a continuous process of construction of temporary dwellings which last until the government clears the land for other purposes or until they are washed away by tropical downpours. Thus, as the value of land close to the city centre increases, squatters are forced to move towards the expanding periphery away from employ-

[17]Ibid., p. 132.
[18]*Housing*, World Bank Sector Policy Paper, p. 15.

ment and other opportunities, never along the way having
had the opportunity to build up equity in a house.

The housing scheme designed by ASAG in Ahmedabad
stands in stark contrast to the demolition of slums and squatter
settlements in Delhi and the eviction of the urban poor. As
Shah notes,

Instead of bulldozing the poor out of their houses, a negotiated settlement based on the voluntary choice of the people
has been attempted. Instead of being passive recipients of
dole, people have been made active partners in a process
designed to foster their entry into the mainstream of the
city's life from their previous illegal and marginal existence.
Instead of providing uneconomic and culturally undesirable
multi-storey houses, modest shelters have been built to suit
their life-style. Recognising the futility of exclusive housing
in bringing about the desired social and economic transition,
social, educational, organisational and motivational objectives
have been integrated into the housing and environment
improvement schemes.

URBAN PLANNING

The consideration of the various dimensions of urban poverty
leads to the conclusion that the causes of slum formation and
squatter settlement are neither industrialisation nor the size of
the city but urban poverty and the socio-cultural marginalisation
of the urban poor.[19] Hence, it is important that the planners
who are preoccupied with technocratic models of urban planning
should develop a greater understanding of the structural aspects
of urban poverty such as slums and shanty towns, unhygienic
environment and ecological deterioration through over-crowding
and the lack of basic services and facilities. As we saw earlier,
the problem of urban housing is not a question of finance so

[19]On this point see Victor S. D'Souza, 'Urban Development in
India: Demographic Functional and Socio-Cultural Perspectives' *Indian
Journal of Social Work*, XXXVI, nos. 3-4, October 1975-December
1976, p. 291.

much as the consequence of the social stratification of the urban population and the elitist values which determine the structural elements of housing policies embodied in building codes and the unrealistic standards enforced by urban authorities and city planners.

Urban planning is basically concerned with decisions regarding the organisation of space and land use. These decisions are based on an ideology of development and professional models of planning that reflect the social and economic system with its pattern of unequal distribution of power and varying systems of social and cultural values. The tendency of urban planners in India, with a few exceptions, is to accept without examination models of urban planning inherited from the colonial past. Delhi is a good example of the way in which British colonial assumptions regarding housing influenced their perceptions of the needs of different social groups. Colonial urban planning was incapable of evolving models of urban development responsive to the needs of the urban poor because the only value system that had any validity for it was totally different from the social, cultural and economic values associated with the traditional institutions of caste, kinship, ethnic identity and region.

In what way could unrealistic and elitist models of urban planning, to which planners and architects are so committed, change? Basically, two approaches have been suggested for the formulation of a urban policy and planning design that will take into consideration the massive fact of urban poverty. On the one hand, there is a strong trend that urban planning cannot be carried on as a professional technocratic exercise in isolation from the social and cultural values and patterns of behaviour of the urban poor. To bridge the gulf between the planner and the urban poor there is the need of developing anthropological documentation on the social groups who comprise the urban poor so that comprehensive urban planning will then have adequate knowledge for the setting of goals which can be achieved by the majority of the urban population which is poor, rather than by a small minority of the social, economic and political elites. As Unni points out,

Middle-class projections of goals and objectives have to be

used very cautiously in dealing with our city planning, problems and issues, since the majority of urban households (over 60 per cent) cannot afford to own a house of minimum standards except with aid in one form or another.

The significance of sociological information for urban planning can be seen from the studies by Majumdar and Menefee Singh of Delhi squatter settlements; the analysis of the informal urban sector in developing countries and Ranchi by Sethuraman and Van den Bogaert; the complexity of the relationship between migration, employment and slum improvement in Calcutta by Lubell and Sivaramakrishnan; the studies of the urban poor in Madras by Wiebe and Katona-Apte, and the developmental approach to urban housing in Hyderabad and Ahmedabad by Cousins and Shah.[20] Whether these sociological studies of the value systems and patterns of behaviour of the urban poor will have any impact on the elitist and technocratic bias of urban planners is uncertain. Nevertheless one can derive hope from the fact that some of the most influential urban planners in India and other countries are moving away from colonial inspired models of urban planning to alternative approaches to the development of a planned environment responsive to the housing, employment, educational and health needs of the urban poor.

The second approach is to enable the urban poor to participate in planning decisions affecting them by organising them to manage effectively the political, social, bureaucratic and ecological dimensions of the prevailing structures of modern urban life. This theme of the participation of the poor in the process of urban development is widely recognised as one of the most significant changes that has to occur if the situation of the urban poor is to improve. A recent study of community participation in the planning of human settlements has developed a typology of modes of participation and has assessed them according to type of participation, its function and the locus

---

[20]I was unable to get an acceptable paper on the slums of Bombay. For a penetrating study of the slums of Bombay see Owen M. Lynch, 'Political Mobilisation and Ethnicity among Adi-Dravidas in a Bombay Slum', *Economic and Political Weekly*, IX, n. 39, Sept. 28, 1974, pp. 1657-1668. Earlier versions of the papers in this book appeared in *Social Action*, Special Number on the India City, July 1977.

of power.[21] Another typology of the associations commonly found in squatter settlements has been developed by Majumdar. He distinguishes five types of associations based on caste, kinship, regional or religious identities as well as common interests. In his view these associations 'provide an institutional framework for the articulation of demands and rights of the inhabitants and thus link the *basti* community to the rest of urban society and through it to national institutions'.

These associations are managed by different types of leaders whose primary function is to manipulate the institutions of the urban economy to the advantage of the urban poor and also to act as communication channels for the specific groups they represent to the wider society. The importance of associations as focal points of the interest and needs of different social groups among the urban poor has been well brought out by Shah, Menefee Singh and Unni. Menefee Singh shows how the sex segregated character of Indian society prevents women from participating in urban institutions, even in the informal sector, for their own benefit. Thus, the women in the squatter settlements 'not only lack the machinery or power to press for their demands, but they also lack a medium through which their most urgent problems and grievances can become publicly known and comprehended by those in power'. In the housing project for relocated slum dwellers in Ahmedabad a great emphasis was placed on the 'social action component' which would ensure that the resettlement process would enable community participation in decision making, problem solving and the raising of resources; this was to be accomplished by promoting community level organisations and institutions to foster a culture of self-reliance and self-respect. The importance of organising the poor in associations for the development of community housing so that local initiative and self-determination can be exercised, is also discussed by Unni and contrasted with urban planning which conveys the idea of objectives and legislation imposed by bureaucrats, planners and the elites.

[21]See Mary Racellis Hollnsteiner, 'People Power: Community Participation in the Planning of Human Settlements' *Assignment Children* 40, Oct-Dec 1977, pp. 11-47.

In this paper I have outlined the basic themes that underlie the challenge posed by urban poverty not only to the professional planner and bureaucrat but also to the social scientist and social worker. Several interrelated themes recurred. First, there was a consensus on the immense contribution of the informal sector to the urban economy. Second, it was assumed that slums and squatter settlements are a permanent, not a transitory, feature of modern urban life in the less developed countries of Asia. Third, urban poverty was not viewed as a problem of people but of structures maintained by an elitist and technocratic value system that keeps large numbers of men and women poor and powerless.

1

The Informal Urban Sector in Developing Countries: Some Policy Implications

S.V. Sethuraman

The urban population in the Third World has tripled in a short span of only twenty-five years, from 273 million in 1950 to 819 million in 1975 even though its total population (rural and urban combined) increased by only 75 per cent over the same period.[1] Over the next twenty-five years, it is expected to increase further, reaching a level of over two billion by the year A.D. 2000. As the World Bank paper cited here observes:

> Urbanisation by itself is no cause for alarm; what is alarming are the gross inefficiencies and inequities that characterise urbanisation in the developing world.[2]

Needless to say, migration from the rural to the urban areas has played a vital role in the urbanisation process. Evidence from the developing countries shows that the migrants are young and have only a few years of schooling, if at all; they have very little previous work experience, if any; they possess

The responsibility for this paper is the author's; publication does not constitute an endorsement by the ILO of the opinions expressed.

[1]George Beier *et al.*, 'The task ahead for the cities of the developing countries', *World Development*, 4 (n. 5, 1976) Table 1.1, p. 363.

[2]Ibid., p. 363.

very little capital, if at all, to start their own business in urban areas. Yet the migrants seem to have significantly improved their employment and earning opportunities, as the evidence from the Third World suggests.

Though it is heartening to note that the urbanisation process has opened up new opportunities for the growing labour force, such evidence conceals more than it reveals. It is common knowledge now that a vast majority of the urban population lacks the minimum necessities of life such as shelter and access to water besides other basic needs like food and clothing. In this context, it is pertinent to ask the following questions. What factors explain the existence of urban poverty on such a massive scale? On what activities do they depend mostly for their income? What are the bottlenecks that contribute to their low level of income? Perhaps more important from the long-run point of view is the question whether the existing and emerging urban areas will have the capacity to absorb the growing labour force as in the past and if so, with what consequences?

THE FORMAL AND THE INFORMAL SECTORS

The heterogeneous nature of the urban economies in the developing world is well-documented in the literature. At the risk of simplification, it has been suggested that there are two parallel sectors of activity which provide employment to the urban labour force. The two in turn are popularly labelled as the formal and the informal sectors. What are the distinguishing features of the two sectors? The informal sector, as its name suggests, is not formal in its character. The enterprises in this sector are hypothesised to have virtually no access to credit, skills or technology from the formal private and public institutions such as commercial banks and training institutions. Or, as it frequently happens, the enterprises may not be able to afford the price for such needs. Accessibility could itself be a function of certain constraints inherent in these enterprises; the low level of education of participants in these enterprises may prevent them from getting admission to certain training programmes; likewise, the enterprises may not be able to offer any collateral against credit sought from formal credit institutions.

Whatever may be the reasons, the informal sector enterprises are subject to severe constraints which make it difficult, if not impossible, to expand into viable units capable of competing successfully with other formal sector enterprises. As a result, the informal sector enterprises lack access to adequate business premises and tend to be small in terms of volume of output, employment and investment. They also resort to indigenous technologies that are accessible; they seek simple skills through informal sources and methods of training. They frequently occupy space illegally or resort to variable locations for operating their business. The consequence of all this is that their products and services are generally labour-intensive and often lack sophistication and quality finish which in turn limits their access to a wider market. The average income and earnings of the participants in this sector thus tend to be low as compared to the rest of the labour force in the formal sector.[3] The formal sector enterprises, on the other hand, have no such problems with regard to accessibility to various facilities; they have free access to credit, training, technology, markets, foreign exchange and so on. They have formal relationships with the Government, with the banks and other formal institutions. They have direct access to imports and exports. As a result, they tend to be more capital-intensive and their products are more sophisticated and have the capacity to cater to a wide range of taste. The volume of output, employment, investment and earnings of workers, therefore, tend to be higher than in the informal sector.

In reality, however, the enterprises in the economy do not fall neatly into the two sectors, for there are always enterprises which fall somewhere in between the two. In other words, it would appear that there is a continuum with enterprises ranging from the informal to the formal sector. Nevertheless, if there is going to be a choice in favour of a target group of enterprises deserving direct assistance through special policies and

[3]For further discussion on the concept, see S.V. Sethuraman, 'The urban informal sector: concept, measurement and policy', *International Labour Review*, 114, (n. 1, July-August 1976), pp. 69-81.

programmes, it will naturally be the lower end of the spectrum or the informal sector as described here, assuming of course that the policy objective is to promote employment and the incomes of the urban poor.

THE ROLE OF THE INFORMAL SECTOR

Why is the informal sector important? First, the accumulating body of empirical evidence suggests that not only is the base of the formal sector in developing countries small, but also that the rate of growth of employment in this sector is so low that it fails to generate enough jobs to absorb the additions to the urban labour force because the commodity produced and the technology used are such that they are highly capital-intensive. Second, many of the new entrants to the job market are ill-prepared to be absorbed into the formal sector notwithstanding their expressed preference for a secure wage employment in the formal sector including the Government. Third, even though the number of jobs in the Government sector increased rapidly in many of the developing countries in the wake of independence and because of the expanding role of the Government, the rate of increase in Government employment has tended to slow down, if not stagnate, in recent years.

As a consequence, it is not surprising to find that many of the new entrants to the labour force choose to establish their own enterprise, however small it may be, in spite of the odds against them noted earlier. There is a growing feeling in the developing community in recent years that the informal sector is not a transitory phase but is going to be a permanent feature of the urban economies of the Third World. Further, the dependence on this sector for employment opportunities will grow over the years for the simple reason that no conceivable rate of growth of the formal sector will be sufficient to absorb the projected increases in the urban labour force. Under the circumstances, it is imperative that a search be made for ways and means through which employment and productivity in this sector can be promoted which in turn will lead to an amelioration of urban poverty. The ILO, under the World Employment Programme, initiated in 1974 a series of case studies pertaining to the informal sector in several large and medium sized cities/towns of the developing world. The purpose of the paper is to describe the kind of evidence that emerges from some of these completed studies with a view to drawing appropriate lessons for other developing countries such as India.

THE URBAN INFORMAL SECTOR: SOME EVIDENCE

The informal sector[4] is an important source of employment in many developing countries, particularly in the urban areas: perhaps 60 to 70 per cent of the employed persons in Kumasi city (Ghana), 41 per cent in Jakarta (Indonesia), are employed in the informal sector however defined. The informal sector enterprises are typically located in or near slum areas; often they have been forced to move from one location to another through public policies either because they contributed to over-crowding and congestion in the city or because they occupy land that does not belong to them. Not infrequently, they have been harassed and moved to other locations because their presence mars the beauty of the city. A vast majority of these enterprises either have no structures or building premises, or have only temporary structures; some do not even have a fixed location.

It should not therefore come as a surprise that most of them do not have access to either water or electricity. Frequently, they are far removed from the market place where they must sell their goods and services. Neither is it surprising to know that only a small fraction of the informal sector enterprises are registered with the appropriate authorities. Besides the ones mentioned, a variety of restrictive policies has been applied to this sector, arising out of a concern for either traffic congestion or public health and safety or other environmental considerations. This is not to say that the attitude of the governments towards this sector has been exclusively a negative one; rather it ranges from an absolutely negative to a neutral or mildly positive attitude depending on their understanding and concern for the informal sector.

---

[4]This section is based on the findings reported by the respective studies which are still under preparation unless otherwise stated.

Goods and Services

Notwithstanding the hostile conditions described, the informal sector has not only thrived but is also growing. The reason for this is obviously the existence of demand for the goods and services produced by this sector, as is also borne out by empirical studies. The goods produced by this sector range from the production of instantly consumable food products to light industries; the services provided by this sector range from simple personal and household services to the repair of vehicles and consumer durables. Thus, the activities of this sector (excluding agriculture) include manufacturing, transport, construction, trade and services.

The extent to which these activities are important varies with the case in question. For example, the manufacturing and repair services in the informal sector are more important for male employment in Ghana as compared to trade and services for women in the same country. In Indonesia, on the other hand manufacturing is relatively less important, both for men and women. What is perhaps more interesting is the finding that it is not the demand factor alone which determines the relative importance of various activities within the informal sector; more important are factors like the availability of skills, the opportunities for acquisition of new skills and access to financial resources. Where specific skills are lacking and capital limited, the enterprises facing such constraints tend to produce goods and services that are similar, if not the same, and as a result compete against each other for a limited market which in turn drives down their earnings. In contrast, enterprises with specific skills and some capital are not so severely threatened by competition owing to barriers in acquisition of skills and credit; it is also true that the demand for goods and services produced by them is not limited in absolute terms but grows with the general development in the urban economy. For example, some of the traditional and simple handicrafts, preparation and sale of food and other consumable items, household services, etc., are all activities fostering severe competition between the enterprises, and since they require simple skills that can be acquired easily and need little capital, there are virtually no barriers to entry by new enterprises. By contrast, the metal manufacturing and repair activities require a considerable amount of skill and some capital; and the demand for such goods and services is growing.

Access to Credit

It is, therefore, clear that not only market opportunities but also access to skills, credit, raw materials and intermediate inputs and technology play a vital role in the development of the informal sector. Looking at access to capital, the studies generally show that the informal sector enterprises have virtually no access to credit facilities from formal sector institutions; and where credit is available from informal sources, the interest rates are exorbitant. The enterprises mainly depend on their own savings which again amount to very little, given their low level of income. For example, only 2 per cent of the enterprises in Freetown (Sierra Leone) obtained credit from the banks as opposed to 75 per cent who depended on their own savings, the rest depending on other sources of finance such as friends, relatives, etc. Some entrepreneurs in this sector (e.g., Ghana) who have acquired employable skills do seek wage employment for a short while and the lucky ones who successfully obtain such employment save a substantial part of their current income in order to establish their own enterprises. The remaining unlucky ones, as in the case of engineering enterprises in Calcutta's informal sector,[5] depend on the formal sector enterprises for their working capital needs at the cost of surrendering their freedom not to sell their output except to those advancing the capital.

In the case of Indonesia, it even takes the form of loans in kind; for example, a migrant from the rural to the urban area who chooses to become a *betjak* (three-wheel rickshaw) driver does not have the necessary capital to buy the vehicle and hence depends on an intermediary who either sells the vehicle at twice the market price and recovers the dues over a period of eighteen months or so, or rents the vehicle on a daily basis in return for a share of his daily revenue which is usually 50 per

[5]A.N. Bose, *The Informal Sector in the Calcutta Metropolitan Economy*, Geneva: ILO, WEP Research Working Paper WEP 2-19, WP 5, 1974.

cent or more of his daily earnings. In some cases, the individuals entrusted with the task of enforcing city laws are themselves the lenders who lend a petty sum of, say, US $ 1.50 in return for an interest of 15 cents (or 10 per cent of the principal) on a daily basis.

Education

Let us look at the human resources engaged in the informal sector. A vast majority of the participants are migrants, often from the regions not far from the urban centres where they are now. Besides limited employment opportunities in the formal sector, their age, level of education, skills and experience would seem to explain why they enter the informal sector in such large numbers, notwithstanding their expressed preference for a secure wage employment. In Freetown (Sierra Leone), two-thirds of the informal sector employees never attended school; 12 per cent were dropouts from primary school and 6 per cent did not go beyond primary school. In the case of Jakarta, 87 per cent of the heads of the informal sector enterprises had fewer than six years of schooling. In Kumasi city (Ghana), the situation seems to be slightly better; about 40 per cent of the informal sector entrepreneurs had below primary education while 58 per cent had up to middle school education. Further, these participants are young, usually below thirty years of age. In Kumasi, 72 per cent of the heads of the enterprises were below thirty-five years. In Freetown, two-thirds of the owners of the enterprises were below thirty-nine years. If we look at the new enterprises, the participants are much younger.

Skills

What about their skills? Most of them do not possess any skill when they enter the informal sector. A substantial number of them enters activities which require virtually no skills. For example, 40 per cent of the participants in Freetown reported that they did not have to learn any skills, and these were exclusively engaged in the trade sector. In other activities that do require skills, most of the participants acquired them through on-the-job training from within the informal sector itself. In Kumasi, for example, 90 per cent reported having had their apprenticeship in the informal sector in contrast to 5 per cent in a formal sector training institution. In this context, it is worth noting that Ghana has a very well-organised and developed apprenticeship system which provides access to skills at very little cost in comparison with the formal systems of training. Typically, the master of an informal sector enterprise (be it a metal manufacturing, fitting and repairs of vehicles or tailoring) recruits new entrants who usually have some schooling and trains them on the job for a period ranging from two to five years, depending on the nature of the skill and the trainee for a small fee payable at the end of the training period.

What makes this system attractive to youngsters is that they not only do not pay any fee during the training period (which in any case they cannot afford) but actually receive a token sum from the master for their daily food and sometimes transport expenses. It suits the master well insofar as he has more labour at his disposal at a wage far below the going market wage. Another merit of the system is that it emphasises the practical aspects of training, unlike the formal sector training institutions which emphasise the theoretical aspects, and thus the apprenticeship system in the informal sector prepares the trainee to become self-employed rather than encouraging him to seek an uncertain wage employment in the formal sector. No doubt there are some transfers of skills, and to some extent, technology, from the formal to the informal sector through flows of personnel between the two sectors on a limited basis, as another study on the informal sector in Ghana shows.

Linkages

Are there linkages between the formal and the informal sectors? What is their nature? Are they favourable or not to the informal sector? Some of the linkages were already alluded to in the context of marketing, hiring labour and acquiring capital. In the case of Kumasi, the informal manufacturing and repair enterprises depend, to a considerable extent, or imports for their raw material and spare parts needs, even though the direct linkages with formal sector firms are surprisingly small—only about 10 per cent of the intermediate inputs were directly bought from the modern sector. Such linkages, however, show a significant strengthening as the size of the informal sector firm increases. Thus, the backward linkages with other informal sector enterprises are much stronger. Many of the informal sector firms with somewhat more capital at their disposal specialise in stocking and selling small quantities of imported and local raw materials and spare parts and in this sense they are easing the bottleneck resulting from the lack of working capital for other informal sector enterprises. But, of course, this means that the firms using the inputs must pay higher prices besides facing the uncertainty of timely input availability, i.e., out of stock.

More frequently, at least in the case of Ghana, the linkage takes the form of sub-contracting to other informal sector enterprises. For example, certain aspects of automobile repair or metal manufacturing are sub-contracted to other informal sector enterprises which possess the necessary capital equipment and/or skills and are hence specialised. Such linkages are quite strong in Ghana and the inter-relationships between themselves are truly impressive. This implies more efficient use of available capital and other resources. It also explains to some extent why the informal sector enterprises are clustered together within a given city. The backward linkages with the rural areas are virtually absent. The forward linkages are mainly with individuals, households and informal sector enterprises and only to a small extent with the formal sector; this is explained partly by the pattern of goods and services produced (which are mostly consumer goods oriented) and partly by the inability of the informal sector enterprises to reach out to the formal sector clientele, their inability to stock and sell, and the poor finishing quality of their products.

Ability to Innovate

One of the interesting things about the informal sector is its ability to exploit discarded and scrap materials ranging from cigarette butts to waste paper to scrap metals from automobiles etc., for profitable use. In fact, the demand for such materials is so great that it is a limiting factor in expansion for some of the enterprises, e.g., manufacture of die-cast utensils from discarded aluminium sheets in northern Ghana. Needlto to add, such 'recycling' of waste materials, besides contributing to employment generation, also promotes efficient use of resources. Another point of interest about the informal sector is its ability to innovate. This is particularly noticeable in the case of Ghana, where import substitutes are manufactured in the informal sector at a fraction of the cost of importing the same. Some enterprises even have significant export potential but not fully exploited owing to distortions in exchange rates and market prices.

Capital Requirements

Turning to some of the quantitative measures, the most striking fact is that the informal sector is not homogeneous as one might expect—far from it. The amount of capital available per person varies enormously and yet the capital-labour ratio for this sector is only a fraction of that prevailing in the formal sector. The Kumasi study showed that the average amount of fixed capital per person in the informal sector is about 206 ccdis (i.e., about US $ 200) though it is subject to considerable variation. It is higher for smaller enterprises (i.e., with one person only) than for larger enterprises (with more persons per enterprise). But another study of Ghana showed that the average capital-labour ratio in auto related metal industries in the informal and formal sectors were respectively 225 dollars and 7,713 dollars; similar figures in the non-auto related metal industries were respectively 78 dollars and 1,006 dollars. These figures demonstrate how little capital is required to create a job in the informal sector as compared to its formal counterpart. Likewise, capital per unit of output was estimated to be 6.1 for the formal sector and 4.2 for the informal sector, in auto related industries. In non-auto related industries, the respective figures were 9.3 and 1.9. If these quantities were cast in terms of shadow prices, the disparities between the formal and informal sectors would become more glaring since capital and imported inputs used by the formal sector are usually underpriced.

Earnings

Notwithstanding the relatively low capital-labour ratio, the informal sector seems to generate a reasonable level of earnings and productivity per worker. However, as in the case of capital-labour ratio, these quantities are subject to enormous variations depending on the nature of activity. As one study of Jakarta shows, the informal sector generates a level of income that is sufficiently attractive for the migrant from rural areas to be better off, no matter what his earlier level of income was. In other words, even the lowest paid worker in the informal sector in Jakarta was better off in relation to his income earlier in the rural areas.

Growth

How rapidly has the informal sector been growing? In Jakarta (Indonesia), the number of informal sector enterprises seems to be growing at the rate of about 12 per cent per year; in terms of employment, it is slightly less at 11 per cent. In Kumasi (Ghana), the number of enterprises seems to be growing by about 12 per cent per year. In Freetown (Sierra Leone), the number of enterprises seems to have grown at an incredible rate of 25 per cent per year. The bulk of the new enterprises are small, having one to three persons. In what activities are they growing? In Kumasi, though it is spread in all activities, the growth is faster in shoe, leather and related manufacturing. In the case of Jakarta, however, the fastest growing activities are trade and services (13 per cent per year), then comes transport with 10 per cent and industry with 5 per cent per year.

SUMMARY AND CONCLUSIONS

The findings represented here, though based on limited evidence and hence preliminary in nature, nevertheless reveal the range of problems and potentials within the informal sector. They do not only provide clues but also raise new questions as to the nature of development policies required to develop the informal sector. For example, will the informal sector grow as rapidly as it has done in the past and absorb future migrants? What factors limit the growth of this sector?

Human Resource Development

Several conclusions emerge from the evidence presented in the foregoing paragraphs. The informal sector has played and continues to play a vital role in employment generation in urban areas notwithstanding the generally hostile attitude of Government policies. It has also contributed to higher levels of income for its participants, however small it may be. Imperfections in the capital market have severely limited the income opportunities of this sector. The empirical evidence from Ghana suggests that the informal sector can play a crucial role in human resource development by providing appropriate training and thus develop skills in a relatively inexpensive way. This does not mean that there is no room to improve the apprenticeship system that now prevails in the informal sector. The need for skill development becomes more obvious when we consider the fact that lack of skills is a major constraint limiting the scope for diversification of goods and services produced in the informal sector, which in turn contributes to a low level of income for participants in certain types of activities. Further, skill development within the informal sector is likely to promote greater self-employment rather than wage employment.

Infrastructural Facilities

In addition, the findings point to the desirability of introducing other new policies and programmes such as the following. First, the provision of minimum infrastructural facilities including provision of land in appropriate locations to the informal sector enterprises. Second, the introducing of credit facilities that are accessible to the informal sector enterprises. Third, the provision of raw materials and spare parts, imported or otherwise, through appropriate channels. Fourth, to forge new forward linkages with the formal sector and explore new market opportunities for the informal sector goods and services. Fifth, to eliminate price distortions that discourage the production of import substitutes and exportable goods, particularly in the informal sector. Finally, to introduce a mechanism through which the innovative enterprises can be identified for further encouragement.

Perhaps one can think of various other measures to promote development in this sector. From the implementation point of view, a complicated question is what should be the vehicle for channelling assistance to such small enterprises. The answer to this will have to be found through appropriate pilot projects and presumably it will depend on the country in question. In any case, the essence of the strategy should be to facilitate the flow of investment into the informal sector with a view to increasing its employment and income potential.

Relevance to India

Can one draw from the preceding account some lessons pertinent to India? First, it is obvious that the number of cities will increase substantially over the years to come for the simple reason that many of the present towns will develop into cities by virtue of population growth. As a result, the informal sector activities are likely to increase very substantially, which in turn will intensify the concern for the urban poor. Why? Experience to date with regard to the large metropolitan areas such as Calcutta, Bombay and Delhi suggests that the urban authorities in these cities are already facing formidable problems in providing decent housing and other urban amenities to their population; besides inadequate resources, the capacity to administer a comprehensive programme of informal sector development is indeed a formidable constraint. This being the case with large metropolitan areas, one really wonders what is in store for the emerging metropolitan areas and cities which have relatively little experience in the field of urban development. It would appear that there is an urgent need to expand the capacity (or rather the quality) of local administrations in urban areas to recognise and solve the problems of urban development such as migration and the informal sector. Perhaps the setting up of a national urban management institute, with specific focus on multi-disciplinary training and concern, would go a long way in filling this lacuna.

Second, besides improving the capacity of urban administrations, there is an urgent need to acquaint them with the problems of the informal sector enterprises and encourage them to take necessary steps to solve them. Third, though there have been some scattered efforts to help informal sector enterprises in selected activities (e.g., credit facilities), there is neither a comprehensive programme to assist the informal sector enterprises nor the machinery to implement such assistance programmes. Thus, there is an urgent need to collect the relevant information, analyse it, draw policy conclusions specific to various activities and formulate appropriate assistance programmes. The problems of the urban informal sector are, in many respects, similar to those of marginal farmers and agricultural labourers in rural areas.

These are indeed radical steps to undertake; nevertheless, it would appear that they are necessary for the target population affected by these measures is likely to be around 50 per cent of the urban population, or about sixty million. Yet these are but initial steps towards a national policy concerning the urban informal sector. Experience gained through this will no doubt also pave the way for promoting similar activities in the rural areas as well.

2

Interdependence not Duality: Slum Perspectives

Paul D. Wiebe

In my book, *Social Life in an Indian Slum*,[1] I present a picture of social life as it occurs in a selected Madras slum (pseudonym Chennanagar), from the perspectives of the people themselves. However good this picture is, and however meaningful in either scholarly or practical terms, it is limited. The very fact of focus allows for a detail in analysis that is not possible given a larger context of research explication. But simultaneously, such a focus tends to under emphasise the importance of viewing the particular locality within its more general setting. This eventuality is unintended, of course, and so I state:

> ... it is not possible to delineate fully any of the local patterns that occur without reference to similar or related patterns in the Madras, Tamil Nadu and Indian environments. . . . In India . . . where both 'old' and 'new' cultural forms emphasise continuity across strata and classes, the poor consider themselves only as poor, not also as people outside the society and its 'shared rules of interpersonal decency'.[2]

[1] Paul D. Wiebe, *Social Life in an Indian Slum*, Vikas Publishing House, New Delhi, 1975.

[2] Ibid., pp. 160, 162.

Yet the problem remains. Thus, herein I simply emphasise again that an analysis of such a setting in its own terms alone, though reasonable in the definitions of a sociological case study, in no way allows a comprehensive picture of the examined context. Reviewing first the materials relevant to this argument, I conclude briefly with comments pertinent in general.

RESEARCH FINDINGS

A reciprocity in relationships among the various groupings of people that constitute Indian society has often been described. It is pronounced in the ways in which villages and small towns merge together in the social networks that characterise a particular region, labourers and land-owners relate themselves in producing the land's yields, service groups work in relation to patrons and patron groups, marriages are arranged, family relationships are made meaningful, political support is mobilised, 'little' and 'great traditional' religious groupings inter-relate, and so on. The unities and continuities of Indian civilisation are most certainly very well-established[3] and whether or not the 'traditional' and the 'modern' are disjointed anywhere else, the polar use of such adjectives in the examination of the process that characterise Indian social life is largely incorrect.

And so it is in reference to Chennanagar. Here too we cannot but see local processes in consideration of contextual processes. Poor the people unmistakably are in their access to outside political and economic institutions, public services, their material and personal conditions of life. A family here is often forced to get by with as little as one bucket of water a day; its handicaps are as easily recognisable when the access of its children to schools and elementary health provisions are considered. Yet the patterns of living of the people tie them intimately, both culturally and socially, into those that characterise the living conditions of their more well-to-do neighbours.

OCCUPATIONAL IDENTIFICATIONS

The occupational identifications of the 376 Chennanagar

[3]W. Norman Brown, 'The Content of Cultural Continuity in India', *Journal of Asian Studies*, 20 (August 1961); Milton Singer, 'The Social Organisation of Indian Civilisation', *Diogenes*, 45 (April 1964).

household heads are varied; thirty-four of them work as sales people (selling fruits, vagetables, cloth pieces, food items, utensils and so on); fifty-two in skilled and semi-skilled occupations; fifteen in factories; 172 as casual labourers; thirty-five in various household industries (for example, in making *beedis* [leaf-rolled cigarettes], weaving, tanning, and in making cardboard boxes), eight as shopkeepers; forty-seven in lower class miscellaneous activities (as watchmen, rickshaw pullers, bus conductors and so on); and thirteen are unemployed.

A major portion, and often all, of most family incomes in Chennanagar is contributed by the household head. Additionally, about a third of the married women and many of the older boys work irregularly as coolies or in other part-time jobs, thus adding to the income of a household. Then too, in 19 per cent of the Chennanagar households, at least one adult other than the household head also reports a relatively regular income, and some of the people own at least a little property (a draft animal, a milk cow or a few chickens) in relation to which they are in a position to earn a little additional income.

None of this can imply that the people are fairly well-off. They aren't. The *per capita* income figures for the Chennanagar people show that 80 per cent of them are below the 'absolute poverty' level—the level at which incomes are sufficient to secure provisions for a minimum adequate diet (in terms of calories alone), under local environmental conditions—identified by V.M. Dandekar and Nilakantha Rath in their excellent study of poverty in India.[4] Very few indeed are more than just a little over this level. Simultaneously, the levels of expenditures, savings, investments and indebtedness of the people[5] buttress a conclusion identifying their poverty.

But the Chennanagar people work and are far from

---

[4]V.M. Dandekar and N. Rath, 'Poverty in India', *Economic and Political Weekly*, 6 (2 January 1971), pp. 25-48; See Wiebe, op. cit., p. 87: 'Whereas in urban India in 1960-61, only a little more than two per cent of the people were in the monthly per capita expenditure class, Rs 0-8, in Chennanagar, more than 10 per cent even today report incomes in this category. About 86 per cent of the people make less than the average per capita consumer expenditure (Rs 33.67) for the state.'

[5]Wiebe, op. cit., pp. 95-100.

apathetic in seeking and maintaining whatever jobs they can. The variety of their occupations speaks for the nature of their general urban employment in which it is extremely difficult for people at such socio-economic levels to find secure employment (given their low levels of education, their acquired occupational skills, etc.); a context in which traditional patron-client linkages (as defined, for example, in the *jajmani* system) have broken down, a context in which the problems of underemployment are severe. It speaks also for the ingenuity of the people in their willingness to take whatever jobs are available.

Finally, the nature and variety of their occupational identifications indicate clearly that it is impossible to think of the city's economic processes going on without an appreciation of the kinds of work such people do. They are primarily engaged in the trade and service sectors of the city's economy—in the 'informal' urban sector,[6] in the city's 'bazaar economy',— wherein an 'incredible volume of *ad hoc* acts of exchange occurs', rather than in the city's 'firm-centred' economic sector wherein 'trade and industrialisation occur through a set of impersonally defined social institutions which organise a variety of specialised occupations with respect to some productive or distributive end'.[7] As such, they are engaged primarily in occupations that commonly have a 'multiple of the number they need',[8] with the result that they face severe problems of underemployment, if not of employment *per se*. But such people are simultaneously engaged in the kinds of occupations that play a critical role in the economy of Madras.

POLITICAL RELATIONS

Harold A. Gould, recognising the influences traditional features have on modern features in Indian political organisation, has

[6]S.V. Sethuraman, 'Urbanisation and Employment: A Case Study of Jakarta', *International Labour Review*, 112 (August-September 1975), pp. 191-205.

[7]Clifford Geertz, *Peddlers and Princes: Social Development and Economic Change in Two Indonesian Towns*, University of Chicago Press, Chicago, 1963, p. 28.

[8]W. Arthur Lewis, 'Economic Development with Unlimited Supplies of Labour', in H.N. Agarwala and S.P. Singh (eds.), *The Economics of Underdevelopment*, Oxford University Press, Bombay, 1958, p. 402.

constructed what he calls a *jati*-model of Indian politics. He outlines this as follows:

> The *jati*-model . . . is an operative feature of the mental life of most Indians. Its origin lies in the fact that most Indians are socialised in socio-religious *jatis* whose persistence depends upon the survival of the social structures and cultural values which support it. Its specific relevance is to group formation and participation. In many domains of modern Indian social life, including politics, where caste in its traditional forms is not a legitimised, sanctioned basis for role recruitment, patterning and interaction, Indians tend to model the informal and *ex-officio* group structures which form and become the viable bases for determining power relations and reward distributions in these domains, on the principles of solidarity, reciprocity, exclusiveness and ethnicity which this *jati*-model codifies.[9]

Now caste (or *jati*) *per se* has little direct influence on the political processes of Chennanagar. True, area-wide political life is still to an extent channelled by caste considerations.[10] But leadership in the Chennanagar setting is not correlated with particular caste groupings and there is little evidence that political associations of any kind have emerged here on the basis of caste identifications alone. Nevertheless, the Gould analysis remains compelling, for a caste-related mentality and procedure of the kind he outlines strongly influences political relations in Chennanagar.

On their own, the people of Chennanagar have done and can do many things. They settled the land on their own without legal right. They built their temple and employ a priest with their own funds. They go to hospitals for help when they feel they need it, vote in elections, and participate in the local self-help associations (*mandrams*). These associations are in part simply units within the State's various political party systems of

[9]Harold A. Gould, 'Toward a Jati-Model for Indian Political Relations', *Economic and Political Weekly*, 4 (1 February 1969), pp. 296-7.
[10]Robert L. Hardgrave, *The Dravidian Movement*, Popular Prakashan, Bombay, 1965; Wiebe, op. cit., pp. 103-9.

organisation, part the product of the local need to organise in the pursuit of whatever advantages their combined efforts can effect.

But in many situations, self-help is not possible or even appealing as an option. In a general context in which jobs, space and goods are scarce, the people often lack the power and influence necessary to accomplish what they want on their own.

Knowing this lack, the people seek help wherever they can find it, generally relating themselves as 'clients' with persons more powerful than themselves. Thus, the largest *mandram* had as its president in 1970 the Labour Minister of Tamil Nadu; the second most important *mandram* had an important lawyer in the area as president; the last, still seeking a president at the time this study was conducted, hoped to develop a direct association with Kamaraj Nadar, one of the most influential Congress politicians in the State and the country. And, thus, individuals in their attempts to get things done seek to the extent possible to develop personalistic ties with potentially helpful outsiders.

The fact of such associations is not enough to guarantee services. But it has helped and certainly it always offers the possibility of help. Through such contacts, the people have been able to help guarantee that tank trucks bearing water to their slum will actually show up and that their claims to the land on which they live will at least be granted a hearing. Through the patronage such relationships identify, the people plan to further develop their community, knowing that to gamble in investments of any kind without reasonable backing is to risk more than they can afford.

The Chennanagar people, in their relationships with patrons, whether or not through their *mandrams*, can seldom make demands on the basis of right or precedent. Involving only particular persons as such relationships usually do, particular questions are decided on the basis of their particular merits and hold good only for particular times. But the implications are clear. While the Chennanagar people can thus help guarantee things for themselves, their patrons can mobilise support. This political-ecological reciprocity speaks well for the grass-roots authenticity of the local political process. Certainly neither level can be divorced from the other. And certainly both traditional and modern elements are closely interwoven in the relationships that occur.

SOCIAL ORGANISATION

By no stretch of imagination can it be said that caste and family patterns in Chennanagar resemble closely those found in villages of the area. Dravidian and modern Indian ideological emphases have made far more extensive inroads here. The conditions of slum living make the concepts of pollution and ritual separateness locally difficult to apply. Systems of transportation, recreation and housing make stereotypical responses in behaviour or attitude impossible. And some of the older correlations between *jatis* and families, and such things as occupations and ceremonial participations, are far from possible, given the shortages the people know.

Yet it is nonsense to assume that the influences underlying such patterns no longer have an effect. No person in Chennanagar of an accountable age has any difficulty in giving his *jati* identifications. Only fifteen Chennanagar households can be classified as mixed-caste households, and preferences for intra-*jati* marriages remain very strong. Interests in the processes and implications of Sanskritisation remain meaningful, stereotypes still often follow *jati* lines, and however variant the local conditions of life have become when contrasted with an ideal-typical model, the general contextual influences of such configurations remain strong.[11]

Coping socially in their conditions of scarcity, the Chennanagar people are developing new political, economic, social and cultural forms. Adaptations of various kinds have been necessary. At the same time, the people persist in their participation in many of the social forms that are part of their heritage. On the one hand, such forms have always proved adaptable in the continuities of the civilisation; on the other, the people continue to find in participation the kinds of social securities such forms have always enabled.

[11]Joan P. Mencher, 'A Tamil Village: Changing Socio-Economic Structures in Madras State', in K. Ishwaran (ed.), *Change and Continuity in India's Villages*, Columbia University Press, New York, 1970; Hardgrave, op.cit.

SYMBOLS AND IDEA SYSTEMS

The religious traditions that occur in India's villages have resulted in general from a continuous process of interaction between little, local traditions, and greater traditions which have their places partly inside and partly outside the village.[12] Only residual fragments are separable and distinct.

The patterns of household and temple worship, and life-cycle ceremonial observances, are distinct in Chennanagar in numerous ways. Of necessity, numerous formalities and ritual observances associated with such activities have been truncated, moulded in relation to the needs and social and financial abilities of the people.

Yet many traces of the greater cultural traditions of Hinduism can be quickly found here. The names of the deities the people approach are names familiar in the pantheon of Hinduism. Local temples fit into the general ecological organisation of temples in the city. Some of the people know Sanskrit chants. Almost all of the people know that should they be interested, their own interpretations of life and meaning can be interpreted further for them by others in their more general environment who are more versed in the abstract meanings of their general religious system. And almost all of them have gone on pilgrimages to regional centres, given particular reasons to do so.

As in most other Indian settings, in short, local as well as great traditional religious influences—both 'low' and 'high' religious patterns—characterise the Chennanagar idea and symbol setting, and in the local configuration of these, neither set really persists at the expense of the other.

Finally, even as caste, the 'Church of Hinduism' in a sense at least,[13] retains its importance here. It is only reasonable to expect that the related, more general philosophical underpinnings of this system simultaneously exercise a local influence. And so it is.

[12]M. Marriott, 'Little Communities in an Indigenous Civilization', in M. Marriott (ed.), *Village India*, University of Chicago Press, Chicago, 1965.

[13]M.N. Srinivas, *Caste in Modern India and other Essays*, Asia Publishing House, Madras, 1962.

Numerous social patterns in addition to those already specified also link the Chennanagar people to their Madras, Tamil
Nadu and national environments. The people know of the
advantages in gaining education and some of them make valiant
efforts to guarantee for their children the abilities that will
ensure them better life chances than they themselves have had.
Family planning programmes exercise an influence here. Police
officers, court officials and lawyers are occasionally approached
for special reasons. And the cinema attracts many, especially
among the younger males.

ANALYSIS AND CONCLUSION

From an external point of view, people in Madras from places
like Chennanagar have an important resource: their numbers.
As estimated by the President of the City Corporation in 1971,
approximately one-third of the Madras people live under such
conditions.[14] Comprising such large numbers, the potential of
such people for 'disorder' and confrontation are enormous.

The 'repression' of this potential, to the extent it is effective—
and it has generally so far been very effective in Madras, less
effective in certain North Indian cities (as evidenced recently in
the reactions of the electorate in the 1977 elections to some issues,
including the issue of slum clearance as this was undertaken in
certain areas)—obviously has to do with the extent to which the
reciprocity in relationships between people like those in
Chennanagar, and the others in positions of power and authority over them is mutually beneficial. And the implications here
(however viewed) are very important.

But these cannot concern us directly in this paper. More to
the point: What is the nature of the relationship? And what
does this mean?

Reciprocity

As evidenced by our data, the linkages between the Chennanagar people and outsiders are clearly reciprocal. Whatever the
asymmetry in the advantages that accrue to the slum people,

[14] *The Hindu*, 5 January 1971.

they are active participants in the social life of their surrounding social environments. Like their fellows in other such contexts, they perform menial tasks essential in Madras. They pull the carts used in the transportation of goods. They work as coolies in construction projects. They sweep the streets and clean latrines. They collect garbage. In return for the advantages they seek under the patronage systems they develop, they back those who help, with their enthusiasm, votes and other supports. They buy things. They attend festival celebrations. In sum, only a few if any social patterns are unique to the local setting.

Interpreting such findings, I have written[15] that 'culture of poverty' and similar definitions of slum mentalities and capacities are inapplicable in the understanding of the Chennanagar people. I have also argued[16] that slum clearance, when this is necessary, can never be premised on the assumption that in one way or another the communities of such people are 'cancerous growths' on the body social, growths somehow overwhelming negatively the essential fabric of society. Poverty is their problem; it cannot be related to supposed personal or social deficiencies.

Concluding more generally, an analysis of this kind brings us inescapably to the conclusion that unilinear descriptions of social transformation like those advanced by Rostow[17] and Black[18] are, at the very best, misleading. Viewing contrasts in living standards, differences between rural and urban conditions of life, developed and underdeveloped countries, slum settlements and developed city centres, the rich and the poor, and proceeding on the assumptions basic to an earlier evolutionary evaluation of change, such conceptualisations tend to view the reasons for poverty, 'backwardness', underdevelopment and so on, as lying primarily within the segments of society so affected, not in the features of surrounding environments. As a result, emphases in dealing with the more disadvantaged are usually placed on attempts to alleviate the problems such people pose

[15]Wiebe, op.cit., pp. 154-61.

[16]Ibid., pp. 161-6.

[17]W. Rostow, *The Stages of Economic Growth*, Cambridge University Press, Cambridge, 1960.

[18]C.E. Black, *The Dynamics of Modernization*, Harper and Row, New York, 1966.

for the better-off, attempts to improve local educational standards, attempts to encourage the people to do more for themselves, attempts to ease transitions from more 'backward' to
more 'advanced' styles of life, and so on.

There is nothing practically wrong with much of this. People
like those in Chennanagar need to be understood in their abilities to
do much for themselves. They also need to be guaranteed effective
access to public utilities, public services and good education.

But to come too readily into the conclusion that people are
somehow responsible by themselves for their problems is
irresponsible. Social segments in a context like Madras are not
isolated from each other. They cannot be viewed as arranged in
a sequence that transitionally leads through successive stages in
the process of development. In fact, their problems have very
much to do with the ways in which their environments act in res-
training them, however much existing inter-relationships are
reciprocally meaningful.

Dominance-Dependency Model

Andre Gunder Frank writes of dominant centres and dependent
regions in his analysis of the socio-economic system of Brazil.[19]
At the most general level, he contends that certain international
centres (and at this time, particularly, the United States) dominate major regional centres such as Sao Paulo. In turn, he sees
the regional centres dominating more local centres, the overall
effect being that chains of interdependency, under dominance,
link together the entire system. As David G. Epstein[20] notes in
his cogent analysis of Frank's model, the entire system so
describable:

> is a single, integrated system: the impoverishment and
> backwardness of each dependent unit relative to its domi-
> nating centre is accounted for as a product of the dynamics
> of the system as a whole.

[19]Andre Gunder Frank, *Capitalism and Underdevelopment in Latin
America*, Monthly Review Press, New York, 1967.

[20]David G. Epstein, *Brazilia, Plan and Reality*, University of California
Press, Berkeley, 1973.

There is no reason to assume that Frank's model, applicable though it certainly is in providing a framework according to which Brazilian economic and political relationships can be analysed, is automatically relevant in the understanding of Indian society in general. Historical and contemporary circumstances obviously differ here. Second, too much emphasis on aspects of social life such as dominance can lead to a neglect of the mutuality that often underlies social relationships. And third, such a framework can lead to the postulation of more manipulation in the relations between dominant and subordinate groupings than is empirically justifiable.

Given the reciprocity that characterises all the social relationships examined, however, *plus* the fact of an asymmetry throughout that works to the disadvantage of the slum peoples, it is clear that the local patterns of 'dominance' are not in the hands of people like those in Chennanagar. Such people always find it difficult to find economic security. Their schools, teachers and facilities are inferior to those of the more wealthy, and the education their children receive often prepares them at best only inadequately for the kinds of occupations for which they can compete. Curtailed in their contacts and social opportunities by their conditions of life, they are compelled to rely on the services patrons can and might provide.

Such people most certainly are integrated into their larger social environments. But they are integrated in a system that places them as unequals in almost every way. Thus, what happens to them depends both on what they can do for themselves and what the elements in their social environments will enable. Slum people need help, of course. But the conditions that result in their subordination to outsiders must also be changed if basic improvements in their standards of living are to be realised and maintained. The impoverishment and the difficulties of slum people, in short, can only be understood and dealt adequately if the conditions of their inter-relationships in their more general social environments are taken into account. These conditions involve mutuality and reciprocity; they also involve the dependencies of the slum people.

3

The Urban Poor and Social Change: A Study of Squatter Settlements in Delhi

Millions of people in the large and metropolitan cities are living in self-built homes on illegally occupied lands. In Calcutta, Bombay, Madras and Delhi, approximately five million out of a total of nineteen million live in *bastis* or spontaneous settlements. It is estimated that about 15 to 20 per cent of the other thirty-nine cities with a population of 3,00,000 or more live in such settlements. The inhabitants of these settlements are the new urbanising groups reflecting the process of change in the social structure of the cities. The proportion of such settlements in the cities has increased over the decades. In Delhi, in 1951 the ratio of squatter to non-squatter households was 1:20; in 1973 it was 1:4.5. The population of these *bastis* has been growing at an overall

This paper is based on a survey of a sample of 21,000 households out of a total of 142,000 in 1,375 spontaneous (squatter) settlements scattered all over the city of Delhi; it also makes use of an in-depth study of a sample of 1,100 households that was conducted from October 1973 to the end of 1974. These spontaneous settlements have since then been demolished and all the residents relocated on the outskirts of Delhi during 1976. See *Jhuggi Jhonpri Settlements in Delhi*, Part I, Town and Country Planning Organisation, Delhi, 1973; *Jhuggi Jhonpri Settlements in Delhi*, Part II, A Sociological Study of Low-Income Migrant Communities, Town and Country Planning Organisation, Delhi, 1975.

annual rate of 10.8 per cent, twice that of the growth rate of
the city's population since 1951. The increase in the number
of *bastis* accounted for 16.3 per cent of the total increase in
the city's population (Delhi's population increased from 1.5
million to 2.36 million during 1951-61) as compared to their
proportion of 20.3 per cent of the increase of the total population of the city during 1961-71. (The population of Delhi
was 3.6 million in 1971.) The population added to the *bastis*
during 1971-73 constituted 30.9 per cent of the estimated
increase in the city's population during this period.

These settlements accommodate 5.52 lakhs of inhabitants
comprising about 60 per cent of the rural migrants of the
city. Excluding refugee workers (those who came from
Pakistan), they house 31 per cent of the migrant workers of
urban Delhi. Seventy-two per cent of those earning Rs 3,000 or
less per annum in the city live in spontaneous settlements. Whatever may be the rate of migration to the city in future, the most
effective and dynamic forces will not be simply the increase
in the number and size of the cities, but their progressive
proletarianisation. The future city will be one of the working
classes recruited largely from the rural migrants and it is they
who are likely to shape the social profile of the city. This study
of the urban poor refers to those living in the spontaneous
settlements in Delhi. It is intended to provide a better understanding of the social transformation in which the poor are
involved and from which the development planning of the
Indian city may benefit.

SOCIAL CHARACTERISTICS

The urban poor are similar to those in the rural areas—both
lying at the bottom of the social structure, and suffering from
cumulative inequalities. Their social origins are the same, 93
per cent of the urban poor coming from the villages. Of the
total number of households studied, 35 per cent of the heads
of households were formerly marginal farmers (owning one
to three acres of land), 20 per cent share-croppers, 24 per cent
landless labourers, 15 per cent artisans and occupational castes,
and the rest belonged to a variety of urban based occupations.
Sixty-five per cent of them belonged to the scheduled and

lower castes. The difference that lies between the two social categories is that the urban poor sell labour in the urban market as casual and regular workers; the rural poor are tied to agricultural occupations that are dependent on land and, to some extent, as rural artisans.

There is another basic qualitative difference between the urban and rural poor. Those living in the urban areas are located in an open and large community whereas those in the villages are encapsulated in 'closed' and small communities where their status and position are identified on the basis of caste and fixed, and the relationships between various castes depend upon the ownership, control, and use of land as well as on the *jajmani* system (patron-client relationship) which specifies inter-related rights and obligations between groups at different caste levels. In any case, the relationships of the rural poor with the rest of the social groups of the village community are governed by the 'obligations' that bind them to the classes or castes on whom they depend for their employment, social recognition and to a large extent, for their survival. There is no scope for social mobility or for achievement. Their status is ascribed not only in the present, but has been so in the past and will remain so in the future until radical changes occur in the social structure of rural communities and the ownership of land resources.

It is in the urban complex that there are possibilities of overcoming the limitations of caste, of finding employment on the basis of skill, of acquiring education and new skills, and organisational methods which could fundamentally alter their life pattern, and offer scope for mobility, achievement and the development of social capabilities. It is another matter whether they achieve what they aspire to. We are only referring to the availability of alternative choices which the urban social situation offers. People can become other than peasants, landless labourers or share-croppers. Their children need not live in a society where there is no escape from the ascribed status to which they may have happened to be born.

Having indicated the qualitative differences between the social conditions of the urban and rural poor, it may be emphasised that the urban poor do not constitute a separate world but are linked with the rural world through visits, remittances of money, the continuity of social, cultural and economic networks, and most important, through recruitment of people. Adaptation to the new conditions of city life do take place, but at the same time the cultural traditions are reinforced, being expressed in life-styles and values which reflect an amalgam of rural-urban culture.

The other important social characteristic of the urban poor is that a large majority among them works in the informal and service sectors where entry is easy, requiring less skill, less education and less capital. The scale of operation is small, labour-intensive and based on adaptive technology and skills acquired outside the formal school system. Of the 32,035 earners in 21,000 households, 42 per cent were engaged as construction workers, 8 per cent as hawkers, vendors and petty traders, 9 per cent in the traditional artisan trades and skills, 29 per cent in miscellaneous occupations comprising porters, loaders, cooks, waiters, domestic workers, unskilled office workers, workers in transport and repair shops and other low level service personnel. Analysing the occupational structure in terms of skills it was found that 60 per cent were unskilled, 31 per cent skilled (based on adaptive technology and acquired outside the formal school system), while 9 per cent possessed cultural or inherited skills. Seventy-one per cent of the households had monthly incomes of Rs 250 or below, while 24 per cent fell in the income range Rs 250-450, and the remaining 5 per cent earned over Rs 450. The average income of the households was Rs 237 per month with an average income of Rs 149 per earner per month. There were 1.6 earners in these households of the urban poor with 1.5 dependents per earner.

Forty-six per cent of the adult male population among them were illiterate, 4 per cent literate, 47 per cent with less than high school education, 2 per cent had higher secondary education and 1 per cent were degree holders. Among those who had less than high school education, more than 80 per cent had got themselves educated outside the school system. Among the adult females, 90 per cent were illiterates, whereas 9 per cent were literate or with less than high school education and the remaining 1 per cent had higher secondary education. The population of the urban poor is dominated by the young with the 15-34 age group having the largest percentage. Persons in the age group 45 and above constituted only 10 per cent while children under the age of 15 years accounted for 42 per cent. The rest belonged to the age group 36-45 years. Among the adults, the sex ratio was as low as 730 females per 1,000 males.

Among the migrant households, 5 per cent had lived in the city for two years or less, 20 per cent for three to seven years, 22 per cent for eight to twelve years, and 53 per cent for over twelve years. Sixty-five per cent of the urban poor belonged to the Scheduled Castes, 16 per cent to the high castes, 12 per cent to cultivating and artisan castes, 3 per cent were Muslims, 3 per cent Sikhs and 1 per cent belonged to other religious groups like Christians and Buddhists. In respect to their regional origins, 3 per cent came from the southern and eastern States, 75 per cent from Uttar Pradesh and Rajasthan, and the rest from the Union Territory of Delhi, Haryana, Punjab and Himachal Pradesh.

PROCESS OF SETTLEMENT

Faced with a situation of seeking secure and cheap shelter which is not available in the conventional land and housing market or through other institutional means, the urban poor improvise their own ways of occupying land generally without the consent of the owners. This they do by first prospecting unusable or undeveloped land in the areas near their place of work. Having found such land, information is passed on to the groups and a few families then put up their huts or make-shift structures and test it for two to three days for the possibility of their being evicted from the site. Subsequently, the other members of the group put up their huts, again on a temporary basis. But as some time elapses (generally four to eight months), the settlement gradually acquires a relatively stable character. Once the nucleus of a settlement has been in existence for about a year, other groups arrive and occupy the vacant areas. The settlement at this stage

grows very fast and the process of aggregation and accretion
goes on until it reaches its full size.

There are certain key aspects of this process of securing
land and shelter. The initial clustering or nucleus of the settlement is formed by smaller groups consisting of kin, relatives,
fellow villagers, or caste or community fellows or those intimately known to each other, and its subsequent expansion takes
place by the clustering of similar groups in compact residential blocks. Generally speaking, the aggregation pattern of
the total settlement also manifests homogeneity in terms of
region, village, caste or community and occupation. Even in
large heterogeneous settlements with over 300 households, the
heterogeneity is not made up of unrelated households, but
consists of small homogeneous social groups though different
from each other in social composition. Excluding factors like
nature, size and availability of land near the places of work, it
is social homogeneity that controls the size of the settlement
which normally does not exceed 300 families. The typical
settlement consists of between 100 and 150 families. Each of
the small groups occupies only as much land as is required
for the minimum needs of individual households (between
twelve and fifteen metres). They do often occupy some extra
space to accommodate future additions to the group. The
size of such groups normally consists of fifteen to thirty
families, and rarely exceeds the outside limit of fifty families.

Though the whole process of occupying land is 'illegal', the
rights of the various groups to the portions of land occupied
by them are scrupulously respected by other groups and once
an individual family has chosen a piece of land, nobody else
would encroach on it. There are rarely different claimants for
the same piece of land which may result in conflict. The
sharing, regulation of the allocation of parcels of land and
the 'self-legitimisation' of individual ownership rights of land
are made possible through the mechanism of homogeneous
social groupings of the urban poor. The dwellings are self-
built and individually owned but the ownership of land is
secured through the shared objective of the group and the
larger community of the poor guaranteeing the occupation of
land. The settlement as a physical entity exists only as a
community.

HOUSING AND SPATIAL ORGANISATION

The spatial structure of these settlements, which is closely related to the pattern of social organisation of the rural migrants, consolidates them as social and economic units. The overall physical pattern of these settlements that emerges thus depends on the serial composition of the inhabitants that comprise them. Since there are no premediated layouts to be followed by the inhabitants, they reproduce the physical form which they had in the village and the organisation of space indicates housing patterns that are found in the villages of the various regions of India. The frequency of any single pattern that occurs depends on the proportion of residents of any single region in these settlements. The settlements are thus formed spontaneously by their inhabitants and organised independently of public authorities.

Construction methods and use of housing are ingeniously adapted to minimum costs. Around 60 per cent of the households had dwelling units with walls of mud-mortar and rubble and a thatch roof or other material costing them from Rs 200 to Rs 400. However this type of housing is built when the migrant is in the stage of finding a foothold in the urban community. Location has priority at this stage which is sought nearest to the places of employment. A job and steady income are the main concern at this stage of settlement which, though it remains provisional, provides the initial stage for acculturation in the new urban environment. The migrant attaches little importance to housing amenities and during this period, his shelter takes care of the minimum needs of sleeping and storing of a few possessions. There is hardly any interest in improving the shelter or in the broader concerns of the community.

After a period of five to seven years, when he has secured more or less regular employment and a reasonable degree of security of tenure (in the sense that he does not expect to be evicted), he begins to invest in the construction of a better home, progressively, according to his own values of space and amenity and within his income. Forty per cent of the households reflect this tendency of investing Rs 800-2,000 in various types of improved housing. Once the urban poor have reasonable assurance of tenure, they view their community as their permanent home and not as a temporary shelter. The settlements become future-oriented and are perceived as offering sufficient incentives to the residents for their involvement in its development. The urban settlements for all their shortcomings and deprivations with regard to public services and community facilities are self-improving communities. The additions of an improved house, brick-paved roads, school, or hand-pumps provide new facilities and services where none had existed before.

A spatial organisation which provides for the communal use of space is effectuated by the existence of a coherent group life and value commitment to the joint ownership of the land of the settlement by the community as a whole. It also enables spontaneous settlements to achieve a high density of 400 to 600 persons per acre. The grouping of dwelling units and their accessibility to some common space thus become the governing factors in not only determining the use of space but also in regulating the range of social relationships between the families. It is in this sense that spatial social systems are integrated with each other, facilitating the accommodation of the varying needs of different families. In a situation where the availability of land to the urban poor for residential settlement is extremely difficult, they make use of the available space most intensively and efficiently by providing a high degree of spatial flexibility in accommodating various activities. The spatial configuration that thus evolves expresses a functional relationship between social needs and environmental forms.

In the absence of low-cost housing alternatives for the urban poor, the establishment of spontaneous settlements through self-built homes on illegally occupied lands is a rational response which corresponds to their needs for shelter, economic security and social status. The process also reflects a participatory approach in the formation of settlements and housing systems. First among the participatory modes that evolve in this process is the very act by which the urban poor come together to occupy the land on which they proceed to build their homes and create a community. In the face of great hostility by the public authorities and the fear of eviction, to establish a spontaneous settlement requires a collective decision involving voluntary participation and group solidarity which are vital to the success of the enterprise.

Generally speaking, the selection of the site, the timing of its occupation and preparations for settling and forestalling possible eviction are well planned. Where tenure to the land is uncertain, this perceived external threat serves as the single most important unifying force in the community. Success in establishing a community is the most tangible sign of the benefits that accrue to the people as a result of their collective efforts. It gives them a sense of being able to control their fate. Using the techniques of popular participation, the urban poor, in an effort to solve their housing problems, are in effect contributing to the solution of the problems of urbanisation. This form of self-help housing in spontaneous settlements is an important source of capital formation. The spontaneous settlements are formed as a response pattern of low income and under-privileged rural migrants to the process of urbanisation. They serve not only as entry points for the rural migrants to the city but also manifest the process by which population growth and social change are effected in the city under the circumstances of a highly inadequate allocation of resources for housing and social development.

PARTICIPATIVE PROCESS

It is evident from the foregoing analysis that the process of seeking shelter by the urban poor promotes a development-oriented self-image. Participation in establishing the spontaneous settlement gives its founders a sense of being able to shape their own physical and social environment. The image is further reinforced by building and improving their own shelter. Through such processes as self-help, mutual aid and community action, the inhabitants of the sponteneous settlements deal with a wide range of collective and individual problems that affect community improvement and individual betterment. The spontaneous settlement provides scope for traditional mutual aid activities which strengthen the development-oriented characteristics of the residents.

By moving into a settlement and building a house, the urban poor demonstrate a rational-instrumental view of the world rather than a fatalistic one. This is reflected in the disposition to defer immediate gratification, organise local institutions, trust in others and the readiness to assume moderate risks. These attributes correlate positively with a strong development outlook. By working co-operatively with others to improve their own lot and that of the community through a participative process, the inhabitants of these settlements improve their competence in dealing with the political and administrative authorities. The initial act of organising the settlement is generally significant in terms of its future development. It is during the formative phase that leadership comes to the fore and begins to assert itself; while both formal and effective power may centre in a single individual or a group, leadership is a key factor in promoting popular participation in settlements. The ability of local leaders to articulate and aggregate community demands, in a large measure influences the way the public authorities respond to these demands.

To find a place to live and survive in the city, demands of the poor a very high degree of initiative, ingenuity, tolerance and pragmatic co-operation. The spontaneous settlements of the urban poor are not merely aggregations of shacks and huts but communities of fellow migrants. Each is based on a network of primary affinities of language, region, village, caste or kin. It enables the rural migrants coming from small village communities to become socialised and acculturated in the complex and diversified environment of a metropolitan city. Traditional loyalties and obligations are essential references and it is these primary affinities which bring about the articulation of the rural social structure with the urban. This leads to the creation of a rural world in the city, the result of a functional relationship between the social needs of the urbanising poor, environmental forms and new settlement values.

The poor do not want to live permanently as they do now but their choices and opportunities to improve are limited. It is a conscious decision on their part to live as they do in the present by optimising the resources available to them. Their priorities go on changing all the time as their social situation improves. Within the constraints of their life in the city and the choices available within their resources, they are evolving new settlement values and with them a new type of settlement which is processual or incremental in its development. The essence of the emergence of the new society of the urbanising poor is that it is taking place through a coalescence of the traditional rural world and the modernising city. The new society, spontaneous as it is, opens up a new realm of vast resources and opportunities that are to be found in the constant interflow of cash, consumer goods, produce, life-styles and values between the city and the village. It is the spontaneous settlement, which is not only a participatory mode of settlement but a co-operative non-exploitative social order evolved through collective effort and sharing, that is giving shape to the evolution of a natural Indian city—a city which is rural and urban at the same time.

EMPLOYMENT PATTERNS

The relationships between the city and the urbanising poor are reciprocal. The rural migrants seek opportunities for social mobility through employment in urban-based occupations and the city in turn needs their labour. The jobs done by the urban poor provide the most important link for interaction with the wider urban society and also a new environment for enculturation in modern and urban values. The occupational roles of the urban poor have their structural concomitants which determine social relationships by bringing them into contact with multiple reference groups and enlarging the possibilities for both social and cultural mobility.

The urban poor are involved in diverse occupational roles. First, there are the unskilled and skilled construction workers. While some among them move back and forth between the city and their villages of origin, the majority stays on in the city moving from one construction site to another. In a growing city like Delhi, construction is a major industry and workers always find or hope to find work. Second, there are those employed in low paid jobs as unskilled workers, porters and loaders in the markets, shops and railway stations, rickshaw pullers, horse— and bullock-cart drivers, domestic servants, cooks and hawkers, and other miscellaneous service occupations requiring no specialised skills. Third, there are those engaged in public undertakings, Government and semi-Government agencies and private offices as peons, watchmen, other unskilled office workers, semi-skilled technical and service personnel. In the manual occupational categories are included those who work as mechanics, fitters, metal workers, scooter, bus and taxi drivers, electricians, plumbers, wiremen, moulders, painters, tailors and other manual occupations requiring some skill or vocational training. Fourth, there are hawkers, peddlers, wayside restaurant owners, vegetable and fruit sellers, grocers and other petty retail traders. Fifth, there are those engaged in traditional occupations and cultural trades as scavengers, leather workers, potters, carpenters, blacksmiths, basket-makers, weavers, doll-makers, washermen, barbers and others occupied in various household and cottage industries. Sixth, there are those employed in various industries and repair workshops as skilled, semi-skilled and unskilled workers. Lastly, there is a small proportion among the urban poor who are semi-professionals like compounders, midwives, school teachers and white-collar workers like clerks and accountants. Thus, the workers among the urbanising poor are integrated in the urban economy at the lower levels in the trade and labour-intensive service sectors. Nonetheless, they are all essential for the efficient functioning of the urban economy at its present stage of development and the use of technology. They can only be replaced at enormous additional cost to the city's economy.

The arrival of the rural migrant in the city is not due to a random search for employment but largely depends on the presence of friends, castemen, relations, fellow villagers or those from the neighbouring areas. Our study of Delhi revealed that 75 per cent of the workers among the urbanising poor had friends, relations, fellow villagers or those from the same region working in the city and it was through their assistance that they were able to get jobs in the city. Only about 6 per cent got jobs through employment exchanges while another 4 per cent found jobs through their own efforts. Recruitment to occupations in which the majority is employed does not take place by impersonal and institutional means but by informal methods.

Vacancies are mostly advertised by word of mouth and, therefore, territorial, kin, and caste affinities play a predominant role in the recruitment of workers to the urban labour force. Our study revealed that over 60 per cent of the workers were engaged in the same occupational categories as their relations, fellow villagers, castemen, friends or people from the same region. Fifteen per cent of the rural immigrants got jobs through the contractors. In the case of contract labour or labour recruited through similar methods (mostly construction labour), recruitment is through the *jamadars* (foremen) who procure labour from the regions to which they themselves belong and mainly from their own kin and caste groups. Thus, though migrants may move to the city individually, they are not among strangers but are supported by a network of social relations built on ties of kin, caste, regional affinities and friendship.

Our study of Delhi *bastis* revealed that about 46 per cent of the heads of the households were regularly employed: 19 per cent were working for twenty-six days or more in a month, 17 per cent for twenty-one to twenty-five days, 10 per cent for sixteen to twenty days and 8 per cent for less than fifteen days. Though 54 per cent of the heads of the households worked as casual labourers, a substantial proportion (about 30 per cent) of them had two or three casual jobs. It was found that on an average a casual worker got employment for 240-260 days a year, more than twice the working days they had in villages. Further, though their wages were low in the city, their average earnings over the year were two and a half times more than what they could earn in the rural areas.

CONSUMPTION PATTERNS

The average income of the *basti* settler in Delhi was Rs 61 per capita per month. This relatively high per capita income is due to the fact that among the urban poor the average family consists of 4.3 members with 1.6 earners per family. Most single earner families are concentrated in the income group of Rs 150 and below (constituting 34 per cent of the total number of households) where the majority of the households are of 1-2 member families. The disposable income available to the households is not the total sum contributed by the head of the household. On an average, another Rs 20 per capita per month is contributed by the additional earner to the per capita monthly income. It also needs to be emphasised that a large proportion (about 44 per cent) of *basti* households in the city are a part of families that remain in the villages. Therefore, in the case of these families a substantial proportion (about 30 per cent) of the earned income in the city is repatriated to their families in the village.

It is in this social context that the economic life of the urban poor has to be viewed. Among those who repatriate part of their income to the villages (9,240 households) the average disposable income is Rs 3.50 per day for an average household size of 2.8. Ninety-five per cent is spent on food and fuel and the remaining 5 per cent on transportation and occasional recreation. These are the families who live perpetually in debt and need credit and aid from kinsmen, relatives and friends. For the rest of the families, the disposable income available is Rs 11 on an average per day for an average household size of 5.4 members. Sixty-eight per cent of this income is spent on food, 4 per cent on fuel, 2 per cent on health care, 5 per cent on education, 6 per cent on clothing and 15 per cent on other items including transportation and recreation. There are other items which are not included in the regular family budget since these relate to occasional expenses. The occasional expenditures include those on ritual ceremonies, marriages, housing improvement or repairs. Expenses on these items are considered socially essential and are sometimes heavy enough to force them into debt. The purchase of the necessities of life is made on a daily basis, even among those who are regularly employed.

The urban poor pursue a dual strategy of maximising resources and minimising expenditures. Specifically, this entails several techniques: employment of the household labour force including children; dependence on kin, friends, castefolk and money-lenders and other people (generally employers) with resources for credit and aid in cash or kind; buying on credit from grocers, and small, less than standard quantities of retail goods; pawning possessions; and tolerating cheap, free or low quality of goods and services in food, health, housing utilities, clothing and transportation, education, recreation, etc. While these adaptive mechanisms enable the poor to cope with the present situation, certain negative costs are manifested in poor health and malnutrition, insufficient education for children, lack of training for acquiring skills, indebtedness to usurious money-lenders, insecurity of residence and a general absence of the amenities of life. Yet, for all this, they display a dogged determination to remain in the city. Despite their poverty, they continue to feel that Delhi will provide the hoped-for opportunity, if not for themselves, then at least for their children.

OCCUPATIONAL MOBILITY

The analysis of the occupational structure of the heads of households in relation to the duration of residence in the city will help to understand the nature of occupations new migrants enter and of the changes that take place as a result of greater exposure to city life. If such changes occur on a large scale, they appear to indicate occupational mobility among the urban poor. The effects of duration of residence on changes in the proportion of heads of households among the hawkers, vendors and petty traders and shop-keepers has increased with duration of residence. Over 65 per cent of them have been living in the city for over seven years. The same trend is noticeable among skilled construction workers, skilled manual workers, skilled industrial workers, semi-professionals and white-collar workers, where the proportion of those with residence of over twelve years range between a minimum of 53.5 per cent for skilled construction workers and the maximum of 16 per cent for semi-professionals. Among industrial workers, though unskilled, 63 per cent had been in the city for eight or more years. It is among the unskilled manual (miscellaneous occupations) and construction workers that we found that over 60 per cent of them had lived less than eight years in the city.

A comparison of the occupational structure in different time periods reveals that among those with two years or less of residence, the three occupational categories of unskilled construction, manual work and industrial labour accounted for 82 per cent of the heads of households while it was 55 per cent among those with over twelve years of residence. The proportion of heads of households in the occupational categories of hawkers, vendors, petty shop-keepers, skilled construction and manual workers, traditional trades and skills, skilled industrial workers, and semi-professionals was less than 16 per cent among those with two years or less of residence in the city whereas it is more than 45 per cent among those living in the city for more than eight years. It may seem that the occupational structure of the heads of households among the *basti* settlers is more or less static; but when it is seen over a period of time, a certain degree of change and mobility is discernible. The longer the duration of stay, the greater is the tendency to move out of unskilled and low paid jobs to self-employment or better paid and skilled jobs. Thus, with longer exposure to city life, a gradual improvement in the occupational status of the heads of households is noticeable. The improvement and changes observed in the occupational status among recent arrivals and those who had been for several years in the city, though not yet very extensive are significant, especially when we consider their impact on the children of the urban poor.

When we analyse the occupational structure of the various castes and communities, we find that there is considerable occupational diversification among them in spite of a tendency in the various caste and community groups to take up particular occupations. However, where the skill and educational levels are low, the choice of occupations is limited. Many high caste heads of households have taken to manual work and other low status occupations. The two most important occupations among the caste Hindus are petty trade and hawking and unskilled manual work. This change also represents a new attitude towards work. The lower and the Scheduled Castes who form the majority of the urban poor present an overall picture of change in their occupational status. Though they are still found clustered in the lowest status occupations consisting mostly of unskilled workers in industry, construction, miscellaneous manual work and low paid service occupations, the urban situation has led to changes from their traditional occupational pattern of agricultural labour to a wider network of occupational opportunities.

There is also considerable evidence of a strong motivation among the lower castes, to take up skilled jobs so that they can improve their social status. In the case of the Scheduled Castes, the majority of whom continues in the traditional occupations of scavenging and street sweeping, higher income has made an important difference since it enables them to imitate the life styles of better placed status groups. Thus, economic improvement also makes more visible their status vis-a-vis other caste and social groups in a multi-caste situation. Those engaged in traditional crafts and inherited skills do so for greater profit-ability and also become a part of the urban market system different from the village *jajmani* system of inter-related obligations and rights. The urban situation provides a wider spectrum and a secular axis for occupational choice and scope for a considerable degree of horizontal social mobility. Horizontal mobility within the same occupational status is thus becoming increasingly possible for the low caste groups, though vertical mobility as a movement from one stratum to another is still very limited.

In the closed system of village society, not only are occupa-tional roles limited but they are ascribed and embedded in kin, caste and community groups. Specialisation of tasks tends to be by households and social categories. The approach to recruitment to urban occupations is achievement-oriented and a given occupational role and its occupant are distinct and separable so that one can move from one occupation to another. However, due to lack of social capabilities, education and skills, the urban poor have only been able to enter low status occupations and social mobility has been very limited. But there have been considerable changes from one occupation to another at the same status level with the possibility of wider opportu-nities for learning new skills and earning higher incomes. This horizontal mobility should be seen as part of a process of upward social mobility through which backward and under-privileged social groups become aware of new opportunities and, with continued urban residence, are able to grasp. This process also enables them to achieve individual mobility which is only possible at the group level in the villages.

It is true that kinship, caste and regional affinities are no longer essential in determining the choice of occupation *per se*, but the personal obligation system helps to link together as many individuals as possible. Through a feedback process of linkages, the obligation system influences the recruitment of per-sonnel to various occupational categories so that, even under

persistent secular urban pressures, preferential access to employment opportunities are assured by kinship, regional, caste or
community ties. This suggests that both the traditional and
modern axes are operative in bringing about occupational
change and social mobility.

TYPOLOGY OP SOCIAL NETWORKS

The urban poor constantly move back and forth from
the world of association based on kinship, ethnic and regional
ties to participation in groupings which cut across such
affiliations, particularly in economic and occupational activities,
education and other social services. To understand this, one
must have a clear appreciation of two important networks of
contact and reciprocal relations which are at work. Family,
kinship, caste and regional ties are all constituted and bounded
by a small-scale social field which comes into existence to
meet the needs of those who form these groupings. The larger
scale field, the world of goods and services, of employment,
of mobility and change, of opportunity and failure, has a
different network of relations. These two social fields through
constant convergence and separation provide the basis of the
social life of the poor in the city.

What forms of groupings typically occur among the urban
poor? The concept of social network helps to chart the channels
of interaction between persons and the extent of regularities
which give a minimum of order to communities which, as
discrete groups, have no clear structure. Since more than 90
per cent of the urban poor are rural migrants, their community
as a whole resembles the village community since they bring
with them not only a network of relations but also corporate
institutions which make up the total structure of their rural
communities. However, the social network does not operate
as a replica of the social system of the village but rather
functions as an adaptive mechanism and as a guide to behaviour
and social identity to which even children are able to respond.

At the core of the social networks lie kinship relations, communal or regional affinities which link together large numbers
of individuals in several groups and introduce an element of
stability in a fluid situation. The basic social units comprise

small scale groups constituting fifteen to twenty-five families on the outside limit whether based on kinship, caste, village, religious or regional ties. These are the groups which function as units of effective relationships. The basis on which these groups are formed is increasingly becoming dependent more on personal choice than on conventional affinities, and although choice is still influenced by kinship, caste or village considerations, it is the mutuality of interests that conditions the choice.

The second type of grouping is larger, looser and somewhat more extensive than the first. However, it resembles the first type in that the bonds of solidarity are strictly based on social homogeneity characterised by caste, village, regional or religious identities. All those belonging to the same caste, region, religion or community are potential members, although only in a few instances do all those eligible actually become participants. It is a community of cognitive recognition and not so much of participation. These groupings function as resource bases for the constituent participants in the first type of grouping. Their functions are broadly the same as those of the first type but involve a larger number of individuals.

The third type of grouping found is that of caste *panchayats*, mainly the evolution of the second type of grouping in a structured form. The *panchayat* acts as a representative body for its members at the residential level and to the wider society.

The fourth type of grouping is based on common interests and is associational rather than ethnic, regional or communal in structure. The individual's involvement is voluntary. Having a formal structure in the sense that it has membership and officials, this type of association is still not popular with the urban poor and only 30 per cent among them belonged to these associations. The kinship, quasi-kinship and caste basis of relationships is supplemented by the association formed on the basis of relationally derived interests. These associations exist at the local residential level, at the zonal and city level. They are gradually emerging as surrogates of kinship, regional, caste and communal networks. The main functions of these associations are political, economic and developmental and they are used to mobilise community resources for the improvement of living conditions of the *basti* settlers. Another major role that these associations play is to provide collective security against eviction or the demolition of the *bastis* from the present sites. The associations also provide an institutional framework for the articulation of demands and rights of the inhabitants and thus link the *basti* community to the rest of urban society and through it to national institutions.

The fifth type of social network consists of loosely organised friendship groups based on reciprocal interests generally limited to four to six members. They are not based on ethnic or communal considerations but are voluntary. They function as small credit groups, recreation, card-playing or gambling groups, or they may be formed at work-places because of shared occupational interests. Most of these networks are transitory and only serve immediate or short-range needs.

Finally, there are at the city level large-scale regional associations, caste associations or *panchayats* like the Bhojpuri Samaj of those belonging to eastern U.P., Prajapati Samaj for potters, Dhobi *panchayats* for the washermen, Bhairvan Samaj for the Bhairvans of Rajasthan, the Balmiki Sangh and the Harijan Welfare Association for the Scheduled Castes, South Indian Workers Association for the South Indian workers in the city and many other associations representing various caste and regional interests with which the poor in the city can affiliate. Besides, the urban poor also participate in occupational associations and trade unions which are meant to promote the economic interests and employment prospects of those engaged in particular occupations. Participation in such unions is limited to construction labour, factory workers, domestic servants, and those employed in public agencies.

It is thus seen that the urban poor are involved in some kind of network of relations based on ties of kinship, caste, community or region. These networks emerge both by necessity as well as by choice since, excluded from the formal urban institutions, the poor need the security these networks offer. They provide social security in times of emergency, sickness and unemployment, secure shelter in the city, arrange for jobs, take care of relatives, disseminate news and provide information. They serve the purpose of providing access to credit, job training and sponsorship and of giving political power shape and meaning. While there are certain restricting features in the network of relationships based on particularistic affinities, in the highly complex situation of the city, these relations are transformed into active and useful associations. They enforce social control and provide security and familiarity, so that for the poor they are structures in which they can trust. It is the remoteness of secular urban institutions that reinforces the traditional ties of *basti* settlers.

Though the basic social networks keep the traditional form, they are modified by taking up the functions of voluntary and secondary groups. These networks also increasingly begin to depend upon the mutuality of interests of the constituent participants. On the other hand, the associations partake of some of the characteristics of kin and caste groups, as their function is to serve the needs of these groups. What does take place in this process is the widening of the base of institutional organisation in which, on the one hand, particularistic and narrow loyalties take on new forms of articulation, thus changing the very ethos of the social system by making it more secular and universalistic; on the other hand, more diverse forms and interest identification emerge, both of which contribute to increasing participation in the broader network of relationships. This enables those still submerged in the traditional society and culture to transcend the political illiteracy which would otherwise handicap their ability to participate in the larger urban community and gain access to its sources of power.

TYPES OF LEADERS

To understand the pattern of leadership among the *basti* settlers, it is important to recognise the varied contexts in which it operates. We have already analysed the organisation of social life and the pattern of groupings among the poor. All these groups have a stable core whose participants change but slowly, and when they do, they are replaced by others with similar characteristics. These groups form the social base of the leadership structure. The leaders that emerge at various levels of groupings are tied to the particular problems and conditions of that group and the amount of support they can

muster from the urban society or local community in handling
the varied and complex problems that arise in the course of
urban living. The authority of the leaders and the way they
exercise their influence are also confined within the specific
context of groups at different levels.

First, there emerge what can be called 'grassroots' leaders
who are drawn from the different kin-cum-caste or village
based social groups whose members reside together in compact
areas in the various *bastis*. Such leaders draw their strength
from traditional mutual bonds that exist between them and
other members of the groups. Recruitment to this type of
leadership role, though based on traditional principles is not
strictly ascribed, and is achieved by consensus and acceptance
by the members of the group.

The second stratum of leaders is found at the level of larger
groupings of a single caste, religion or region whose members
may or may not form a compact spatial unit in the *bastis*. These
leaders may be drawn from the leaders of the small groups
at the dwelling cluster level or may be in close touch with
them. Leadership at this level is not confined to a single
individual but consists of a few individuals. If there exist
formalised caste *panchayats* in the *bastis*, their members are
regarded as leaders of the caste or community groups. They
generally consist of a council of six to eight members and are
elected democratically or through implicit acceptance on the
basis of consensus by the members of the concerned caste
community.

Even among the castes among whom *panchayats* are formed,
leadership exists outside them. In both cases, leadership depends
upon the support and allegiance that it can muster from the
leaders of the primary groups. It may however be mentioned that
solidarity of the caste or community group is structured into a
diffuse network of various segments of the caste depending
upon its numerical strength. Therefore, the leadership of
a single caste group consists of leaders of the various segments
of the caste although they share in the corporate power of
the entire caste. Another aspect of the caste leaders is that,
unlike what happens in primary groups, the mobilisation of
group support follows rather than precedes. The leadership
roles at the level of regional groupings are patterned in the

same manner as those of the caste or community groupings. The leaders of the regional groupings are drawn from the caste leaders and the strength of the leaders of regional groupings depends upon the alignment of caste leaders. As in the case of caste group leaders, the leadership consists of few individuals, but it is much more broad-based.

There are also a few leaders whose social base is secular, cutting across caste, community and regional alignments, and who have influence over the entire community of the *basti*. In the settlements where the associations exist, they are democratically elected by the members. The emergence of such leaders depends on the support and acceptance they get from the various regional and caste group leaders, and this largely depends on the influence that they command with government officials, local authorities and political parties or inter-settlement associations in securing benefits of various kinds for the inhabitants of the *bastis*.

Leadership among the urban poor is thus not only variegated, but depends on the complex structure of its social base. However, in all cases, except that of the leaders of the small groups, it is still undeveloped and dispersed with the result that the effectiveness of leaders in social mobilisation and group action is confined to a limited numbers of families. The bases of leadership support and organisation are still segmented rather than collective. In such a situation, the leadership structure articulates the special interests of homogeneous segments and, through them, the interests of the local community as a whole are expressed.

FUNCTIONS OF LEADERS

The functions of the leaders of the small social groups at the residential unit level relate to the maintenance of the internal unity of the group and the continuity of on-going inter-relationships between the members of the groups. The effectiveness and the acceptance of the leadership role depends upon the ability to solve the problems the group faces. These involve helping the members to get a ration card, employment, giving them credit, securing shelter and services and other benefits from government officials, local authorities and leaders of the *panchayat*. They must be able to manipulate the world external to the group to its advantage. They also have to act as communication channels for the group whom they represent to outsiders in all matters.

The leaders in the caste, community or regional groupings serve as mechanisms for mobilising support and collective action to secure maximum benefits, allocation of resources and social power within the settlements. By enlarging the effective range of relationships based on caste, regional, or community lines, these leaders impart an associational framework to these groups through which they can bargain or negotiate with government officials and political leaders in securing social and economic advantages and facilities to improve the living conditions of their particular groups in the settlements. The effectiveness of these leaders lies not only in the internal integration of their caste, regional or community groups, but also more importantly through an external integration of these groups in the more inclusive field of opportunities, facilities, services, economic prospects and social development in the urban community at large. The caste and regional group leaders perform all services similar to those of primary group leaders but for a larger number of individuals. If they fail to manipulate the urban system in resolving some of the problems of the groups they represent, their position is relegated to a nominal and ceremonial role.

The functions of leaders at the community level as informal leaders or office-bearers of formal associations mainly consist of obtaining basic amenities and services for the settlement, securing permanent tenure of the land occupied and in promoting the improvement of the living conditions of the *basti* through lobbying with local authorities and other agencies. One of the important and primary functions is that of preventing the demolition or 'clearance' of the *bastis*. They also perform functions similar to those performed by leaders of primary caste or regional groups, but for the community as a whole and not for particular segments of it.

Leaders at all levels promote group or community improvement organisations and provide important psychological support to the urbanising poor when they make demands on public authorities. Participation in collective demand-making greatly reduces the individual's initiative and provides the *basti* settler with a clear strategy for articulating his needs and influencing the behaviour of government decision-makers. Moreover, to the extent that community-based organisations are successful in securing benefits through the collective presentation of demands they strengthen the *basti* settlers' perception of the political system as being vulnerable to manipulation and increase the sense of political efficacy. Such attitudes and perceptions increase the propensity to engage in collective demand-making.

SOCIO-ECONOMICS CHARACTERISTICS OF LEADERS

We attempted to locate leaders in individual spontaneous settlements, where the 21,000 families surveyed lived, by finding out to whom people turned for help and problem-solving, whose judgment was respected, who took the initiative in doing things for the community, and who were involved in decision making, organisational participation and social mobilisation. On the basis of these criteria, 250 leaders were identified, comprising those at the primary, regional, and caste group levels and at the settlement community level of participation. A majority of these leaders functions at larger and more inclusive levels of participation. We analysed their socio-economic characteristics and important leadership traits.

The leaders belonged to higher income groups among the poor, the average income of the leader being Rs 261 as against the average income of Rs 149 of the heads of households. Sixty-six per cent of the leaders belonged to the occupational categories of skilled manual or industrial workers, shop-keepers and petty businessmen, and semi-professionals. Only 34 per cent were engaged as unskilled workers. Twenty-eight per cent of the leaders had high school and more education whereas 47 per cent of them were educated up to middle school. Only 25 per cent of them were illiterate. Forty-two per cent of the leaders were thirty-five years or less while only 24 per cent were more than forty-five years of age. The rest belonged to the age group thirty-six to forty-five years. Sixty-five per cent of the leaders had lived in the city for more than fifteen years. Fifty-four per cent of the leaders were Scheduled Castes, 35 per cent caste Hindus belonging to artisan and cultivating castes, and the rest were Muslims and Sikhs. The leaders were more or less equally spread over the various regions from where the *basti* settlers come except in the case of Uttar Pradesh which contributed 41 per cent of the leaders.

It can be seen from the analysis of the socio-economic characteristics of the lead   that education, income and occupation are considered important attributes for recruitment to leadership since these qualities enhance the range of interaction, participation and communication with urban institutions. These attributes help the leaders in manipulating the urban conditions and in mustering support from the various segments of the power structure, both of which are necessary to fulfil problem-solving functions. Greater experience and understanding of the working of complex urban institutions and their involvement in the urban socio-economic system helps the leaders in their negotiations with government officials, local authorities, political leaders and outsiders for securing benefits for the urban poor as well as dealing effectively with the problems that arise in the process of adjustment to urban life. This comes with longer and continued residence in the city.

It was observed that an increasing proportion of leaders belonged to higher income groups, had better occupational positions and educational status and longer duration of residence in Delhi. A majority of them came from the younger age groups. Caste and regional affinities as criteria for determining leadership roles are losing their hold in a multi-caste and multi-regional environment. Income, occupation, education and length of residence are very important considerations in the choice of leaders even among particularistic groups based on kin, caste, regional and communal ties. The leaders tend to develop such traits as propensity to plan for the future, a capacity to project one's self into social or political roles of other people (empathy), a felt need for achievement, a sense of control over one's environment (opposite of fatalism) and a tendency to take risks in order to achieve desired goals. All these traits are regarded as indicators of attitudinal modernity. The leaders generally possessed a high level of trust in people and a strong preference for working collectively.

SOCIAL CHANGE

Since the urbanising poor are overwhelmingly rural migrants, the study of the patterns of social change is concerned with what happens to people steeped in the values and social organisation of the village community when they encounter the economic, social and cultural order in a metropolitan city. Although sociologically speaking, the urbanising poor are creating a new society at the interface of the traditional-rural and modernising-urban, for a substantial proportion of them, it involves changes in many spheres of life. They find themselves in an urban occupational environment where modifications in values and behaviour are required by the inherent demands of the situation. Since they live in an interacting system, the multiplicity of reference groups induces changes in the value system, aspirations and styles of life of the *basti* settlers.

Occupational Choice

The new economic opportunities offered by the city provide a wide range of occupational choices that represent a shift from traditional to non-traditional occupations. The occupations available to the urban poor are not only varied but also removed from the context of kin, caste and community. This is particularly true for Scheduled and lower castes, forming a large majority of the poor in the city whose occupational choices in the village society are not only limited but also fixed. Although a significant number among them continue to pursue traditional occupations, they do so for greater profitability and higher incomes. On the other hand, a large number among them have taken to other occupations which was not possible in the village community. This applies to all other castes and communities to whom alternative opportunities and work situations are now available, if they have the required skills. Thus, continuity of traditional occupations persists together with occupational change. The important point to be borne in mind in this context is that ascribed status is not accepted as a conditioning fact of social life and this new element of choice becomes part of the emerging scheme of values.

Self-concept

The study of attitudes towards themselves and their society held by those at the lower job levels, showed that about 63 per cent of them emphasised personal worthiness and considered themselves equal to the other members of society. They, however, rated themselves as belonging to the lower class (the concept of caste for positional evaluation was only confirmed by 37 per cent of the respondents) in terms of income, occupation, education and skills. They were also aware that the prestige of work in which they are engaged is considered low by the urban society at large, though they also emphasised that their labour makes a significant contribution to the efficient functioning of the urban economy. Only 37 per cent had a poor self-image, considering themselves to be powerless and without any opportunity for the good things in life. Yet, a large majority among the urban poor felt that there are new openings for the under-privileged and the overall attitude was one of confidence in their own future and that of their children.

Future Orientation

In the light of their past experience, how do the urban poor view their present and future prospects? Our study revealed that a large majority (57 per cent) considered their life in the city preferable to what it was in the village, because of better education opportunities, transportation and communication, better medical services, more jobs and better wages, more freedom and greater equality. More work, employment opportunities and higher incomes were cited as the most important indicators of improved conditions of life in the city. About 15 per cent of the respondents saw no difference in their situation and 28 per cent considered their situation to have worsened when compared to the past. The reasons advanced for this view were bad housing and environmental conditions, insecure employment, family separation, hard work to earn a living, job competition, less respect, and the high cost of living.

Taking all things into account, how do the *basti* settlers see their future? Sixty-three per cent were hopeful about the future but about 20 per cent were unable to say in what ways the future would be better. About 80 per cent thought about their future prospects in terms of secure employment for themselves, better educational and occupational opportunities for their children, higher social and economic development, better environmental conditions and housing, further development in government welfare and services, greater political power. Only 10 per cent did not believe that the future would be different from the present, whereas 27 per cent thought the future would be worse. The reasons cited for this included unemployment, fewer opportunities for education of their children, more crime, higher cost of living, greater inequality and the worsening of housing and environmental conditions.

The *basti* settlers, though poor, have improved their conditions since incomes have increased over time and it is because of this that they are not generally fatalistic about the future but believe they have some influence in shaping the direction of their life in the city. This future-oriented outlook is underscored by the widespread tendency among the urban poor to save money wherever possible, secure better educational opportunities for their children, and improve their homes. What seems to be crucial is that they consider themselves important to and valued by society.

Family

The family pattern and value-system found among the urbanising poor act as counterforces to environmental degradation and poverty. The family extends beyond the individual unit, being a part of a cohesive, small social group having a homogeneous socio-cultural system. Everything outside this group is seen as a means to its survival in the city. The structure and form of this group is increasingly changing. With a marked tendency towards nuclearisation of families, the network of relationships in these groups revolves round the norms of reciprocity of interests in such a manner that the members of the group subserve the needs of each other. As a part of a group, the family functions as a problem-solving entity, as a mechanism of adaptation to the values of the urban situation and enhances accessibility to urban resources and benefits by providing social stability. Of course, the groups are still based on primary affinities, since it is within this framework that they can be operationally effective. Thus, the orientation and value framework of the urban poor is not so much related to the maintenance of traditional obligations but to the rational ordering of these relationships to meet the mutual needs of the group and deal effectively with the problems that arise in the process of being urbanised.

Changing Life-styles

The process of cultural change that is taking place among the urbanising poor is seen in their changing life-styles, particularly so among the Scheduled and lower castes. This happens through the emulation of the way of life of the more urbanised and better-placed social groups. Since the urban poor live in the context of a multiplicity of social groups, it is not that the way of life of a particular group is imitated, but the reference model comprises many social groups with which they come into contact in the city. The cultural change consists of change in dress, food habits, rituals, vocabulary, material culture, customs and mode of travel and type of conveyance. Factory-made textiles, ready-made garments, terylene shirts and nylon sarees have replaced home-spun and home-made clothes. Women do not make clothes, professional tailors do the job. The mode of dress has changed considerably, trousers and shirts are becoming popular among the men.

Commercial restrictions between the different castes have been relaxed considerably. Tea and soft drinks are commonplace. Small restaurants like *dhabas* and tuck-shops are being used in the same way the better-placed social groups use the tea and coffee houses and better quality restaurants. Lower caste people are adopting the rituals of the upper castes. Bicycles not only form a part of material culture but have also become a popular mode of conveyance. Public transport such as buses and rickshaws are also used. Kerosene stoves, transistors, wrist-watches, aluminium utensils and crockery are increasingly becoming part of the material possessions of the *bast* dwellers.

The significance of these changes in life-styles could be

interpreted as the attempts of the urban poor, who are at the bottom of the status hierarchy, to realise their social and economic aspirations through non-institutional means. It is not so much the extent of actual improvement achieved in the living conditions that matters but the orientation towards change and development. It may be considered as an initial phase of modernisation which, though manifested in the imitation of the life-styles of higher status groups, may lead to greater social and economic mobility, educational achievement, the learning of modern skills and developmental innovations.

Emerging Values

An aspect of the social situation of the urbanising poor is that in the city they live in the midst of a tremendous information system. The various mass media of communication popularise development programmes that are being undertaken to improve the living conditions of underprivileged social groups, the changes that are taking place in the world outside the social context of the *basti* and the whole gamut of new conceptions and values of life. Because of their exposure to the mass media of communication, the urbanising poor absorb these new ways of life through their traditional social patterns.

The democratic pattern of the polity and the corresponding ideal of social equality have percolated to every segment of the poor and have become part of the texture of their social life. The idea of one man one vote has given them a new sense of personal worth and the recognition that even the *basti* settler is as important as anybody else for the functioning of society. The fact that his vote counts in determining the composition of power structure has tremendously enhanced the position of the urban poor as part of a collectivity of the similarly placed persons vis-a-vis other social groups. The increasing politicisation of the urban poor has contributed to their greater integration in the larger urban society.

The urbanising poor as a community of rural migrants stand at the cross-roads of two value-systems, the folk-traditional and the modern. The folk-traditional system of values emphasises social stability, continuity, commitment to normative standards of behaviour; the modern system stands for the values of secularism, functional differentiation, innovation and development. The direction of change is determined by reference models, both traditional and modern, with whom the urban poor interact as they seek to make new lives for themselves and for their children. This will largely depend upon their participation in the common resources and values of the emerging society and its culture.

The urban poor—the hardest working and poorest paid people—can and often do constitute the most important political mass as well as the most significant element in social change. But how their energies and strengths are used will depend on how extensively the process of change is politicised. Just as the strategy of rural development advocates appropriate technologies to meet the twin objectives of increased productivity and labour-intensive employment, so too can planners adopt realistic strategies for urban development. The urban poor have a right to share in the monetary and technical resources so readily available to more affluent sections. As the government initiates development programmes for the rural poor, it is only fair that the urban poor should also be the focus of greater attention and concern, since the unorganised or informal sector of the economy can and does contribute positively to the overall urban economy. Only when urban planners recognise this fact will they be able to tackle effectively the complex relationship one observes between urbanisation and poverty in India and other less developed countries.

4

Women and the Family: Coping with Poverty in the *Bastis* of Delhi

Andrea Menefee Singh

The problem of urban poverty has been explored from many different perspectives, yet most studies in the past have depended on data collected from the household head who, in a large majority of cases, is male. This paper[1] focuses on the central role of women in the family, their responses to conditions of absolute poverty, and the ways in which they adapt and cope with these conditions. There are many dimensions to urban poverty, and the choice of focus understandably depends on the professional orientation and goals of those conducting the study. Thus, we find planners and architects concerned with the cost and utility of housing, labour experts concerned with the role of the informal sector in a modernising urban economy,

[1] I am grateful to the Department of Social Welfare, Ministry of Education and Social Welfare, Government of India, for providing the funding for this research project. The responsibility for the facts stated, opinions expressed, and conclusions reached, however, is entirely that of the author and not of the Department of Social Welfare. I would also like to express my deep gratitude to my research assistants, Sujit Deb, Padmaja Kelkar, and Poonam Narain for their contributions in carrying out the fieldwork, and to Alfred de Souza, who served as Project Director and whose collaboration and support have been invaluable. Doranne Jacobson's comments on an earlier version of this paper were most helpful. The research project was carried out in association with the Indian Social Institute.

and so forth. It is revealing, however, that most such studies
ignore almost entirely the needs and priorities of women and
the family. This is so despite the fact that females make up
nearly half of the population of the urban poor, and the institution of the family, as in other social strata, continues to
provide the underlying basis for their settlement and social
organisation. In India, one of the special characteristics of
urbanisation is that the different values and life-styles of
different social groupings based on kinship, caste, religion and
region of origin influence the migrant's adaptation to the urban
situation in many important ways. These social and cultural
variations thus form a central theme of this discussion, as
indeed they should in any sociological study of migration and
urbanisation in India.[2]

In the following pages, an effort is made to bring out the
consequences of poverty for women and the family, the strategies women employ for coping with these conditions, and
their basic needs and priorities. Throughout, I have attempted
to indicate the policy and programme implications of the
findings for integrated urban development. First, the setting
of the study is described, the extent to which this physical
environment can be manipulated for social ends, and the
consequences of this harsh environment for women and the
family. Next, patterns of migration, kinship networks, and
family structure are discussed, followed by the allocation of
roles and decision-making within the family. This is followed
by a fairly extensive description of the employment and income
of women in the *bastis* (squatter settlements) and a discussion
of health and nutrition (which can be considered a measure of
the impact of poverty on the family). Finally, the women's
hopes for the future and their links to the wider community
are discussed in an effort to present a realistic picture of their
most immediate concerns and the existing channels of
communicating these concerns to the wider society.

[2]For a discussion of the significance of these traditional identities
and nodalities on the neighbourhood life of middle class migrants to
Delhi, see Andrea Menefee Singh, *Neighbourhood and Social Networks in
India*, Marwah, New Delhi, 1976.

SETTING

The present paper is based on a study of women in four unauthorised squatter settlements (*bastis*) in New Delhi which was carried out between April 1975 and January 1976. Along with approximately 600,000 other squatters, these people have since been shifted to resettlement areas on the outskirts of Delhi. However, the problems and processes discussed herein remain relevant to an understanding of the urban poor. The four *bastis* included in the study were selected for the range of caste and regional backgrounds of their migrant populations, and also for the variety of occupations in which women were employed.[3] Let us refer here to these squatter settlements as Pallanpur, Devendrapur, Kaharpur and Hassanpur.[4]

Pallanpur was the largest *basti* included in the study with 252 families and a population of 1,193. Founded twenty years ago, it was located on a narrow strip of public land bordering a housing colony for upper level Government employees. Ninety per cent of the household heads in this *basti* had migrated to Delhi from the far-off State of Tamil Nadu, and the vast majority (84 per cent) belonged to the untouchable caste of Pallans, formerly landless labourers. Pallanpur was physically the most highly developed *basti* included in the study, with roughly 40 per cent of the structures *pakka* (i.e., brick and cement plastered walls with asbestos roofing), brick-paved lanes, and at least a dozen vegetable plots individually cultivated behind the *basti*. The municipality had provided three public

[3]The *bastis* included do not represent a random sample of *bastis* in Delhi, having for example, a much higher representation of Tamil migrants and lower representation of U.P. migrants compared to Delhi as a whole, and also a somewhat higher proportion of working women, especially domestic workers. For a good description of the squatter situation in Delhi in the early 1970s, see the Town and Country Planning Organisation study cited later (fn. 7) and also the article by Majumdar in this book.

[4]*Bastis* in Delhi are generally named after a nearby road, residential colony, or some other important marker. In order to protect the identity of the *bastis* included in the study and also to facilitate the reader's identification of the group under discussion, however, I have chosen here to give the *bastis* pseudonyms based on the name of the major caste group in each *basti*.

taps for safe water supply and two sets of public latrines, while the people themselves had planted dozens of trees and vines for shade, fruit, and the production of fodder for the goats which were kept by about 10 per cent of the families. The social organisation of this *basti* was highly integrated, with social, political and religious structures overlapping considerably. This was possible, at least in part, because of the unusually homogeneous population of the *basti*.

Devendrapur was only seven years old although most of the residents had lived in Delhi for at least fifteen years, moving to this *basti* from other nearby squatter settlements which had been demolished. It was also the smallest *basti* in the study with only fifty-five families and a population of 232. Situated on public land near a school and an upper level government housing colony, twenty-seven of the household heads (49 per pent) were Tamil, and twenty-five were Pallan. All of the other households in this *basti* were North Indians: twelve of these were untouchable Balmiki (sweeper) households, seven were Rajput, and the rest were caste Hindus (i.e., not untouchables) from Uttar Pradesh. The Tamil Pallans in Devendrapur were well-organised with a temple and an informal *panchayat*,[5] but, falling just short of a majority in the *basti*, they did not dominate the social and religious life of Devendrapur to the same extent as the Pallans did in Pallanpur. The North Indian population was too heterogeneous, however, to develop a comparable level of religious or political organisation, and thus usually had to defer to the South Indians in major political decisions. Devendrapur was not as well developed as Pallanpur in terms of housing structures and lanes, but also had more open space and room for expansion due to its recent origins. Although a latrine and two safe water taps had been provided by the corporation, disputes between the North Indians and South Indians developed frequently over their use. Both water taps were situated within the Tamil section of the *basti* and the latrines

[5]The *panchayat* is literally a council of five but may in reality include any number of recognised leaders who meet to discuss local issues and problems. The formation of local *basti panchayats* has been encouraged by local politicians and officials who are reluctant to act on petitions presented by individuals.

near the North Indian section, and both groups sought to exercise control over these facilities.

Kaharpur was basically a Central Indian *basti* with most of its residents having migrated to Delhi from Madhya Pradesh, Rajasthan, and Maharashtra. There were 111 households and a population of 583. The *basti* was first established twelve years ago, but it had twice been demolished and rebuilt in the interim. The majority of the families (58 per cent) belonged to the Kahar caste and had migrated from Madhya Pradesh. In the villages, Kahars traditionally work as boatmen, water carriers, water chestnut cultivators, and domestic servants for the upper castes; in Delhi, in fact, the term Kahar has come to be used as a synonym for domestic servant regardless of specific caste identity, because of this traditional association. There were also sixteen Rajasthani Dhobi families (traditionally launderers), nine Neo-Buddhist families from Maharashtra, five Muslim families from U.P., and a sprinkling of other service castes, mainly from U.P.

Kaharpur was located on public property on the edge of a *nallah* (open drain) next to a housing colony for middle level Government employees. The terrain was very uneven and generally lower than the surrounding areas so that flooding was a major problem during the rains. Since the public latrines were located between the *basti* and the *nallah*, floods would wash excreta down into the *basti* along with other wastes, creating a serious health hazard. There was one public water tap and a hand-pump located within the *basti*. Kaharpur gave the impression of being randomly settled because of its many dead-ends and internal cul-de-sacs, but this actually represented an intentional pattern of settlement which functioned both to express and reinforce the major social divisions within the *basti* by limiting physical access to caste clusters and thereby social interaction. Religious events were celebrated and caste-specific disputes were usually settled within these caste clusters, while the official *basti panchayat*, which included representatives from all of the major caste groups, dealt mainly with outside representations and the occasional issues of concern to the entire *basti* community.

Hassanpur was different from the other *bastis* included in the study in that it included three distinct housing clusters which had been settled at different points in time, the first one being

nearly fifteen years old. Situated on the edge of a large and
relatively new upper class residential area, it had eighty-seven
households and a population of 380. Cluster 1 was dominated
by Muslims who had migrated from U.P., but also included a
number of Hindus of different castes from U.P., including seven
families of U.P. Dhobis. A few Muslim families also
occupied some huts in Cluster 2 immediately adjacent to Cluster
1, but they were constructed in such a way that they faced away
from the rest of the huts in Cluster 2 which were occupied by
Rajasthani Berwas, an untouchable caste of leather-workers and
landless labourers. Cluster 3, like Cluster 2, was also dominated
by Rajasthani Berwas, but had two small sub-clusters attached
to it. One of these sub-clusters was occupied by four Balmiki
households from U.P., and the other by different Hindu castes
from U.P., most of whom worked as *malis* (gardeners) in nearby
schools and residences. Altogether then there were twenty-one
Muslim households, eighteen Berwa households, seven U.P.
Dhobi households, and the rest of the forty-one households
were occupied by other Hindu castes, none of which had more
than four families resident in the *basti*. Hassanpur had the fewest
facilities of all *bastis* included in the study. There were two
hand-pumps, one located in Cluster 1 and the other in Cluster
3, but no latrines or water tap at all. As in Devendrapur and
Kaharpur, the heterogeneity of the *basti* presented certain
obstacles to the development of integrated political and religious
structures. The *basti panchayat* was dominated by Muslims of
Cluster 1 and the Berwas of Clusters 2 and 3 could not seem to
find many grounds for co-operation.

PHYSICAL ENVIRONMENT AND ITS SOCIAL CONSEQUENCES

As the preceding description suggests, the settlement of *bastis*
is not a haphazard process but involves a good deal of
social manipulation of physical space. This manipulation may
strengthen or limit social interaction in many important
ways. Families of dominant castes clustered together in such
a way as to largely exclude interaction with minority castes,
except for the minimal interaction brought about by the
necessity of sharing public facilities. One of the consequences

of this was that families belonging to minority groups in the *basti* had little recourse to social support in time of need and practically no power or influence in local political matters. But the amount of control that *basti* dwellers can exercise over their environment is limited. The physical environment of the *basti* is otherwise harsh and presents many obstacles to growth and development, especially when compared to the planned areas of the city. The most obvious disparity is in the gross inadequacy of public utilities and services.

The few hand-pumps and water taps found in these *bastis* had to supply water to all of the households for their basic domestic chores such as cooking, washing, cleaning, and bathing, and were clearly inadequate for meeting the needs of the population they were meant to support. Some household chores could be carried out at the water source itself, but several gallons of water a day still had to be carried back to the *jhuggi* (hut) and stored. This was normally done by the woman of the household (sometimes assisted by her children), and often required waiting in lines for a considerable amount of time. Even where public latrines were present, they were inevitably overloaded and poorly maintained, thus becoming health hazards themselves rather than promoting a hygienic environment.

The scarcity of water and facilities in the *basti* for bathing also affected social relations. The Muslim women in Hassanpur sometimes constructed small walls behind their *jhuggis* in order to bathe in privacy, but officials tore them down as soon as they came to their notice. Their only alternative was to bathe within the *jhuggi* itself, creating damp and unhealthy conditions since most of their *jhuggis* had only mud floors. Women of other caste groups, however, were accustomed to bathing publicly (fully clothed, of course, discreetly changing into a fresh *sari* afterwards without exposing themselves). These different bathing customs ended up being a source of antagonism between the Muslims and Berwas in Hassanpur since the Muslim men also bathed at the same hand-pump in the evenings when working Berwa women needed to use the facilities. The two groups were unable to reach a compromise over the use of the hand-pump since the Muslims at any rate considered it inappropriate and immodest for women to bathe in the open. Eventually, the Berwa women resorted to carrying water from other more distant public taps for their bathing and household needs.

None of the *bastis* had covered drains, and as a result refuse and children's excreta would collect, attracting flies, and becoming a natural source of infection and disease. The total absence of electricity and lighting facilities in the *bastis* meant that school children either had to do their homework outside in public spaces during the day or in the evenings under street lights. Such an environment obviously put these children at a tremendous disadvantage in school, no matter how highly they were motivated.

There were also special problems related to the housing itself. As the record of repeated *basti* demolition experienced by these people suggests, there was no security of land tenure. The initial investment in building or buying a *jhuggi* which had mud-plastered brick walls and a thatched roof ranged from Rs 300 to Rs 600,[6] a large sum of money for these people to get together at one time. In cases where there was a reasonable security of tenure, as in Pallanpur, the *basti* dwellers themselves gradually improved on their environment and dwellings over time. *Basti* demolition, however, wipes out the initial *jhuggi* investment entirely and requires a whole new investment. This results in mounting indebtedness and less adequate housing than would otherwise have been possible. Consequently, the vast majority of *jhuggis* in the *bastis* studied provided only minimal shelter from the heat, the rain, and the cold of Delhi's extreme climate.

The high cost of even this minimal housing relative to their income meant that families had to live in the smallest possible space, even where a low density of population might otherwise have permitted building more spacious quarters as in Devendrapur. The average *jhuggi* had one room measuring approximately 10'x15' which provided shelter, living space, and storage for an average of 4.7 people, and sometimes one or two goats as well. It is not surprising, therefore, that a very large portion of the daily chores and activities of the family were carried outdoors. This style of living, involving as it does frequent and extensive

[6]The estimated minimum cost of approved housing in the resettlement areas is around Rs 1,500-2,000. Resettled squatters were also required to pay a monthly rent of Rs 8-9 for the plots they were given.

face-to-face interaction and little privacy obviously requires a considerable amount of co-operation and social control. Thus, it could be particularly straining for those minority groups whose customs, beliefs, and values differ from those of their neighbours.

In the sections which follow, I shall focus on the dynamics of family life of squatters as revealed by interviews with 161 adult women (i.e., women fifteen years and older) who were selected by random sample from the 596 adult women residing in the four *bastis* described.

MIGRATION, KINSHIP NETWORKS AND FAMILY STRUCTURE

People who take up residence in squatter settlements are generally people of rural origin and low socio-economic status who have been forced by economic circumstances to look beyond the village for a means to support their family.[7] When we asked the women in our sample why they had left the village, 81 per cent replied that they had left because they could not support themselves or their families in the village. The majority said that this was because of adverse agricultural conditions (e.g., drought) or that there was simply no work available in the village. More than half chose Delhi as their destination, however, because they had relatives, friends or caste-fellows who were also migrating or who already lived in Delhi. At the time of interview, in fact, 92 per cent of the women reported having kin living in Delhi other than those included in their own household. Thus, it can be seen that while economic factors influence the decision to migrate, the ties of kinship, caste and village exercise a strong influence in

---

[7]A similar conclusion was reached by T.K. Majumdar and his colleagues in their macro-study of squatter settlements in Delhi, *Jhuggi Jhonpri Settlements in Delhi: A Sociological Study of Low-Income Migrant Communities*, Part II, mimeo.; Town and Country Planning Division, Ministry of Works and Housing, Government of India, 1975, New Delhi, p. 12. Majumdar stresses social as well as economic reasons for migration, but does not distinguish clearly between reasons for leaving the village and reasons for choosing to come to Delhi as opposed to some other place.

shaping the direction of migration streams from the village to the city.

Extended kinship ties are particularly important to women in the city, for there is a strong reluctance among them to form close friendships with those who are not related by kinship or marriage. Unlike the village situation, however, where the members of a married woman's natal family would normally live in another village, in Delhi these categories of kin were almost as likely to reside in the same *basti* as were the members of her husband's descent group (e.g., HB, HF, HM). In fact, it was found that 41 per cent of the women's own kin living in Delhi resided in the same *basti* as the respondent. This compared to 48 per cent of the kin from the husband's descent group and 62 per cent of the husband's other kin (especially his sister) who would also normally reside elsewhere after marriage. There was also no difference in the frequency of women meeting with their own kin and with their husband's kin (women reported meeting 44 per cent of both categories of kin on a daily basis). Thus, the *basti* setting appeared to provide a setting for the intensification of the extended kinship group beyond what would normally be expected to occur in the village setting.[8] These kinship ties provide valuable friendship and psychological support to women and the family in addition to other more tangible benefits. It is through these networks, for example, that people living in *bastis* generally find jobs, a place to stay in Delhi, help in an emergency, and even loans for such things as starting a business or constructing a *jhuggi*.

[8]There is some evidence that there is considerably more intra-village marriage and migration to villages where the wife's kin or husband's sister reside among low caste groups, especially untouchables in both North India and South India than among upper castes. These urban settlement patterns therefore may not reflect a radical departure from rural traditions, but rather a common response to poverty or crisis situations. See, for example, Bernard S. Cohn, 'The Changing Status of a Depressed Caste', in McKim Marriott (ed.), *Village India*, University of Chicago Press, Chicago, 1955; Kathleen E. Gough, 'Caste in a Tanjore Village', in E.R. Leach (ed.), *Aspects of Caste in South India, Ceylon and North-West Pakistan*, Cambridge University Press, Cambridge, 1960, pp. 42-5 I am grateful to Pauline Kolenda for bringing this to my attention (personal communication, December 1976).

Although the rural migrant has a strong network of kinship ties in the city, joint families are rare. In fact, 90 per cent of the families in the *bastis* studied were basically nuclear in structure.[9] More than half of the women interviewed, however, said that they considered the joint family the ideal, viewing it as a source of togetherness, protection, help in times of crisis, and economic and social security. It could be argued that one reason for the predominance of nuclear families could be lack of space. Some of the families which were classified as joint actually occupied two or more *jhuggis* (and these were not always contiguous) although they shared expenses and ate together. Another factor is that in-laws often stay back in the village, and thus the basis for a full-fledged joint family is not always present even if money and space would allow.

These were not the only reasons, however, for there was a clear tendency for family structure to differ according to caste and region. For example, 82 per cent of the single person households were migrants from U.P. although U.P. migrants comprised only 24 per cent of the total households. Studies in other cities of India have also noted the tendency for U.P. males to migrate to the city alone, leaving their wives and children behind in the village.[10] There was only one joint family among all of the migrants from U.P.,[11] in fact, and among the Muslims, Balmikis, and Dhobis from U.P., there was no joint family at all. Among the Kahar migrants from Madhya Pradesh, on the

[9]The analysis here utilise Kolenda's definition of the nuclear and joint family so that a family classified as nuclear often had widowed, divorced or single kin staying with them in addition to a couple and their children. See Pauline M. Kolenda, 'Regional Differences in Indian Family Structure', in Robert I Crane (ed.), *Regions ond Regionalism in South Asian Studies*, Duke University, Durham, pp. 147-72.

[10]Rowe has found similar patterns for U.P. migrants to Bombay and Bangalore, and Lubell notes this trend in Calcutta. See William L. Rowe, 'Caste, Kinship and Association in Urban India', in Aidan Southall (ed.), *Urban Anthropology: Cross-Cultural Studies of Urbanisation*, Oxford University Press, New York, 1973, pp. 211-50; Harold Lubell, *Calcutta: Its Urban Development and Employment Prospects*, International Labour Office, Geneva, 1974.

[11]Several researchers have pointed out that there may be both regional and caste (or class) based differences in the tendency to have joint families. See, for example, Kathleen E. Gough, op. cit.; Pauline M. Kolenda, op.cit.

other hand, nearly 20 per cent of the families were joint, but the Dhobis from Rajasthan lived only in nuclear families. Thus, it would appear that cultural as well as spatial and economic factors influence the family structure of those settling in Delhi. In the light of these findings, it is perhaps surprising that the majority of the women interviewed supported the ideal of the joint family, but attitudes do not always reflect actual behaviour, and this is a good case in point.

DOMESTIC ROLES AND DECISION-MAKING

Within every family, there are numerous domestic chores and responsibilities which must be carried out on a regular basis, and in traditional societies these are usually carried out according to a fairly strict division of labour which is based on sex. In a nuclear family, these duties must be shared among fewer family members than in a joint family, although the pattern of sex-role allocation probably does not differ much. In order to arrive at an understanding of how these roles are allocated within the family, the women were asked to specify the person in the family who had the primary responsibility for performing each of fifteen common domestic chores, and also the person (if any) who helped the most in a secondary capacity.[12]

The findings reveal that there are certain chores which could be labelled 'female tasks' since they were almost always allocated to females, whereas most other chores were either shared by husband and wife or were allotted to males in some families and females in others without any consistent pattern emerging. The tasks which were performed almost exclusively by women were cooking, washing utensils, washing clothes, cleaning the house, and preparing tea or coffee. About 20 per cent of the respondents said that daughters carried either primary or secondary responsibility for these chores, while less than 2 per cent of the women said that sons were given any responsibility

[12]The domestic chores listed were: cooking meals, cooking when you are ill, preparing tea or coffee, washing dishes, washing clothes, cleaning house, shopping for cereals, shopping for vegetables, buying the children's clothing, buying the husband's clothing, buying your own clothing, taking care of the children, taking care of children when you are out, medical aid for children, house repairs.

for these chores. Women also assumed the primary responsibility for caring for the children, and 73 per cent of them said that there was no one in the family who carried a secondary responsibility for this task. Forty per cent, in fact, said that there was no one to care for their children when they left the house (their children were left 'in the care of God', as they frequently said), and another 30 per cent said they never left the house without their children. The findings indicate clearly a great need for child-care arrangements in the *basti*, especially if we consider that 65 per cent of the women interviewed were employed. It should also be noted, however, that 9 per cent of the women said that their husband carried the primary responsibility for child-care and another 18 per cent said that the husband carried a secondary responsibility. Although a minority, it appears that males are ready to assume more responsibility for this critical domestic task than for other kinds of household work that are considered basically a woman's responsibility.

Surprisingly, there were no chores in which husbands were attributed the primary responsibility by a majority of respondents, although in some cases the husbands were given the primary responsibility somewhat more often than wives. The greatest responsibilities of husbands turned out to be buying their own clothing (48 per cent), shopping for cereals (43 per cent), buying the wife's clothing (39 per cent), buying the children's clothing (39 per cent), and taking care of house repairs (35 per cent). In the other chores listed, either the wife carried the primary responsibility or the responsibility was shared by both husband and wife. These findings indicate that the husband's major domestic responsibilities relate directly to the economic aspects of running a household and very little else. Thus, women carry an especially heavy responsibility for the domestic work of the family among the urban poor even though a large percentage of them work.

Comparing the responsibilities of sons with those of daughters, the findings indicate that role allocation based on sex begins very early in life and daughters carry far more responsibility for household tasks than sons. Sons were somewhat more likely than daughters to be given some responsibility for shopping for cereals and vegetables, and for house repairs, but even so, less than 6 per cent of the respondents reported assigning any domestic responsibility to sons compared to about 20 per cent who assigned primary or secondary responsibilities to daughters. The most common responsibilities of daughters were washing dishes, washing clothes cleaning, house, cooking meals normally or when the respondent was ill, preparing tea or coffee, and child-care when the mother was out. Daughters appear to be an especially valuable domestic resource for women who live in predominantly nuclear families. As a consequence, however, the daughters' opportunities outside the home are more limited than sons' for such things as education or training.

While women are assigned the greatest responsibility for carrying out domestic chores, they do not exercise the major authority in making decisions in family affairs. When asked who makes the decision with regard to thirteen common domestic decisions,[13] women said that they themselves make the decision in a majority of cases for only two items — planning the daily menu (78 per cent) and deciding whether or not to take up employment (57 per cent). The second item is of particular interest, however, since it indicates that women who work have in most cases assumed a personal responsibility to help support their families.

Surprisingly, husbands also were not credited with making the decision in a majority of cases for any item, though comparing only husband and wife, they were said to exercise sole authority far more often than the wife with regard to financial decisions (i.e., purchase or sale of property or jewellery, money spent on festivals or weddings). They also exercised somewhat more authority than women in deciding the age at which a son or daughter starts working, and the use of family planning methods.

On all items other than deciding the daily menu and wife's employment, more women said that the husband and wife make the decision jointly than that either the husband or wife makes

[13]The decisions listed were: planning the daily menu, wife taking up employment (or not), purchase or sale of property, purchase of jewellery, son's education, daughter's education, visiting relatives outside Delhi, visiting friends in Delhi, money to be spent on weddings, age at which son starts working, age at which daughter starts working, use of family planning methods (or not).

the decision unilaterally. This was especially so with regard to decisions about visiting relatives outside Delhi (65 per cent), visiting friends in Delhi (62 per cent), money to be spent on festivals (53 per cent), and money to be spent on weddings (50 per cent). Thus, while the allocation of sole responsibilities for common household tasks according to sex was fairly clear-cut, the process of decision-making turns out to be far less so. In fact, there appears to be a considerable amount of sharing in the decision-making process of squatter households with men and women both exercising an influence in many of the critical decisions within the family, but men generally holding the upper hand with regard to financial affairs.

EMPLOYMENT AND INCOME

The majority of the adult women in the *bastis* included in this study were employed and earning a cash income. Of the total *basti* population studied (including children), 40 per cent of the females were employed compared to 48 per cent of the males, and in the interview sample (which included only adult women), 65 per cent were employed. This female work force participation rate is unusually high when compared with Delhi's total population; only 5 per cent of Delhi's total female population were classified as workers in the 1971 Census. Participation in the work force, however, is not necessarily a consequence of *urban* poverty, for exactly the same percentage of women reported working prior to migration as reported working in Delhi. Women in slums, as in the village, were also more likely to take up employment in middle age than when they were young and newly married.[14].

Urban migration requires both men and women to seek out new types of employment since the majority were engaged in

[14]In Madras it was found that women above thirty years have a significantly higher rate of employment than those fifteen to thirty years. See Rama Arangannal, *Socio Economic Survey of Madras Slums*, Tamil Nadu Slum Clearance Board, Madras, 1975. A similar pattern of work force participation among rural female workers has been reported by Rama Joshi, 'Socio-Economic Conditions of Women Agricultural Workers', in S.M. Pandey (ed.), *Rural Labour in India: Problems and Policy Perspectives*, Shri Ram Centre for Industrial Relations and Human Resources, New Delhi, 1976, p. 80.

agricultural activities prior to migration, but the urban occupational structure offers far more limited opportunities to women than to men at this level of society. Table 1 shows the extent to which the employment of females differed from the employment of males in the *bastis* studied.

TABLE 1 : OCCUPATION ACCORDING TO SEX

Occupational category	Males		Females		Per cent female out of total workers
	Number	Per cent	Number	Per cent	
Domestic	57	9.33	372	84.35	86.7
Unskilled labour	211	34.53	32	7.26	13.2
Semi-skilled	160	26.19	10	2.27	5.9
Skilled	80	13.09	2	0.45	2.4
Household industry	13	2.13	6	1.36	31.6
Business	62	10.15	11	2.49	15.1
Technical/Manager	16	2.62	2	0.45	11.1
Agricultural	6	0.98	4	0 91	40.0
Others	6	0.98	2	0.45	25.0
Total	611	100.00	441	100.00	41.9

As can be seen from this table, 84 per cent of the women workers were engaged in domestic service of some kind. This occupational category included the occupations with the lowest status and pay in the urban occupational structure such as utensil cleaners, launderers, sweepers, etc. Their next largest representation was in unskilled labour (7 per cent), business (2.5 per cent), and semi-skilled labour (2.3 per cent). It is particularly instructive that in terms of labour-intensive occupations the representation of women within each category of workers falls dramatically as one climbs the ladder of prestige and income from unskilled labour (13 per cent) to semi-skilled labour (6 per cent) and skilled labour (2 per cent). Their representation among the self-employed, however, was considerably better. They comprised 32 per cent of all those in household industry, and 15 per cent of those in business.

There was also considerable variation in work force participation rates of females according to caste and region. Table 2 gives the percentage of males and females who were employed and the ratio of female workers per 1000 males for each of the major caste categories included in the study.

TABLE 2 : PERCENTAGE OF WORKERS ACCORDING TO CASTE AND RELIGION FOR TOTAL POPULATION

Caste category	Male (Per cent)	Female (Per cent)	Female workers per 1000 males
U.P. Muslims	58.82	12.28	209
U.P. Balmikis	47.02	31.58	659
U.P. Dhobis	31.82	31.58	992
U.P. Others	48.98	19.60	400
Rajasthani Berwas	45.28	47.06	1039
Rajasthani Dhobis	41.30	42.86	1038
Rajasthan-U.P. others	55.17	23.82	432
M.P. Kahars	44.57	41.38	931
Other Central Indians	50.00	25.00	500
Tamil Pallans	47.73	45.37	951
Other South Indians	55.56	45.10	812
Christians	28.57	33.33	1167
Not ascertained	45.00	43.59	969
Total	47.85	39.69	829

As this table shows, women in some castes are just as likely to work as men. Such castes include the Berwas, Dhobis, Kahars, Pallans and Christians.[15] They are somewhat less likely to work than men among the Balmikis and other castes, though a substantial portion of the women of these castes were also employed. Among the Muslims from U.P., however, none of the women said that they had worked before migration, and in the city they had the lowest participation rate of any of the groups studied.

Not only do work force participation rates vary according to caste and region, but so also do ideas and attitudes concerning the appropriateness of different types of work for males

[15]Although Christians and Muslims do not properly constitute a caste, they have been grouped together here as a caste-like category in order to facilitate analysis. The reader should also bear in mind that the number of Christians included in the study was very small and, therefore, cannot claim to be representative of this community as a whole.

and females. This functions to limit the possibility of social
mobility for both sexes, but especially for women since their
opportunities are already far more limited than men's. As a
result of these preferences, there is also a certain continuity
from the rural to the urban setting in types of employment
taken up by many of the castes included in the study. For
example, most Balmikis, traditionally sweepers and scavengers,
continue to follow this occupation in the city, but males often
get jobs with the municipality or offices in Delhi which assure
them of better pay, more benefits, and job security, while
women generally get work only as sweepers in private homes.
Berwa men and women, traditionally landless labourers, both
get work in the city as unskilled labourers, but the women are
not given a chance to rise above the status of coolie while the
men often move up to semi-skilled or skilled positions. Pallans
are also landless labourers in the village, but while most Pallan
men find work in Delhi as unskilled labourers, Pallan women
have shifted to domestic service in the *bastis*. This actually
implies a rise in status for Pallan women, however, since
domestic work such as cleaning utensils for caste Hindus
was denied to them in the villages because of their untouchable
caste status.

Some examples of the women's attitudes towards different
types of employment may help to demonstrate how the process
of limitation works. Women working as domestics said that
utensil cleaning would be degrading for a man, but it seemed
all right for a woman since she has to do this work for her own
family anyhow. The Kahar women who worked as domestics
considered domestic work more appropriate for women than
daily wage labour, or, as they put it, 'outdoor work'. Berwa
women, on the other hand, felt that coolie work was good
paying work for a woman, but considered domestic work to be
degrading and polluting. Even among the Dhobis (launderers),
there were regional differences regarding attitudes towards
work. Dhobis from Rajasthan would iron clothes but refused
to wash them since washing is the more polluting work; Dhobis
from U.P. did both, but assigned the job of washing to the
women, while men did the ironing. With one exception (a
domestic), Muslim women only took up work that they could
do within their own homes such as tailoring. But women who

tailored for other residents of the *basti* were paid less than the market rates; even when they demanded higher prices it was found that their clients would simply refuse to pay more after the work was done. Thus, it can be seen that while the urban occupational structure offers highly limited employment opportunities to women, caste and regional values function to limit their options still further.

An understanding of these values, preferences and traditional skills is clearly important for the design of effective programmes for enhancing the employment potential of women at this level of society. Such programmes must also take into account the massive illiteracy and lack of modern, adaptable skills among the women. In the *bastis* studied, it was found that 88 per cent of the females were illiterate compared to 63 per cent of the males, and that females had lower rates of school attendance and attainment than males long after migration to the city.

In terms of income, women also fared very poorly when compared to men. It was found that working women worked an average of forty hours per week compared to the forty-eight hours per week for men, yet their average monthly income was only Rs 76 compared to Rs 192 for men. In other words, they earned less than half as much as men per unit of time worked. The low earning capacity of women reflects in part the fact that they are in a lower status and lower paid jobs than men, but it also reflects the fact that even when they are in the same occupation, they are usually paid less (e.g., domestic work which is one of their main sources of employment), and that their chances of promotion in occupations where men find some mobility (e.g., construction) are practically nil. Efforts to increase the earning capacity of *basti* women would thus seem to require a multi-dimensional approach which would take into account the complexity of the situation. In addition to long-term efforts to increase educational and literacy levels, more immediate and direct measures might include legislating a minimum wage for domestics and others in the unorganised sector, encouraging the development of women's workers associations and co-operatives, and requiring Government

80

contractors to lead the way in promoting women to semi-skilled and skilled positions.[16]

Few women actually liked their work, even though they did appreciate the income. Utensil cleaners complained of the polluting nature of their work, their lack of holidays (the majority worked seven days a week), and their employers' attitudes; Dhobi women complained of unpleasant experiences in going from house to house to deliver clothes and collect payments; unskilled labourers complained of the tremendous physical demands of their work. Nearly all of them complained of the difficulty and strain of working and also having to do all of their own family's domestic work. It is little wonder then that daughters are pressed into assuming domestic responsibilities within the household as early as possible.

Despite the highly limited employment opportunities of women in squatter settlements and the exceptionally low pay that they can expect to earn, it was found that they considered it necessary to work in order to provide for their family's most elementary needs. Ninety-one per cent of the working women interviewed said that they were working out of economic necessity. Even more interesting is the fact that 74 per cent of the non-working women interviewed reported that they had been employed at some time in the past and over half of these said that they would like to work again sometime in the future. Non-workers thus cannot be considered permanently out of the work force. The majority had left work because of such reasons as health (including pregnancy and childbirth), child-care responsibilities, or lack of employment opportunities, while only 18 per cent reported that they did not work because their husband's income was sufficient.

In fact, there was definitely a positive female work ethnic in most castes in which women had a high rate of work force participation. Thirty-seven per cent of the working women said that they would continue to work even if their husband's income increased. Interestingly, positive responses to this question were highest among the women with the highest

[16]For a more detailed analysis and recommendations, see Andrea Menefee Singh, 'Women in the Unorganised Sector: The Need for Minimum Wage, Hiring and Promotional Guidelines', *Law and Society Quarterly*, 6 (nos. 1-4), 1976.

individual incomes indicating that the psychological rewards of working increase with income. Furthermore, 87 per cent of all respondents, including both working and non-working women, said that they expected their daughters to work after marriage. Reasons varied, but the most common responses were that they would like her to be able to stand on her own feet (32 per cent) and that it would probably be necessary due to poverty (22 per cent).

Given the expressed economic necessity for women to work, and the very small amount of income which they derive from their work, it is valid to ask just how they spend their money. The findings show that the earnings of women workers go almost entirely towards the most basic necessities of life for the family. Seventy per cent of the women workers interviewed listed food as their major item of expenditure[17] and about 22 per cent said that their income was pooled with that of their husband and spent jointly on the family's basic necessities. Forty per cent also mentioned clothing, 22 per cent simply their children's basic needs, and 5 per cent their children's education. No other item was mentioned by more than 3 per cent of the respondents and none of the items mentioned could be considered personal luxuries. Most women expressed surprise, in fact, when asked who decides how their earnings were to be spent since they did not consider this a matter of choice. Considering the woman's stated spending priorities, it would seem that a substantial increase in women's earnings would go a long way towards raising the family's standard of living and resolving the conditions of absolute poverty in which squatter families live.[18]

[17]Most women gave more than one response to this question, so that the above percentages add up to more than 100. According to data on monthly food expenditure, however, the average family spends 85-95 per cent of their total monthly income on food.

[18]This argument is also developed further in the article cited— Singh, op.cit. A relevant question which has now been answered here, is just how male and female spending priorities differ. Observation suggests that a higher proportion of female earnings is spent on the essential needs of the family than of males.

HEALTH AND NUTRITION

The inadequate public facilities and services, and the unhygienic conditions of the *basti* environment which have been described earlier obviously have severe consequences for the overall health of the community. I would like to focus here on a few indicators of just how critical the problem of health and nutrition is among the urban poor, namely the quality and quantity of food consumed, the nutritional status of children, the incidence of illness in the family, and the unusually high rates of infant and child mortality. Together, these provide a good indication of the consequences of poverty for human growth and development.

Let us first discuss the quality of the diet of the poor. The women interviewed were asked to recall the number of times they ate on the day immediately preceding the interview and what food was consumed in each of these meals. The results are summarised in Table 3 according to the number of times each item was mentioned for all meals.

TABLE 3 : FOOD ITEMS CONSUMED IN DAILY DIET

Food item*	Respondents mentioning at least once (N=161)		Total times mentioned (all meals)	
	Number	Per cent	Number	Per cent
Wheat	150	98.68	278	34.62
Rice	96	63.16	148	18.43
Corn/sorghum	3	1.97	4	0.50
Leafy green vegetables	5	3.29	6	0.75
Potatoes	24	15.79	26	3.24
Other vegetables	103	67.76	156	19.43
Dal (lentils)	124	81.58	173	21.54
Meat/eggs	12	7.89	12	1.49
No food	9	5.59	—	—
Total	—	—	803	100.00

*Chutney, coffee, tea and milk not included in this analysis.

As with slum dwellers elsewhere,[19] the majority of the *basti*

[19]See, for example, Arangannal, op.cit., p. 23. This study found that although 99.57 per cent of the slum dwellers were non-vegetarian, few could afford to include animal protein in their daily diet.

dwellers included in our study were non-vegetarian, yet this table indicates that meat and eggs (both high-protein animal foods) were only rarely included regularly in the diet of the poor. Meat and eggs were mentioned by only 8 per cent of the respondents and were consumed in less than 2 per cent of the total meals described. Animal protein was simply too expensive for regular consumption. The most common items in the poor person's diet turn out to be wheat, *dal* (lentils), vegetables and rice respectively. In fact, further analysis showed that 26 per cent of all meals included only one cereal and nothing else. About 70 per cent of the meals, however, included some combination of a cereal (most often wheat) *dal*, and/or other vegetables. This demonstrates good economics in a sense, since recent research has shown that if wheat and *dal* are consumed in sufficient quantities, the basic protein and calorie needs of an individual can be met as well as most of the vitamin requirements. Therefore, it is also important to evaluate the quantities of food consumed, and their protein and calorie values.

The analysis of the nutritive value of total monthly food purchases as estimated on the basis of recall indicates, however, that the majority of the families did not get sufficient quantities of proteins or calories in their diets, especially the latter. The fact that nine respondents (6 per cent of the sample) said that they had starved the day before because they did not have enough money to buy food suggests just how marginal the existence of many squatter families can be. Further evidence of the inadequate diet of the population studied was provided by an assessment of the nutritional status of children under five. On the basis of anthropomorphic measurements (i.e., the upper arm circumference measurement),[20] it was estimated that at least 40 per cent, and possibly as many as 60 per cent, of the

[20]Weight-for-age and height-for-age are generally considered the most accurate anthropomorphic measures of nutritional status, but these require time and equipment which were beyond the scope of this project. For a discussion of the upper-arm circumference measurement in community surveys of nutritional status, see Maurice King, Felicity King, David Morley, Leslie Burgess and Ann Burgess, *Nutrition for Developing Countries*, Oxford University Press, London, 1973. See also Murray Laugesen, 'Child's Bangle for Nutrition Screening', *Indian Paediatrics*, 13(n. 3), 1975.

children between the ages of one and five suffered from various degrees of malnutrition.

The problem of malnutrition, of course, is complex since it may be the result of an unbalanced diet, insufficient quantities of food, or even diseases (e.g., worms or dysentery) which reduce the body's ability to absorb the full nutritive value of the food which is consumed. Frequently, a combination of such factors is involved, which means that in order to be effective, the treatment must be intensive and complex. Thus, supplementary feeding programmes by themselves rarely make much of a dent on the problem of malnutrition. Environmental improvements, regular medical attention and non-formal education in nutrition and hygiene are measures which also need to be integrated into any programme meant to raise the nutritional status of the poor. Malnutrition is clearly a fact of life for the poor and is in need of immediate attention, for it has severe consequences for the life expectancy of the children of the poor, and also for their growth and development.

Although malnutrition is certainly a great problem in urban squatter settlements, there is some evidence that it is less severe than among the rural poor where an estimated 80 per cent of the children suffer from malnutrition.[21] Life in the city, insecure and marginal as it is, is not as subject to fluctuations in food supply caused by drought and seasonal shortages that often interrupt the supply of food to the poor in the villages. In fact, many *basti* dwellers commented on the better quality of their diet in the city as compared to the village noting that they were able to eat more prestigious foods, had a greater variety of foods in their diets, and did not have to face periods of shortage in the city. Rice, for example, is generally considered a rich man's food in the village, yet 63 per cent of our respondents mentioned eating it in at least one of their meals the day before.

[21]See C. Gopalan and K. Vijaya Raghavan, *Nutrition Atlas of India*, National Institute of Nutrition, Indian Council of Medical Research, Hyderabad, 1971, pp. 74-75. We should point out, however, that there is some indirect evidence based largely on macro-level statistical data and inference, that urban diets may be less adequate than rural diets, especially in North-West India. See V.M. Dandekar and Nilakantha Rath, *Poverty in India*, Indian School of Political Economy, Bombay, 1971, pp. 9-10; and also the article by Judit Katona-Apte in this volume.

Nutrition plays an important role in community health, but the findings also indicate that environmental factors such as unsafe water, poor drainage and overcrowding are also related to morbidity patterns in the squatter community. Respondents were asked to recall the illnesses during the past one year of all members of the family. While this method may underestimate the actual occurrence of disease, the findings nonetheless reveal some disturbing patterns. For one thing, it appears that women are more prone to illness than men. Of all illnesses reported, females were afflicted in 75 per cent of the cases whereas males were afflicted in only 66 per cent. The most frequently cited ailments were fever, cough, malaria and diarrhoea, and females suffered from all of these symptoms and diseases more than males. In terms of households mentioning these ailments at least once, 56 per cent mentioned fever, 48 per cent mentioned cough, 40 per cent mentioned malaria, and 27 per cent mentioned diarrhoea. Thus, the unhygienic environment and crowded conditions of the *basti* could be held directly responsible for a large number of the afflictions cited, especially water-borne diseases such as jaundice, typhoid, dysentery, and gastroentritis which together accounted for 14 per cent of all illnesses reported. Malaria accounted for 19 per cent of all illnesses and its emergence can be attributed at least in part to the collection of stagnant water because of poor drainage in the *bastis*. Twenty-seven per cent of the illnesses were described simply as 'fever' without further diagnosis, and we may assume that many of these cases were malaria which had not been properly diagnosed. Furthermore, in 26 per cent of the illnesses cited, no medical specialist was consulted. Limited public health services and the high cost of travel, consultation, and medicines relative to their income made it difficult for them to avail of proper medical care when ill. Inadequate treatment, in addition to constant re-exposure to the same sources of infection assures that illnesses tend to be chronic in nature.

The lack of a State-supported system of social security and the lack of personal savings or other resources for the poor to fall back on in their old age thrusts a major responsibility for their future maintenance on their children. As is well known, in India this responsibility falls almost exclusively on sons. This places a special importance on having enough children, and especially sons, to assure one's sustenance when one grows old or is no longer able to work. Therefore, infant mortality becomes a matter of special concern, especially in the light of the recent sterilisation drive which was directed at the poor in particular. Maternal histories of the women interviewed revealed that the overall child mortality rate was 221 per 1000 children born live, and that female children were more likely to die than were males. All but three children died before the age of five. Altogether, sixty-seven females were reported to have died out of 283 female births compared to fifty-eight males out of 284 male births. In other words, the poor have little assurance of the survival of their children. Most women said that they wanted to have at least two sons lest 'something happen' to one or 'one turns out bad', but one daughter would be enough. Hence the tendency to continue bearing children until the minimum number of sons has been assured.

It was also found that mortality rates varied considerably according to caste. This probably reflects a combination of factors subject to cultural influences such as diet, weaning practices, child-care practices, pre-natal care, mother's employment, and so on The highest mortality rate (444 per 1000) was found among the Rajasthani Berwas, a caste in which nearly all mothers may expect nearly half of their offspring to die at an early age.[22] This is a particularly tragic finding and suggests that the large number of urban female unskilled labourers and their children deserve the special attention of welfare agencies. It also suggests a need for more critical research evaluating the reasons for variations in infant mortality rates among the urban poor.

HOPES FOR THE FUTURE

Considering the tremendous hardships and disadvantages the *basti* family must endure in the urban environment, it is revealing to consider what the women would like to see the future bring. Seventy-one per cent of all responses related directly to

[22]In a study of female Rajasthani construction workers in Delhi, Ranade also found that child mortality was around 40 per cent. See G.P. Sinha and S.N. Ranade, *Women Construction Workers: Reports of Two Surveys*, Indian Council of Social Science Research, New Delhi, 1975, p. 11.

economic concerns, with 30 per cent of the respondents saying simply that they would like to be well-fed, 27 per cent well-clothed, 21 per cent to live well or in more comfort, 12 per cent to increase their income or salary, and 12 per cent to own their own house or some property.[23] Other economic concerns mentioned were the ownership of gold or jewellery, securing a good job, or acquiring other material comforts. The rest of the responses related mainly to the future happiness and well-being of their children and husbands.

Women's hopes for the future also varied according to caste. For example, none of the Berwa or Dhobi women mentioned economic concerns at all. This was particularly surprising since these groups had the highest proportion of female workers of any of the groups included in the study, and also because the Dhobis had the lowest income of all groups, taking home an average monthly household income of Rs 186.73 compared to the overall average of Rs 280.93. This raises some interesting questions about the relationship between caste-specific values and social mobility.[24]

When asked specifically what they would like to see happen to their sons and their daughters in the future, some further differences emerged. Over half of the responses regarding sons, for example, related to their education (33 per cent) and employment (24 per cent) and only 15 per cent related to their future marriage. For daughters, on the other hand, 51 per cent of the responses related to their being married well or getting a good husband, while daughter's education and employment were mentioned by relatively few respondents (11 per cent and 7 per cent respectively). This may appear illogical, considering the fact that 87 per cent of the respondents had indicated that they expected their daughters to work after marriage. Yet, it also reflects the reality of their experience, that is, that a woman's well-being depends heavily on her husband's income, which is so

---

[23]Most women gave more than one response. Therefore, percentages add up to more than 100 per cent.

[24]See Satish Saberwal, *Mobile Men: Limits to Social Mobility in Urban Punjab*, Vikas Publishing House, New Delhi, 1976, for an interesting discussion of the psycho-historical factors involved in the social mobility (or lack of it) among low caste groups.

much larger than her own, no matter how hard she works.[25] These attitudes of women probably play a critical role in shaping and limiting a young female's self-perceptions and goals, thereby helping to perpetuate her dependence in later life.

LINKS TO THE WIDER COMMUNITY

This description of women and the family in the squatter settlements of Delhi would be incomplete without at least some reference to their links to the wider social environment. These linkages (or lack of them) influence the way in which they cope with their problems and the control that they can exert over their future.

In terms of the more formal political, economic and social institutions of the *basti* and of the city, it was found that the participation of *basti* women was highly limited. Although 60 per cent of the respondents who were twenty-one years or older reported voting in the last election—a figure which compares very favourably with the all-India voting participation rates of women which was 49 per cent[26]—their participation in the local political structures and processes was practically nil. They had no representation on local *panchayats* or associations, and were not allowed to participate in discussions at public meetings; in Hassanpur they were not even allowed to attend public meetings of the *panchayat* as observers. Community conflicts, therefore, even if they originated with disputes between neighbouring women and involved women directly, were eventually resolved through the *panchayat* by males. Similarly, the task of making representations beyond the *basti* to patrons, politicians, or administrative officials was considered men's work, even when the petition represented the interests of women.

Participation in the urban labour force is significantly higher, on the other hand, among *basti* women than among middle or upper class women. But the jobs *basti* women hold are at the bottom of the urban occupational structure, i.e., those with the lowest status and pay, and predominantly in the unorganised

[25]Doranne Jacobson, personal communication.
[26]Ashish Bose, 'A Demographic Profile of Indian Women', in Devaki Jain (ed.), *Indian Women*, Ministry of Information and Broadcasting, Government of India, New Delhi, 1975, p. 170.

sector. The content of these links is, therefore, highly limited. According to a study by Sharma,[27] the vast majority of urban female workers are in occupations that require no education at all. In fact, only 12 per cent of the female population (including children) in the *bastis* studied were literate compared to 37 per cent of the males, a fact which reflects their low levels of participation in the educational institutions of the society compared to men. As a result of these complex factors, the economic power and influence of women is small at the individual or family level; the fact that they are unorganised and unrepresented at the institutional level also limits their power and visibility within the wider society.

In terms of the normal everyday activities of women, it was found that the caste and kinship groups provide the most common basis for organising community activity. Weddings and festivals are the most frequent occasions for community action, and participation in these events is largely limited to the caste and kinship group. Caste endogamy restricts marital arrangements across these boundaries, and rural caste traditions often dictate the form of expression of festivals and ceremonies, effectively precluding the participation of neighbours of differing religions, castes or regions in these important events. It is relevant to mention here that the four most frequently mentioned items in response to a question on self-images were family, gender, caste and occupation.[28] These identities accurately reflect the major social activities, linkages and interactions of women in *bastis*. Caste and kinship give needed social support to the individual, but in the process also function to insulate them from wider associations and interactions in the urban setting.

[27]O.P. Sharma, 'Operational Structure of Urban Working Women', *The Economic Times*, New Delhi and Bombay, 15 June 1975. Sharma found that 66 per cent of the total employed females in 1971 were illiterate.

[28]This question was based on a model of analysis developed by Viktor Gecas in his work with migrant Mexican-Americans. I would like to express my thanks to him for sending me some useful advice on the use of this technique and the code lists which he had developed in his study For further explanation of this technique, see Viktor Gecas, 'Self-Conceptions of Migrant and Settled Mexican-Americans', *Social Science Quarterly*, 54, December 1973, pp. 579-95.

To sum up, this paper has attempted to present a broad view of the consequences of urban poverty for women and the family, and to delineate some of the processes through which they adapt to the urban environment and cope with their conditions of poverty. Each of the four *bastis* included in the study was found to have its own unique internal social and political organisation which was influenced by the major caste, religious and regional identities of their populations. While *basti* dwellers can manipulate their physical environment to a certain degree in order to accommodate their differing values, customs and group identities, the harsh physical environment of the *bastis* was found to create special problems for the work and well-being of the family, especially for women who carry out most of the domestic work of the family, and children whose vulnerability was demonstrated by their high rates of mortality.

Nonetheless, arriving in Delhi from a background of crushing rural poverty, these migrants find themselves in some ways better off than they were in the villages. A large majority of those included in this study lived in nuclear families, but they maintained extensive kinship and caste networks within the city and in the *basti*. Within the home, women and their daughters carried out the majority of household tasks, but there was considerable sharing between husband and wife in decision-making, with the husband maintaining an upper hand mainly in matters pertaining to the financial affairs of the family. It was found that most *basti* women went to work out of sheer economic necessity (as they had in the village before they migrated), but that they earned less than half as much as men per unit of time worked. Discrimination against women in hiring and promotional practices was seen as one reason for their limited employment opportunities, but caste-specific values regarding the type of work considered appropriate for women to pursue, and their lack of skills and education also limited their options. Nonetheless, women were found to make an important economic contribution to the family, spending nearly all of their income on food, clothing and the most basic needs of the family. Still, most families could barely make ends meet. At least 40 per cent of the children under five suffered from malnutrition, and there was an exceptionally high rate of child mortality. It was also found that preventable diseases such as malaria and water-borne diseases were common, largely due to environmental factors. Women viewed their own most critical needs for the future as economic, while they wanted to see their sons get a good job and education and their daughters married well. The limited participation of *basti* women in the major social, economic and political structures of the city and the community was seen to result in a low degree of visibility and a poor understanding of their needs and priorities by the wider society.

CONCLUSIONS

This brief portrait of family life in Delhi squatter settlements makes it possible to make a few generalisations about the problem of urban poverty. For one thing, it is clear that the problem of urban poverty must be viewed within the context of the larger environment of the city and the wider rural society. The transplantation of the urban poor from rural poverty to urban poverty derives from a combination of factors, including the agrarian crisis of the countryside, the burgeoning need for workers in the low-paid jobs of the unorganised sector, and an accumulating shortage of housing in the fast growing cities of India. The cost of 'authorised' housing is beyond the means of these workers and yet the city at India's present stage of development apparently cannot continue to grow and develop without them. Thus, the growth of slums and squatter settlements must be considered but a natural consequence of the process of urbanisation in India. For the city, these migrants provide perhaps the strongest social and cultural links to the countryside as they bring many of their traditional customs to the city and maintain regular communication and contact with their kin in the village. In fact, it is these caste and kinship networks which shape the direction and size of migration streams to the city, and this is one reason for ethnic concentrations in squatter settlements as well as in occupations. Squatters in Delhi comprise more than 20 per cent of the city's population while slum dwellers comprise at least a third of the populations of Calcutta, Bombay and Madras. There is every indication that the proportion of urban poor will continue to grow, regardless of rural development efforts. It is within this larger functional context that the problem of urban poverty must be viewed and tackled.

It is clear that women play a major role in the family's efforts to cope with conditions of absolute poverty in the city. Few women in this study felt that they could afford the luxury of sitting at home, and it was clear that the women themselves had accepted the responsibility for finding a job and providing for the family. They also expected that their daughters would work after marriage to help to meet the basic needs of the family. Although our sample apparently included a somewhat higher percentage of female workers than is found generally among squatters in Delhi or in other cities, there is plenty of evidence to show that a significantly higher proportion of women in the lower income groups are employed than in the urban population as a whole.[29] Although their options are highly limited, it is the problem of under-employment, especially when defined in terms of low pay, that is far more severe than the problem of unemployment. This points to the rather inelastic market in which they compete for work. Raising their income would appear to be the most critical short-term need, while raising their levels of education and training them in new skills might be considered as long-term goals. Even if the females' average earnings were to equal that of the males', the standard of living of the family could be expected to rise dramatically since, as was shown here, a woman's earnings go almost entirely towards the basic necessities of the family. It is also generally accepted that as household income increases and the basic needs of food and fuel are met, the family can be expected to divert more of their resources into housing. Thus, by increasing the earning power of women, the poor would be able to invest

[29]The survey of Delhi squatter settlements by the Town and Country Planning Organisation op. cit., p. 105 estimates that 38.4 per cent of the adult women are employed, but this figure apparently does not include part-time workers who, as our study has shown, may work as much as forty hours a week. According to rough calculations based on census data, this means that percentage-wise about ten times as many women in squatter settlements are employed as women in the rest of the population of Delhi. Figures given for the slums of Madras indicate that nearly 30 per cent of the adult female population is employed. See Rama Arangannal, op. cit., p. 24., and Wiebe (this volume). Unfortunately, comparable data for other cities of India are not available.

considerably more in their own housing than is possible at present.

I would also like to stress the important influence of ethnicity on the position of women in the family and the community. Differing values and customs derived from the rural society tend to persist in the urban environment so that it is inappropriate to generalise about women in lower income groups beyond a certain level. Women from U.P., for example, whether Hindu or Muslim, are often left behind in the village to assume the major social, and often economic, responsibility for their families when their menfolk migrate to the city. When they come to Delhi, they are reluctant to move beyond their homes or the *basti*, and tend to have a low work force participation rate. Among other regional and caste groups, however, families nearly always migrate as a unit, and in some groups women participate in the work force as actively as men. Work at least draws these women out into contact with the wider society, even if these contacts are limited in scope and content. Caste and regional values thus function to create a mosaic pattern in the urban female work force, limiting a woman's options even while they provide a ready source of employment because of the well-established social networks through which workers are generally recruited in the unorganised sectors. These kinds of patterns and processes are not unique to Delhi, to the lower class, nor indeed to Indian society. It remains for us to explore in greater depth, however, their precise configurations and consequences for women in India. Development programmes could be more meaningful and effective if such differences were taken into consideration.

Finally, it is necessary to consider the consequences of the prevailing custom of sex-segregation in Indian society for women among the urban poor. This custom expresses itself in different ways and degrees in different ethnic groups, but nonetheless exercises an influence on nearly every dimension of familial or social activity. Of course, this is true of the middle and upper levels of society, too, but there appear to be important qualitative differences in the consequences of sex-segregation for women in the lower socio-economic strata of society. Unlike women in the middle and upper classes, the women in *bastis* have little chance of attaining literacy, much less of getting an education or vocational training which would allow them to compete in the modern sector of urban society. They do not even value education highly since they see little chance of benefiting from it. Their experience tells them that the jobs which are open to them have no such requirements; it is the men, they reason, who need education since all jobs are potentially open to them. In the unorganised sector, even where men and women are engaged in similar occupations such as in construction work, males and females are separated into sex-segregated teams and the women have no opportunity for further training or advancement. Jobs which are considered appropriate for women of the middle and upper classes to pursue such as teaching, nursing, and clerical work obviously require a far higher level of education and training than is within the reach of women in *bastis*. Less obvious, but at least as important, are the consequences of excluding women from the political structures and processes of society, and their failure to have developed alternative structures of their own. This also stands in sharp contrast to the multitude of women's associations in the middle and upper classes and their active participation in politics. As a result, women in *bastis* not only lack the machinery or power to press for their demands, but they also lack a medium through which their most urgent problems can become publicly known and comprehended by those in power.

Only when there is a fuller understanding of the social and cultural factors involved in urban poverty can we expect to make a genuine breakthrough in programmes and plans for urban development in India. This paper has focused on the contribution of women in coping with conditions of absolute poverty, and has attempted to suggest some of the most basic needs and priorities. Although they lack visibility or the political power to press for their demands, the needs of women and the family in such areas as education, training, employment, health, public facilities, and services are critical and urgently in need of attention. Policies which do not take these needs into consideration cannot possibly succeed in achieving the full potential for human growth and development in the cities of India.

5

Urbanisation, Income and Socio-cultural Factors Relevant to Nutrition in Tamil Nadu

Judit Katona-Apte

It is a well-known fact that in developing countries the poor spend a high proportion of their income on food. For example in South India the poor spend approximately 80 per cent of their income on food, while the affluent spend 45 per cent or less.[1] In the case of the poor, increased income is usually associated with a better diet.[2] However, as income transcends the poverty line, a lesser percentage of the additional amount is spent on food.[3] In addition, as income increases, more high status foods which are often less nutritious are bought, such as when polished rice replaces hand-pounded rice, or when refined sugar is used in place of raw sugar.[4] In terms of food intake, the beneficial relationship between income and quality of diet exists mainly at or near the poverty level. But food is

---

[1] F. Levinson, 'The Effect of Income Change on Food Consumption in South India and Ceylon', in A. Berg, *The Nutrition Factor*, The Brookings Institution, Washington D.C., 1973.

[2] John Mellor, 'Nutrition and Economic Growth', in Alan Berg *et al.* (ed.), *Nutrition, National Development and Planning*, MIT Press, Massachusetts, 1973, p. 72.

[3] Alan Berg, *The Nutrition Factor*, The Brookings Institution, Washington D.C., 1973.

[4] David Call and F. Levinson, 'A Systematic Approach to Nutrition Intervention Programme', in A. Berg *et al.* (ed.)., op.cit., p. 167.

not the only item that contributes to improving the quality of life—increased incomes allow populations to live more satisfactory lives. Even in terms of nutritional status, increased purchasing power by itself is not adequate for achieving improvement. Certain changes in the life-styles and food habits of the population are also necessary.

The preceding statements indicate how complex the process of raising the nutritional status of populations in developing countries is. Much has already been written on this topic.[5] It is the purpose of this paper to select a few variables and discuss them in the context of India with special emphasis on the state of Tamil Nadu. The first section starts with a general discussion of rural-urban differences relevant to the dietary intake of the Indian population. It will be followed by an examination of the extent of undernutrition in Tamil Nadu and the effects of inadequate income on nutrient intakes within the context of rural-urban population differences in section two. After demonstrating that either increased income by itself or in combination with an increased degree of urbanisation will not necessarily bring about better nutrition, the final section of the paper will discuss some important problems which need to be brought to the attention of health and nutrition planners for their attempts to provide a better diet for the Indian population.

1. RURAL-URBAN FOOD PATTERNS

Urbanisation in India, as in many other developing countries, may not necessarily improve nutritional status, though it may increase income levels. Urban areas have a more accelerated population growth rate due to the fact that beside the natural increases, there is also considerable migration.

Migrations to towns and cities and the transformation of the peasant into a wage earner constitutes still another context in which problems of malnutrition may be aggravated.[6]

[5] A. Berg, op. cit., Alan Berg, Nevin Scrimshaw and David Call (ed.), *Nutrition, National Development Planning*, MIT Press, Massachusetts 1973; Lester Brown, *By Bread Alone*, Praeger Publishers, New York, 1974.

[6] Karl Knutsson, 'Malnutrition: Macrolevels and Microlevels', in Berg *et al.* (ed.), op. cit., p. 32.

Large numbers of the urban population are poor, and the nature of poverty in urban areas is different from that in rural areas due to any or all of the following factors: (i) Housing is more expensive in urban areas; (ii) Many items that have to be paid for in urban areas are either free or available at very low cost in rural settings, such as housing and some services, along with many food-related items; (iii) There are extra expenses incurred in urban centres for such necessities as transportation; (iv) For the urban dweller, especially in large towns and cities, there are many more temptations to spend money on material goods and entertainment than for the rural dweller. It appears that the higher the degree of urbanisation, the higher the number of the mentioned attributes present.

Economic Conditions

As regards food patterns and their relationship to economic conditions, the differences between urban and rural areas are as follows:

1. In urban areas all the food has to be bought, none is grown by the consumers themselves or given to them by other farmers who have temporary surpluses.

2. In urban areas food purchases often depend on daily income; if work is found, then there is money to buy food. This is often a much less economical way of purchasing food than buying larger amounts at a time.

3. As the *jajmani* system still operates in rural India, the landlord will often provide grain or otherwise assist his tenants when necessary. The urban poor have no one to turn to; if there is no money, there is no food to eat.

4. Feasts and the ritual interdependence of landlords and artisans and others on such occasions in rural areas means that a wider range of persons are fed than in urban areas where such reciprocal arrangements are lacking. There is usually some surplus gain at least at harvest time to share with those less fortunate. The urban individual has no harvests and may feed only his relatives at festive occasions instead of many persons from other castes.

5. In urban settings there may be less time available for food preparation because fewer persons are available to cook in a

nuclear family, especially if the wife also works. A single male is not likely to do much cooking for himself when he has to prepare food in addition to working at a job.

6. There are fewer home-prepared and home-preserved foods consumed in urban areas which makes people more receptive to new foods, especially to those that are quick and easy to prepare.

7. Many food-related items that may be available without cost or at low cost in a rural setting, such as fuel for cooking—picking wood in the forest or using cow dung cakes—or fish which can be caught in local ponds and rivers, have to be bought in urban areas and thus need to be included in the food budget.

Fuel

The issue of fuel is often ignored and not even investigated when food expenditures are considered. It is not unusual to read that some expert recommends the use of food that is 'instant' and 'only' needs to be mixed in boiling water, without realising the relative high cost of lighting a fire. In Tamil Nadu, for example, many low-income families cook only one meal a day because they cannot afford to light a fire twice a day. This means that they eat leftover foods for the second meal, or have no second meal at all. Even tea and coffee are bought from shops because it appears cheaper than boiling one's own water. Some examples of the cost of fuel in Kumbakonam and Tanjore, both towns in Tanjore district in Tamil Nadu, illustrate the extremely high cost of fuel. In some instances, the cost of fuel was higher than the amounts spent for rice, or constituted as much as 25 per cent of the total income.[7]

The urban and the rural residents each has some advantages over the other. The urban resident eats a more varied diet which is likely to include a better variety of fruits and vegetables. There is a higher consumption of animal protein in his

[7]From data collected by the author in 1972. For information on specifics of data gathering, see Judit Katona-Apte, 'The Socio-Cultural Aspects of Food Avoidance in a Low-Income Population in Tamil Nadu', *Journal of Tropical Paediatrics and Environmental Child Health* (forthcoming).

TABLE 1 : WEEKLY EXPENDITURE ON FUEL

Tanjore		Kumbakonam	
Number of persons in family	Rs spent per week on fuel	Number of persons in family	Rs spent per week on fuel
14	7.90	4	3.50
4	5.60	5	3.50
3	7.00	3	4.00
3	3.73	5	3.03
2	2.10	4	2.80
9	0.93		

diet. He is also less affected by the seasonal fluctuations and availability of the food supply.

The villager also has some advantages over the urban dweller. He can often foresee impending food shortages and guard against them. Inflation in food prices is also less likely to hit him as hard as it does his urban counterpart. He can often depend on his landlord, if he is a tenant farmer, to keep him from starving, as well as on other farmers who may come to his aid when they can.

The following section will primarily focus on the State of Tamil Nadu and will discuss the dietary intake of the population within the framework of rural-urban differences. This discussion will be followed by a more general elaboration of the problems involved in improving the diet and general health of the average person in India.

2. NUTRITION IN TAMIL NADU

It appears from all available sources that the State of Tamil Nadu has the lowest ranking in terms of dietary intake.[8]

The major problem facing the state is malnutrition ... more than 99 per cent eat an imbalanced diet.[9]

[8]C. Gopalan, S. Balasubramanian, B. Rama Sastri and K. Visweswara Rao, Diet Atlas of India, National Institute of Nutrition, Indian Council of Medical Research, Hyderabad, 1969.

[9]O.K. Nambiar, 'Food Habits of Madras State', Census of India, Vol. IX, Part XI-B, Madras, 1964, pp. 67-8.

These statements seem to be supported by available data as will be apparent from the following tables. The average Tamil seems to be worse off than the average all-India individual. Table 2 presents a per capita comparison of Indian daily nutrient intakes and recommended allowances with daily nutrient intakes for Tamil Nadu at two periods, 1961 and 1969. In both years, the average Tamil was worse off than the average Indian as specified by Gopalan.[10] Except for the pulses, the consumption of all other food items is lower for Tamil Nadu than that for the whole of India. Additionally, most values are substantially below the recommended allowances.

A surprising point in this table is that according to the data, the diet of the average Tamil does not seem to have improved between 1961 and 1969. All figures in the table are lower for 1969 than for 1961. Many explanations are conceivable for either the apparent lack of progress in nutrient intake, or for the methodological techniques used in collecting the data.

Devadas[11] cites 'ignorance of nutritional needs and lack of knowledge about commonly available nutritive foods' as one of the major causes of malnutrition. However, it appears that under-nutrition is not mainly a result of inadequate information about nutritious or healthy foods. In a survey[12] which elicited information on what mothers would like to give their children, but cannot because of 'expense', the following foods were mentioned most frequently: milk was cited most often, as a matter of fact twice as often as the next item, 'Horlicks' which could also be considered a dairy product if prepared with milk. Other highly desired foods were fruit, egg, biscuit, 'Ovaltine', mutton, and 'general tonics'. (Vitamin supplements would probably qualify under such tonics.) It appears that nutrition education is not as strongly needed as the capacity to be able to purchase the foods that the people already know they should be eating. However, . . . 99 per cent cannot afford to buy a

[10]C. Gopalan, B. Rama Sastri and S. Balasubramanian, *Nutritive Value of Indian Foods*, National Institute of Nutrition, Indian Council of Medical Research, Hyderabad, 1971.

[11]Rajammal Devadas, *Nutrition in Tamil Nadu*, Sangam Publishers, Madras, 1972, p. 3.

[12]*The Tamil Nadu Nutrition Study*, Vol. 1, Sidney M. Cantor Associates, Haverford, 1973.

TABLE 2: PER CAPITA CONSUMPTION OF DAILY NUTRIENT INTAKES IN GRAMS AND RECOMMENDED ALLOWANCES FOR INDIA AND TAMIL NADU

Food Item	ICMR recommended allowance[1]	Composition of average Indian diet[1]	Composition of average Tamil Diet	
			1961[2]	1969[3]
Cereals	370	540	439	356
Pulses	70	12	28	16
Vegetables	235	99	60	16
Fruits	37	5	43	5
Milk	180	80	52	26
Sugar and jaggery	40	13	39	6
Oils and fats	38	15	—	6
Meat, fish and eggs	35	5	13	13

[1]C. Gopalan, et. al., Nutritive Value of Indian Foods, National Institute of Nutrition, Hyderabad, 1971. ICMR is the acronym for Indian Council of Medical Research.

[2]Census of India 1964. This amount is given in 'consumption units' which is computed on the basis of 100 of the population being equivalent to 76 consumption units (p. 6). The values in the table have been adjusted to be equivalent to per capita units.

[3]C. Gopalan et. al., Diet Atlas of India, National Institute of Nutrition, Hyderabad, 1969.

balanced diet . . . .'[13] The reason for this may be the fact that even in the early 1960s a minimum income of Rs 400 per month was a prerequisite for a balanced diet. Only 1 per cent of the State's population earned it, as a matter of fact only 2.8 per cent earned more than Rs 200 per month.[14]

A comparison of protein and energy intakes yield similarly poor results. Both of these nutrients are far below the recommended levels (see Table 3) and are the lowest among all States in India.[15]

TABLE 3: COMPARISON OF MEAN ENERGY AND PROTEIN CONSUMPTION IN TAMIL NADU WITH INDIAN COUNCIL OF MEDICAL RESEARCH RECOMMENDED ALLOWANCE

	Protein	Energy
Tamil Nadu	36	1498
ICMR recommended allowance	44	2400
All-India	53	1985

Source: C. Gopalan, S. Balasubramanian, B. Rama Sastri and K. Visweswara Rao, *Diet Atlas of India,* National Institute of Nutrition, Hyderabad, 1969.

Urban-Rural Cereal Consumption

When the energy intake is divided into the percentage of calories provided by each food group, it is clear that most of the energy—almost 80 per cent—comes from the staple (see Table 4).

Since the staple is cereal, it has a better protein content than roots and tubers, but it is still inadequate (see Table 3). The energy intakes are also low: this appears to be true at all age levels (see Table 5).

[13]*Census of India,* op.cit., p. 65.
[14]Ibid.
[15]Gopalan *et al., Diet Atlas of India,* op. cit.

TABLE 4: PERCENTAGE OF TOTAL CALORIES PER FOOD GROUP
IN TAMIL NADU

Food group	Per cent calories
Rice	57.90
Other grains	20.60
Total grains	78.50
Pulses and nuts	5.07
Starchy vegetables	1.09
Other vegetables and fruits	1.62
Fish	0.98
Milk products	2.08
Meat, poultry and eggs	0.77
Fats and oils	4.19
Sugar and jaggery	2.62
Condiments and herbs	0.75
Total	97.67

Source: *The Tamil Nadu Nutrition Study*, Vol. 1, Sidney M. Cantor Associates, Haverford, 1973, p. 142.

TABLE 5: COMPARISON OF ICMR (1968) ALLOWANCES FOR ENERGY
WITH AVAILABILITY FROM FOOD SUPPLY BY AGE

Age in years	Allowance	Received
1	1000	600
2	1100	770
5	1400	1050
15 (male)	2600	1700
25 (male)	2500	1900
Female (second half of pregnancy)	2500	1920
Female (lactating)	2900	1970

Source: *The Tamil Nadu Nutrition Study*, Vol. 1, 1973, p. 144.

In terms of per capita expenditure for food, the situation as it emerges from the data provided is summarised in Table 6. Urban residents spend more on food than either the average Tamil or rural residents.

Most of the food money is spent on staples, which in this case is cereal, either rice or any of a variety of millets (see Table 4). Since most of the food intake is cereal, this single item will be used as an example to illustrate the differences between urban and rural dietary intakes.

TABLE 6: PER CENT DISTRIBUTION OF POPULATION ACCORDING TO
AMOUNT SPENT ON FOOD ON THE BASIS OF RESIDENCE

Expenditure per capita in rupees		Residence in per cent		
Monthly	Daily	Rural	Urban	All-Tamil Nadu
Less than 15	Less than 0.50	5.1	2.0	3.9
Less than 24	Less than 0.80	35.6	14.6	27.2
Less than 34	Less than 1.13	66.0	37.3	54.6
More than 34		34.0	62.7	45.4

Source: *National Sample Survey*, Department of Statistics, 24th Round,
1972.

The per capita annual consumption of cereal is as
follows:[16]

	Rural	Urban
1966	381.85	331.38
1971	397.64	337.50

A comparison of staple consumption in terms of amounts
consumed could be misleading. A high amount could either
indicate that the population is worse off than another one consuming a low amount because it is eating grains instead of other
more expensive foods; or that it is better off because it has more
food to consume than another population which is not getting
adequate amounts of the staple. The following data indicate
that in Tamil Nadu the latter is the case. Analysis of the expenditure for cereal yields Table 7.

A comparison of the ratios (see Table 8) shows that the
percentage expenditure on cereals is higher in the rural population than in the urban one.

It is obvious in this case that having a higher proportion of
cereal in the diet of the rural population is not the result of its
being poorer than the urban population because the ratios
increase as income increases. In the developed nations, the ratio
would decrease since affluence means consuming less staple and
more of other foods rather than just eating more staple.

According to the data in Table 7, 58.68 per cent of the

[16]Estimated amount, see *Census of India*, op.cit.

TABLE 7: PER CENT OF TOTAL EXPENDITURE ON CEREAL BY PER CENT OF POPULATION ACCORDING TO INCOME IN RURAL AND URBAN AREAS*

Actual annual income (Rs)	Rural		Urban	
	Per cent of Population	Per cent of cereal expenditure	Per cent of Population	Per cent of cereal expenditure
Below 300	10.01	16.60	2.12	5.77
301-600	33.20	41.80	13.54	28.94
601-900	12.47	11.61	11.07	18.70
901-1200	11.75	9.58	22.78	24.39
1201-1800	15.28	12.51	10.48	10.30
1801-2400	10.06	5.87	4.58	1.56
2401-4800	7.23	2.03	15.69	7.96
4801-9600			19.74	2.38
Total	100	100	100	100

*Projected for 1966-71 in Census of India 1964.

TABLE 8: RATIOS, PER CENT OF POPULATION BY PER CENT OF
EXPENDITURES ON CEREAL BY INCOME

Annual income (Rs)	Rural	Urban
Below 300	0.60	0.36
301-600	0.79	0.47
601-900	1.07	0.59
901-1200	1.22	0.93
1201-1800	1.22	1.01
1801-2400	1.71	2.93
2401-4800	3.56	1.97
4801-9600		8.29
Mean	1.45	1.18
Standard deviation	9.60	9.40
Below 1800		
Mean	0.98	0.67
Standard deviation	0.93	2.80

rural population earn below Rs 900 per year as opposed to
26.73 per cent of the urban. Approximately 40 per cent of
the urban population earns over Rs 1,800 per annum, while
less than 18 per cent of the rural does so. It is not possible to
purchase adequate diets with such low incomes.

To recapitulate : (i) Tamil Nadu is one of the poorest-fed
States in India; (ii) A substantially greater segment of the urban
population is in the higher income bracket than that of the
rural population; (iii) The urban population is spending more
money on food than the rural population; (iv) The rural population, in general, appears to consume more cereal than the
urban population; (v) Almost 80 per cent of the total calories
consumed in Tamil Nadu are from cereals; (vi) Food intakes in
Tamil Nadu are below the average all-India intakes or the
ICMR recommended allowances.

Changes in food habits as a prerequisite to improvement in
the nutritional status of Indians is strongly advocated by Indian
health professionals.[17] Although this is certainly a desirable
and worthy goal, there are numerous problems and difficulties in
achieving it. Some of these are discussed here.

[17]Ibid.; Devadas, op.cit.

IMPROVEMENT OF HEALTH AND NUTRITION STATUS

Problem of Low Income

The target population for such a change in food habits is one that has very little choice in most aspects of life. Ultimately, the income level of most of these people is so low that they have no choice in terms of housing and food, the two most basic necessities for human beings. Yet, they are expected to be educated so they can decide if one food is healthier or better for them than another. It appears that their standard of living needs to be raised first to a point where they can make choices about other aspects of their lives, such as the basic necessities, and only after that, about health and nutrition.

Much of the low-income population in India does not seem future-oriented. When one lives from day to day, one does not have the concept of planning for the future. Many codvert each day's wage into food that same day, understanding full well that if there is no income, there will not be any food. The concept of doing something now, such as eating particular foods so as to avoid illness at a later date is difficult to undertake for a population that does not practise what may be called 'future planning' in many other aspects of their life.

The notion of doing something systematically in order to improve health and nutritional status is also foreign in such low socio-economic classes. Obtaining a nutritious diet for a minimum-income group involves a high level of knowledge of both basic and specific facts. Planning diets on low budgets is much more difficult than planning them with some margin in expenditures. To presume that just by educating the people as to what foods are more nutritious, a change in their food practices would occur is an unrealistic notion.

Besides careful planning, a considerable degree of self-restraint is also necessary in order to get the most nutrients at the least expense. Experience in the West shows that highly-educated, high-income individuals are not able to exercise the kind of restraint necessary for consuming a nutritious diet. To expect that a population which has little enjoyment and entertainment and which may consider its daily meals as the most joyous occasions to look forward to should restrain itself from buying

108

and eating those foods that are not essential to them, is not realistic.

Socio-Cultural Factors

An important point that is often overlooked in several health and nutrition education programmes is how to handle problems of superficial negative causation. Unfortunately, people do not readily accept the fact that the use of a new technique and the occasional negative result may be a coincidence without a causal relation. This means that one negative experience makes the population suspicious about the innovation offered to them; for example, only a few incidences of diarrhoea that may follow the use of a new weaning food will keep not only the affected family from trying it again, but also their neighbours, friends and other acquaintances.

Devadas[18] advocates the combating of malnutrition by also including 'improvement of environmental sanitation'. This is an important point that should be seriously considered and cautiously carried out. It should be remembered that most of India's health professionals belong to the middle class or above. They are highly educated and often far removed from the culture of the people they are working with. After all, even within the same geographical and linguistic area there are many subcultures often quite different from one another. While migrants to urban areas may lose many of the indigenous practices and norms they grew up with, others are acquired in the new urban milieu. They often become partially acculturated while still retaining some of their old practices. Systematic study of such groups is a prerequisite to successful implementation of planned changes including those of sanitation and hygiene.

Often, individuals doing health and nutrition education do not know, or have forgotten the indigenous beliefs that are still ingrained in much of the population. They were taught scientific methodology and they try to do health education according to those principles. This may make it difficult for them to relate to the subculture they are working in to the extent that meaningful communication becomes almost impossible.

[18]Devadas, op. cit., p.6.

CONCLUSION

The foregoing discussion emphasised that urbanisation does not increase nutritional status even when income is increased because the expenses in urban areas are higher than in rural ones. The assumption that, as the rate of urbanisation increases so will the food intake of the population, is not necessarily true. Poor people are, of course, worse off everywhere than affluent people, but they are even worse off in urban areas than elsewhere. Thus, the income levels need to be increased even more for urban than for rural populations in order to provide a better diet.

It is important to remember that in a developing country such as India, food items other than the staples in adequate amounts are still considered to be luxuries. Therefore, ideas, habits, and customs acquired over generations in this important aspect of living cannot be easily replaced by new ones. In the final section, suggestions were offered for more successful planning and execution of health improvement programmes.

The estimate and evaluations used in this paper were based mainly on data from the sixties since comparable data for the seventies are not yet available. It will be interesting to contrast the foregoing with more recent data when they become available in order to evaluate the improvement that may have occurred with regard to dietary consumption.

6

Migration and Employment: The Case of Calcutta

Harold Lubell

Alleviating Calcutta's employment problem requires action on an array of factors which affect both the supply and demand for labour in the metropolitan area.[1] On the labour supply side, the major source of increase is the natural growth of metropolitan Calcutta's already large population. Although in-migration was of prime importance in the 1950s, and 1960s, it was dominated by the flow of refugees from East Pakistan. Normal migration from the rural areas of eastern India is likely to fluctuate with the state of the labour market in the rural areas of origin of the migrants as well as in Calcutta. The spread of the Green Revolution and development of the rural economy of West Bengal and of Bihar can reduce the incentives for unskilled labour to drift into Calcutta.

The demand for labour has suffered from stagnation of the urban industrial economy due in part to the obsolescence of

Responsibility for the views and opinions expressed in this paper is solely that of the author and not of the ILO.

[1]This article is an attempt to reformulate and to bring up-to-date some of the arguments made in a report written several years ago for the World Employment Programme of the International Labour Office. See Harold Lubell, *Urban Development and Employment: The Prospects for Calcutta.* Foreword by J. Tinbergen, International Labour Office, Geneva, 1974.

Calcutta's industrial plant and its inability to shift out of old
lines of production and to meet new patterns of demand for
manufactured goods. It is necessary to reverse these trends by
action at several levels.

MIGRATION AND THE CALCUTTA LABOUR FORCE

The size of the working population in metropolitan Calcutta is
affected both by seasonal immigration and emigration and by
net inflows of persons seeking to settle for longer periods. These
two categories of migratory movement overlap to the extent
that workers who reside in metropolitan Calcutta without their
families return to their places of origin for considerable stretch-
es of time in the course of the year. Many of Calcutta's unskilled labourers return to their villages early in December in
time for the harvest and start coming back to the city after mid-
January. These seasonal movements, to which are added visits
to families in the rural areas, seem likely to provide the rural
sources of labour supply with an effective network of information on the Calcutta labour market.

A characteristic of the Calcutta working force noted in all
the population and labour force surveys of the city is its complex
geographical origin. For that matter, Calcutta has been a city
of immigrants ever since its foundation. Nevertheless, the rate
of immigration has been falling. During each of the two decades
since 1951, the growth rate of the population was considerably
slower in the Calcutta urban agglomeration than in West Bengal
as a whole. From 1951 to 1961, the decennial rate was 25 per
cent for the Calcutta urban agglomeration and 32.8 per cent for
West Bengal as a whole, whereas from 1961 to 1971, the rates
were 22.6 per cent and 26.9 per cent respectively (see Table 1).
In the course of the latter decade, the population of rural West
Bengal increased by 26.9 per cent and of all urban West Bengal
including Calcutta by 28.4 per cent, with a resulting increase of
42.8 per cent in the population of urban West Bengal excluding
the Calcutta urban agglomeration. These growth rates, combined with the fact that there is normally a considerable amount of
migration into metropolitan Calcutta from States bordering on
West Bengal and from eastern Uttar Pradesh, imply that there

TABLE 1: POPULATION GROWTH RATES, WEST BENGAL AND CALCUTTA, 1941-1971

Item	West Bengal			Urban areas		District in which Calcutta urban agglomeration is located*	Calcutta Metropolitan District
	Total	Rural	Urban	Calcutta urban agglomeration	Other urban areas		
	1	2	3	4	5	6	7
Population (millions)							
1941	23.2	18.5	4.7	3.6	1.1	9.5	4.3
1951	26.3	20.0	6.3	4.6	1.7	11.5	5.4
1961	34.9	26.4	8.5	5.7	2.8	15.2	6.7
1971	44.3	33.3	11.0	7.0	4.0	19.1	8.3
Decennial growth rate (per cent)							
1941-51	13.2	8.1	34.0	28.3	54.5	20.9	24.6
1951-61	32.8	32.0	34.9	25.0	64.7	32.0	25.1
1961-71	26.9	26.4	28.4	22.6	42.8	25.6	23.5

*Nadia, 24 Parganas, Howrah, Calcutta, Hooghly.

Sources: Columns 1-6: Census of India 1971. Series 22, West Bengal, Part IIA, General Population Tables Calcutta, 1972, pp. 11, 90-3, 148.
Column 7: Basic Development Plan for the Calcutta Metropolitan District 1966-1986, Calcutta Metropolitan Planning Organisation, Government of West Bengal, Calcutta, 1966 Table 5, p. 10; ibid, A Memorandum on a Perspective Plan for Calcutta Metropolitan District and West Bengal 1971-1989, Calcutta, 1971.

was little, if any, net migration from rural West Bengal into metropolitan Calcutta.

Given the tribulations of Calcutta in the late 1960s, these rates imply that population growth of any specific city responds to the employment and living standard opportunities it offers as compared with other attainable alternatives. Prosperity attracts additional population; stagnation, unemployment and physical and social deterioration discourage it. On the other hand, the rate of population growth is considerably higher in the districts surrounding Calcutta than in the Calcutta urban agglomeration itself, so that the relatively low rate of growth of population in the urban agglomeration itself may conceal a more marked increase in the larger pool of actual and potential members of the urban labour force of metropolitan Calcutta resident in the nearby rural and non-contiguous urban areas of West Bengal.

Since the 1940s, the waves of immigration which have episodically overwhelmed Calcutta have consisted not so much of migrants seeking work as of refugees fleeing from disaster. The flood of refugees who poured into Calcutta in the 1950s was an intensification of a natural movement of persons, particularly middle-class Bengali Hindus from East Bengal, into what had been the capital city not only of Bengal but also, until 1912, of all India. The overwhelming seriousness of Calcutta's problems of unemployment and housing shortage in the 1950s and again in the mid 1960s was created by the accumulating numbers of displaced middle class persons from East Pakistan arriving in Calcutta and other parts of West Bengal.

The traditional migrants from areas other than East Pakistan who came in search of employment apparently either found work of some kind or went back to where they had come from. They also constituted part of the seasonal ebb and flow of the unskilled labour supply of metropolitan Calcutta. Unlike the refugees, they came without their families and could return home.

The situation of migrants to Calcutta city in the mid-1950s was well described in the report of a sample survey, carried out on behalf of the University of Calcutta by S.N. Sen for the

Government of India's Planning Commission,[2] which broke down the Calcutta population into three groups: residents, normal migrants from other Indian States and refugees from East Pakistan. The breakdown showed that the labour force participation rates were much higher for the normal migrants (who arrived for the most part without their families) than for the resident population or for the refugees (who arrived with their families). It also showed that unemployment rates were lower for the normal migrants than for the resident population but much higher for the refugee population.

At the time of the 1961 census, in addition to being the main destination of the refugees of East Pakistan, West Bengal was the largest recipient of net inter-State migration in India: 2.2 million persons from other States were living in West Bengal, while 0.6 million persons born in West Bengal were living elsewhere in India, leaving a net immigration of 1.6 million.[3] Most of the immigrants came from three States: Bihar (60.6 per cent), Orissa (8.4 per cent) and Uttar Pradesh (15.6 per cent). The distribution by sector of work of immigrants to West Bengal from these three States showed the highest concentrations in manufacturing and in services.[4] Manufacturing accounted for 16.0 per cent of the migrants from Bihar, 26.5 per cent of those from Orissa and 26.3 per cent of those from Uttar Pradesh. The proportion of non-workers was highest (40.4 per cent) among migrants from Bihar and lowest (24.6 per cent) among those from Orissa, the latter having come without their families to an even greater extent than other migrants.

The migration status tabulations of the 1971 Census are not yet available. In India's Eastern Region, which is Calcutta's hinterland, migration to metropolitan Calcutta is, for most people, probably due more to a lack of employment opportunities in their places of origin than simply to the prospect of

[2]S.N. Sen, *The City of Calcutta: A Socio-Economic Survey—1954-55 to 1957-58*, Bookland, Calcutta, 1960.

[3]*Census of India 1961*, Vol. 1, Part II-C (iii), Migration Tables, pp. 16, 46.

[4]Tapan Piplai and Niloy Majumdar, 'International Migration in India: Some Socio-Economic Implications', in *Sankhya: The Indian Journal of Statistics*, Calcutta, Series B, Vol. 31, Parts 3 and 4, December 1969, pp. 518-19, quoting *Census of India 1961*, Vol. I, Part II (A).

higher earnings in the big city that would result from higher unit rates of pay: for an employed unskilled worker, unit rates of pay may not be much better than in his place of origin. For the educated in rural areas of West Bengal, the outlook is even clearer. Until modernised agriculture creates manpower demands in the small towns servicing an expanding agricultural sector, there will be few employment possibilities for them except in the big city.

Most studies[5] show that the largest proportion of job-seekers find work in metropolitan Calcutta through friends and relatives, through fellow villagers or townsmen and through caste affiliations. New arrivals seeking factory employment will often stay with an already employed relative and then try to obtain a temporary job at the same place of work, usually as casual labourers who will then gain some skill on the job.

EMPLOYMENT PATTERNS

The breakdown of the population of West Bengal by main activity according to the 1971 census (see Table 2) shows 39 per cent of the working population of the Calcutta urban agglomeration as occupied in manufacturing (including house-hold industry and servicing and repairs), 22 per cent in trade and commerce, 12 per cent in transport, storage and communi-cations and 23 per cent in other services, with construction accounting for 2 per cent and the primary sector for another 2 per cent.

The industrial and occupational employment patterns in metropolitan Calcutta are closely linked with the geographical and linguistic origins of the working population. For example, in the case of large-scale manufacturing, the jute industry is manned to a large extent by Bihari and Uttar Pradesh Muslims, while the labour force in the engineering industry, including the engineering departments of the jute industry, contains a rela-tively high concentrations of Bengali Hindus. Jute and paper show the lowest concentrations of Bengalis, while engineering,

[5]See, in particular, Sen, *The City of Calcutta*, op. cit., pp. 77-8; Reserve Bank of India, *Survey of Small Engineering Units in Howrah*, Report of a survey undertaken by Jadavpur University, Calcutta, 1964, pp. 36, 89.

TABLE 2: WORKERS AND NON-WORKERS BY MAIN ACTIVITY, WEST BENGAL AND CALCUTTA URBAN AGGLOMERATION, 1971 (IN THOUSANDS)

Main activity	West Bengal			Urban areas	
	Total	Rural	Urban	Calcutta urban agglomeration	Other Urban areas
Cultivators	3,955	3,965	50	5	45
Agricultural labourers	3,272	3,172	130	17	83
Livestock, Forestry, etc.	363	338	25	13	12
Mining and quarrying	116	109	7	1	6
Manufacturing, processing, servicing and repairs					
a. Household industry	334	239	95	41	54
b. Other	1,406	332	1,074	852	222
Construction	125	49	76	49	27
Trade and Commerce	981	273	708	514	194
Transport, storage and communications	516	125	391	263	128
Other Services	1,301	524	777	531	246
Sub-total: Workers	12,369	9,066	3,303	2,286	1,017
Non-workers	31,943	24,279	7,664	4,745	2,919
Total population	44,312	33,345	10,967	7,031	3,936

Source: *Census of India 1971*, Series 22, West Bengal, Part II-B (i), General Economic Tables, Tables B-I Part A and B-II; Calcutta, 1973, pp. 2-3, 164-5.

chemicals, rubber and printing show the highest.[6] The proportion of Bengalis among workers in commercial and non-factory establishments is high for banking and insurance, but extremely low in ship-building and inland water transport.

Bengalis traditionally prefer white-collar and skilled jobs. As modern manufacturing developed in Calcutta, they moved into activities requiring greater skills, such as engineering, chemicals and the finer textiles, while the Biharis moved into jute and coarser textiles. At another occupational level, the men pulling the old-fashioned rickshaws in Calcutta are mostly Bihari and Oriya; but among the bycycle-rickshaw drivers in the suburban areas of metropolitan Calcutta, many are Bengalis. Gardeners, plumbers, house servants and *pan* (betel) stall keepers are likely to be from Orissa. Taxi drivers used to be primarily Punjabi, but now include some Bengalis and Oriyas. Tanning and leather working which are low-caste occupations for Hindus, are largely a Bihari Muslim activity in Calcutta.

The occupational concentration of the various groups is reflected in their physical concentration in different parts of the city of Calcutta and of the metropolitan area. For example, the slums on the northern and eastern edges of Calcutta are inhabited largely by Bihari and Uttar Pradesh Muslims, who constitute the majority of the factory hands in the jute mills and, to some extent, in other textile factories. The concentrations of residents within the wards of Calcutta city by language and geographical origin in the early 1960s were mapped and analysed in an illuminating study made by Nirmal Kumar Bose for the Anthropological Survey of India.[7]

An important implication of the pattern of traditional occupational choices is that the progress or decline of the various branches of activity will affect specific groups differently. For example, growth or stagnation of jute processing will influence the flow of Biharis to metropolitan Calcutta; growth or stagnation of the engineering industries will affect the employment opportunities of Bengalis.

[6]See for example, *Labour in West Bengal 1970*, Labour Directorate, Government of West Bengal, Calcutta, 1971, pp. 44-8.
[7]Nirmal Kumar Bose, *Calcutta 1964: A Social Survey*, Lalvani, Bombay 1968. See particularly the maps on pp. 95-8.

DEVELOPING RURAL WEST BENGAL

Today, advantage is being taken of a technological precondition governing the application of policy measures which did not exist only a few years ago: it is now technically possible to transform and modernise West Bengal's agriculture. The effectiveness of the Green Revolution with regard to food-grains—new seed varieties, scientific use of fertiliser, and water control, particularly through ground water irrigation—has already been demonstrated in some parts of West Bengal. It will be only a matter of time before the Green Revolution spreads to all of West Bengal lying in the Gangetic plain and to other crops such as pulses, jute and cotton.

Irrigation in West Bengal has been traditionally carried out by gravity flow of the surface water available primarily during the monsoon season. Besides leaving agriculture at the mercy of floods and drought during the monsoon season, this practice has severely limited crop production during the dry season. As a result of the geographical situation of West Bengal in the basin of the Ganges, the State's ground water resources are enormous; but their exploitation has scarcely begun. By June 1972, fewer than 1,800 deep tube-wells had been drilled in West Bengal; of these, 1,400 were electrically energised.[8] Since 1974, however, more rapid progress is being made despite certain structural rigidities which slow it down. These rigidities include, on the one hand, a social structure at the village level which encourages inertia on the part of the wealthier members of the village society who could afford to make new investments and which blocks any initiative on the part of the poorer villagers and, on the other hand, a fragmentation of land holdings into numerous and scattered small plots which makes it difficult even for the larger land-owners to irrigate enough of their own land with a single tube-well to justify the investment.

One of the more effective programmes for accelerating the installation and exploitation of ground water facilities has been that of the West Bengal Comprehensive Area Development

[8]*Mid-term Appraisal of the Fourth Plan*, Agriculture Department, Government of West Bengal, Calcutta, quoted in West Bengal's *Approach to the Fifth Five-Year Plan 1974-79*, State Planning Board, Government of West Bengal, Calcutta, 1972, p. 41.

Corporation (CADC) which has about twenty projects under way in various parts of the State.[9] The West Bengal Minor Irrigation Corporation, which is active in sinking deep tube-wells and laying underground pipelines for the West Bengal Department of Agriculture, also provides this service on contract for the CADC. The basic approach of the CADC is to effect a 'technological consolidation' of compact blocks of land to provide co-operative facilities, particularly power and irrigation, at minimum possible cost and to make available repair and maintenance services close to the individual peasant. For a shallow tube-well, all the contiguous six to ten acres are dealt with as one unit with respect to irrigation, regardless of the ownership pattern of the particular plots of land covered. Equipment-servicing centres cover wider areas. The unit area development blocks chosen for administrative purposes are of about twenty five square miles which, in West Bengal, implies clusters of twenty-five to thirty villages with a net cultivated area of 10,000 acres.

The creation of a prosperous agricultural sector in West Bengal will ease all of the State's other problems and make both direct and indirect contributions to solving the urban employment problem. The direct contributions will lie in providing increased supplies of food-stuffs and agricultural raw materials to metropolitan Calcutta and its industries and in increasing demand for urban produced industrial products. The indirect contribution will be to provide potential migrants with a viable alternative to moving to the big city.

RESTRUCTURING CALCUTTA'S INDUSTRIAL BASE

Metropolitan Calcutta suffers from a disadvantage faced by many industrial pioneers: an industry oriented towards demands which are often not the most up-to-date and based on raw materials which are becoming obsolete. On the other hand, it

---

[9]This programme was formulated by the West Bengal State Planning Board in *Comprehensive Area Development Programme (CADP): A New Strategy for Development*, Calcutta, 1973. The Comprehensive Area Development Corporation was set up by the West Bengal Comprehensive Area Development Act of 1974; see *State Planning Board, West Bengal 1974-76*, Calcutta State Planning Board, April 1976, pp. 31-41.

enjoys one of the great advantages acquired by the industrial pioneers: a skilled and adaptable labour force.

Metropolitan Calcutta's engineering industry has been one of the victims of shifts in demand. Set up to supply heavy castings, structural shapes, railway equipment and textile machinery, it was badly hit by the reduction in government demands for the output of these industries after 1965 and by the recession in private demand. Meanwhile, the newer metal-working industries producing defence goods, electrical equipment, light machinery and hand tools were being set up elsewhere in Bombay, Poona and Madras. Metropolitan Calcutta's engineering industry will have to adapt itself to new lines of demand: agricultural equipment as the Green Revolution spreads through West Bengal and consumer goods as incomes rise.

Jute manufacturing and pharmaceuticals are two industries suffering from dependence on obsolescent raw materials. Jute manufacturers suffer from fluctuations in the supply of raw jute and the competition of new synthetics which have been encroaching on the international market for jute manufacturers with each downward fluctuation in the supply of raw jute, despite the increased cost of petroleum feedstocks for synthetics. It is hard to see a solution for jute manufacturing other than appreciable improvements in raw jute yields. Pharmaceuticals production in metropolitan Calcutta has the disadvantage of being based on alcohol, whereas modern pharmaceuticals production is based on petrochemicals. Improving Calcutta's position in the production of pharmaceuticals needs the local production of petrochemical raw materials planned for Haldia.

In periods of expansion, the rate of growth of employment in manufacturing normally falls far behind that of output. With productivity per man rising at high rates, the rise in industrial employment may be expected to continue to fall far behind future increases in manufacturing output. The importance of manufacturing for total employment is, however, not diminished by the fact that direct employment in manufacturing may show only moderate increases; the increases in manufacturing output and in total income originating in manufacturing are the catalysts for much of the tertiary sector activity of the metropolis.

The policies which will most directly affect Calcutta's industrial expansion are the investment programmes of the Government of India, its import and raw materials allocation policies and its industrial licensing policies. The rate at which the Central Government increases total investment outlays under the Five-Year Plans is particularly important since West Bengal still contains a considerable share of the Indian industries producing investment goods. The Central Government's decisions in this regard mainly reflect its assessment of the potential inflationary result of investment activity. Similarly, its import and raw materials allocation policies reflect the Ministry of Finance's assessment of the Indian foreign exchange situation. Where there is room for discrimination in favour of, or against, a particular geographical region is in the regional allocation of total investment, import licenses and raw materials in short supply.

At the local level, a development plan which will integrate metropolitan Calcutta's economy into the development needs of the State of West Bengal should be formulated. Such a plan should build on all the human resources available in Calcutta and should include the encouragement of newer branches of activity such as electronics. It should also take explicit account of the production and employment possibilities of the small-scale enterprises of the informal sector.

DEVELOPMENT OF THE INFORMAL SECTOR

An important development during the last several years is a growing awareness of the need to develop what the ILO and other international agencies have labelled the informal sector, which includes the small-scale and household industry units that have been a major focus of attention in India for many years. In the case of Calcutta, the informal sector was the subject of several general studies in the early 1970s[10] and, more

[10]See. A.N. Bose, *The Informal Sector in the Economy of Metropolitan Calcutta*, World Employment Programme Research Working Paper WEP 2-12/WP 5, ILO, Geneva, October 1974, a revised version of which should soon be printed by a Calcutta publisher; Biplab Dasgupta, 'Calcutta's 'Informal' Sector,' in *Bulletin of the Institute of Development Studies*, 5, nos. 2-3, October 1973.

recently, has become a specific area of concern of the World Bank and of the Calcutta Metropolitan Development Authority (CMDA).[11]

Metropolitan Calcutta's informal sector is both the labour market of last resort for those who cannot obtain 'jobs' in the modern sector and an enormous reservoir of productive skills. The goods and services produced by household industries provide a sizable proportion of the incomes generated in the metropolis. With some market organisation and provision of credit and training, much more of the productive potential of the metropolitan area's informal sector could be made a reality.

A start is being made by the CMDA to assist small-scale producers in the slums of the metropolitan area by small bank loans to be made through two of the nationalised commercial banks and by an urban small business extension service being organised by the West Bengal Department of Cottage and Small Scale Industries. Among the target groups already identified by the CMDA are producers of garments, engineering goods, plastic articles, glassware, carpentry products, clay products, etc.

If proposed efforts to deliver credit and extension services to the informal sector bear fruit, productivity and output of the small-scale enterprises will increase. It will also be necessary to encourage sufficient demand to absorb such increases.

The sources of demand for the goods and services produced by the small-scale enterprises of the informal sector in Calcutta are beginning to be fairly well known. In broad terms, they cover the whole range of intermediate and final products: finished goods for household consumption, government purchases and business investment; and intermediate goods purchased by other producers as inputs. Finished consumer goods are sold directly to local household consumers or through normal retail and wholesale trade channels. Consumer goods are also produced on sub-contract for larger enterprises which

[11]See, for example, *An approach to Economic Renewal and Promotion Programme: Informal Industry Sector*, Report No. 44, Directorate of Planning, Calcutta Metropolitan Development Authority, Calcutta February 1977.

124 THE INDIAN CITY

often turn out to be wholesalers rather than producers, the shoe trade in Calcutta being a case in point. With respect to government purchases, a wide range of goods is already 'reserved' for the outputs of small-scale and cottage industry products. Intermediate goods are often purchased on sub-contract to somewhat larger firms which constitute part of the formal sector, as well as for other small enterprises in the informal sector. Inter-industry sub-contracting is particularly widespread within the light engineering industries. Intermediate goods for agriculture (e.g., grain milling machines and tube-well sections) are produced either on sub-contract or sold through normal marketing connections in Calcutta and in provincial centres. Production for export is, at present, also carried out mostly on sub-contract, an example being the increase in production of ready-made garments for export during the last several years.

The task of stimulating demand for the outputs of Calcutta's informal sector producers has to be attacked at both the macro-economic (aggregate demand) and micro-economic (marketing) levels. At the micro-economic level, solutions to a number of marketing problems must be sought aiming at the different elements of demand. At the retail level, direct access to consumers is constrained by lack of space in existing market places. Construction of small local markets to provide additional retail sales space is an option to the town planning authorities. Establishment of an important new centre such as the proposed truck terminal in West Howrah will attract a large enough number of traders to make the construction of a new wholesale market in that area almost certainly a viable proposition. Thought should be given now to the question of how to give informal sector producers access to any newly constructed wholesale markets, perhaps by reserving space for representatives of marketing co-operatives of small-scale producers, which implies a prior (or at least simultaneous) organisation of such co-operatives.

For producers of intermediate goods, marketing can be improved by a combination of information services and additional or improved physical facilities. The existing information network is already an effective one, but it exploits the small-scale producers and benefits the professional traders whose business it is to know the sources of supply and potential customers. It is, nevertheless, important to set a formal sub-contracting exchange in motion and let it develop over time. The West Howrah industrial complex, which should include small industrial estate facilities, will need a sub-contracting exchange (whether formal or informal) to develop linkages between the larger and the smaller producers. One important set of production and marketing linkages which has to be developed is with the expanding Government and quasi-Government agricultural development programmes of West Bengal.

The feasibility of pulling small-scale producers into the export market through sub-contracting has been demonstrated by the ready-made garment export boom. Good possibilities should also exist in other lines of relatively labour-intensive production in which Calcutta is strong and where sub-contracting arrangements can be organised, e.g., metal castings. To realise such possibilities, however, requires the active intervention of profit-motivated private middlemen or an efficient subsidiary of the State Trading Corporation.

A note of caution should be sounded concerning the difficulties and dangers of intervention into the present functioning of the market. The middle man, the *mahajan*, in the Indian marketing system combines serveral functions, among them those of supplying credit, of obtaining raw materials and of providing access to markets (both in the narrow physical sense of space in the market places and in the broader abstract sense of commercial connections to the world outside the *bustee* work place). It is not enough to intervene in only one of these functions—by providing credit, for example. A small producer who gets outside credit but loses his market is worse off than before. To intervene successfully, agencies that want to assist small producers have to take on responsibility for all three of the mentioned functions, in addition to that of providing technical assistance where necessary.

It is the unorganised services in the informal sector which, though the least amenable to policy suggestions, constitute in fact one of the largest users of urban manpower. Laundering, barbering, tailoring, house-cleaning and the other basic services will be provided wherever large groups of people congregate and at whatever income levels the community enjoys. The best guarantee of customers for these services is a multiplicity of household incomes that are too small for the purchase of mechanical household appliances but large enough to command the services of sweepers, laundrymen and tailors. One additional attraction of the metropolis as an employment outlet for unskilled manpower is that it creates a vast demand by both enterprises and individuals for the casual labour and petty services provided by messengers, porters, carters, vehicle pullers and others. It also creates a market for manpower in connection with political rallies, for artisans at religious festivals and for the practitioners of the more questionable activities in which the big city abounds. As long as a large labour surplus exists, all these unorganised services in the metropolis will continue to absorb large numbers of the unskilled at low rates of compensation. The unorganised service sector will thus remain one of the manpower markets of last resort.

7

The Slum Improvement Programme in Calcutta; The Role of the CMDA

K.C. Sivaramakrishnan

Calcutta's problems have received world-wide attention. In recent years, there has been a vast and determined effort to solve some of these problems and to mitigate the effect of others. There is a growing interest in the urban renewal of Calcutta and the lessons it may have for large urban concentrations elsewhere in the developing world. This paper will review the origin, extent and progress of the urban development programme for the Calcutta Metropolitan District (CMD) with special reference to the *bustees* or slums which account for a significant proportion of the city's population.

Calcutta is less than 300 years old. By 1757, it had a population of 4,00,000. Fort William had already been built with an English quarter at its fringe. The discovery of coal and iron in the 1800s, some 150 miles north-west, led to

For more details the reader may consult, 'Calcutta 2001 : Triumph by Survival', in Ashish Bose *et al.*, *Population in India's Development, 1947-2000*, Vikas, Delhi, 1974, pp. 292-305; 'Organising a Metropolitan Development Programme: The Calcutta Case,' July 1972, mimeo; 'Towards a Better Calcutta: Significance for Eastern Region's Economy', Supplement to *Capital*, 26 July 1973; 'Urban Government', *Indian Journal of Social Work*, 36, October 1975-January 1976, pp. 385-9; 'Metro Cities and New Towns', in S.C. Dube (ed.), *India Since Independence*, Vikas, Delhi, 1977, pp. 358-92.

jute and engineering industries being set up on both banks of the river Hooghly. By 1880, a conurbation with settlements scattered over a length of forty miles on both banks of the river had come into existence. The post and railway facilities were set up in the 1850s, and by the end of the century, Curzon could boast of a city of 'a million souls' European city set down upon Asiatic soil, a most striking monument to the energy and achievement of the English race'.

CITY AND REGION

The Metropolitan District of today is only an extension of this conurbation. According to the 1971 Census, this area of 1425 sq. km. (550 sq. miles approx.) held 8.3 million people. Calcutta city itself is about 104 sq. km. (40 sq. miles) with only about 3 million people. The rest of the CMD is fragmented into thirty-five municipalities, sixty-one non-municipal urban areas and 500 semi-urban villages. It is important therefore to note that the Metropolitan District as such is not an administrative entity. As in other metropolitan cities, while the population of the core, i.e., Calcutta city, has remained constant at around three million, the population of the outlying municipal and non-municipal areas has been increasing, as is demonstrated by the following table.

TABLE 1

| | Population in millions | | |
	1951	1961	1971
Calcutta city	2.54	2.93	3.14
Other municipalities	2.01	2.76	3.51
Non-municipal urban and other parts	0.81	1.04	1.69
CMD as a whole	5.96	6.73	8.94

Compared to other metropolitan cities, the CMD experienced a relative decline in the decade 1961-71. While Bombay, Delhi and Madras in this decade had annual growth rates varying from 3.3 to 4.4 per cent, the CMD's growth rate has been less than 2.4 per cent. The notion that hungry migrants are daily pouring into Calcutta from all over its hinterland is unsupported by the data on immigration. Net immigration rates have continued to be low not only in the CMD, but for West Bengal State as a whole, at around 1 per cent per annum.

The eastern region comprising Orissa, Bihar, West Bengal, Assam and other north-eastern States is the least urbanised with an urban component of only 14.3 per cent of its total population of about 138 million, as compared to the national average of 19 per cent or 20-21 per cent in the southern and western regions. Even this 14 per cent drops down to about 9 per cent if the CMD is excluded, as Calcutta Metropolitan Development Authority (CMDA) dominance in the region is overwhelming. Of the twenty old major cities in the region with more than 1,00,000 people, Patna, with less than half a million is the next largest city after Calcutta. Demographic primacy apart, the CMD continues to be the economic centre for this region, the principal port for its exports and imports, the main source for its corporate and income taxes, the region's focus for business and educational institutions and facilities for medical care. Since investments in mining, steel and heavy industry were stepped up in the eastern region after independence, Calcutta has remained the pivot for servicing the new urban centres such as Rourkela, Bhilai, Durgapur and Bokaro.

IMBALANCES

Economic

Despite its primacy in the region, the metropolitan district is affected by some serious imbalances. To take up the economic issues first. Out of about 2.6 million jobs in the CMD, the primary sector accounts for 5 per cent, the secondary sector for 41 per cent and the tertiary sector for 54 per cent. In the secondary sector, the bulk of the employment is in the jute and engineering industries which have been affected by a fluctuating market and obsolescence. While a strong growth of industry in the CMD was noticed in the 1950s, stimulated largely by public investments, the recession which swept the country in 1965 persisted longer in West

Bengal. Registered factory employment declined by 2.6 per cent. Over 700 units, mainly in the engineering industry, closed down. Traffic at the Port, already affected by siltation in the Hooghly fell to 8.9 million tons by 1968 from 11.06 million tons three years earlier.

About 1,20,000 jobs were lost in the closed units (of which about 1,02,000 jobs were restored by 1971 through governmental support). Taking other sectors into account as well, employment in the CMD increased from 2.4 to 2.6 million jobs in 1961-71 compared to the population growth from 6.7 million to 8.3 million (24 per cent). The situation is further complicated by the fact that a significant portion of secondary and tertiary employment is marginal or informal in nature such as petty manufacturing and trade and services. In both sectors, the informal component accounts for 82 per cent of the units and 30 per cent of the employment. It is to be noted that low wages and gross underemployment are pronounced features of the informal sector. To a large extent, the stagnation in industry is to be explained by the colonial nature of the economy in the metropolitan district which had been sustained mainly through cheap raw materials, low wages and production for export.

Sex Ratio

As in other major cities in developing countries, the CMD's demographic profile is also characterised by age and sex-selective migration. Over the years, migration into Calcutta has occurred in waves, especially in the second half of the eighteenth century, induced by a series of famines in Bihar and Uttar Pradesh. Since these migration movements have been mainly of adult males, they brought about a demographic imbalance in the CMD's population. Compared to the national average of 930 and West Bengal's 891, the female-male ratio in the CMD is only 721 for 1000 males: in Calcutta city, it is even less at 636. This is also borne out by the fact that nearly 1.5 million people in the CMD live in single-member households. There is also a preponderance of adult males in the age group 20-50 accounting for 48 per cent of the city population. Children in the age group 0-14 constitute 32 per cent in the Metropolitan District and 29 per cent in Calcutta city compared to the national average of 42 per cent. On the occupational side, compared to 2.11 million male workers, there are only 1,18,000 female workers in the Metropolitan District. The bulk of these women, about 81,000 are listed in the category 'other services', such as domestic jobs, petty trading, education, health services, etc. There are less than 20,000 women engaged in industry, mainly in the jute mills. It should, therefore, be apparent that in the demographic and occupational sense, Calcutta is a 'male' city.

Haphazard Growth

Much has been said and written about the haphazard growth of the city and the metropolis. As in other industrial cities of the colonial era, in Calcutta too, the best locations were pre-empted by industry. Lines of communication developed to serve industry and the port, human settlements grew and expanded close to the work centres. Since the river itself was for long the major corridor for communication, much of the metropolis has been built on its banks. Besides, the river bank was high while the rest of the land sloped down and away from it. The built-up parts of the CMD thus form a ribbon clinging to the river-side. In course of time, urbanisation has spread farther to the east and west of the river. The ribbon has bulged at places but it is still hard to define the form in the usual pattern of inner core, outer core, suburban or fringe. Densities vary from 2,00,000 persons per sq. mile in parts of Calcutta city to less than 2,000 in other parts of the district. Another important feature of Calcutta's morphology is that there is no clear distinction between the *pakka* and *katcha*. *Pakka* is what is built up with good materials, planned to endure and well-finished. *Katcha* is make-shift, flimsy and half-or unfinished. Storeyed tenements of brick and mortar or concrete are *pakka*; *bustees* or slums are *katcha*. One index of the extent to which the two are interposed in Calcutta is that out of the city's 100 municipal wards, 97 have slums.

SERVICES

The level of civic and other services has never been adequate
to meet the needs of the city. Still, it had to bear the brunt
as a supply base for the eastern theatre in the Second World
War. In the wake of independence in 1947 came partition with
consequences more severe in Bengal and Calcutta than elsewhere. Out of a total of about eleven million refugees who are
estimated to have come to India from erstwhile East Pakistan
between 1947 and 1970, nearly four and a half million are
accounted for within West Bengal and at least one million
within the CMD. The poor infrastructural base just could not
sustain this influx of refugees. The Calcutta Metropolitan
Planning Organisation that had been set up in 1961, published
a Basic Development Plan in 1966. Making a case for the
urgency of massive investments in infrastructure to arrest
further deterioration, the Plan set forth in detail the desper-
ate conditions prevailing in the metropolis. Water supply,
once around fifty gallons per head per day, had come down
to less than twenty, and in some parts of the city, it was not
even ten. The drainage and sewer networks laid in the central
city by 1910 had to cater to three times the area and five
times the population; in many parts of the metropolis, even
removal of human wastes remained a problem. Of the total
stock of 1.6 million houses, over a third was *katcha*, only 15
per cent had independent tap water and 11 per cent had
separate toilets. Nearly 2.5 million, i.e., one out of every three
or four persons, were living in slums.

Partition had also removed, at one stroke, Calcutta's hinterland to the east. With the business district, port and bulk of
the employment on the east bank, the city had to devise better
links with the rest of the country and, more particularly, the
vast coal and mineral complex that was opening up on the
south and north-west, beyond the Hooghly. With only two
road crossings for a length of nearly fifty miles, the river
became a major communication barrier. Within the city itself,
circulation space was less than 6 per cent and on this, buses
and trams with a total capacity of two million trips a day
strained to carry thrice that number of passengers.

SLUMS

While wants were many and neglect pervasive, the effects were more severely felt in the slums of Calcutta than elsewhere. The size and spread of slums has been mentioned earlier. The nature and form of the *bustees* are such that the problems of infrastructure are rendered even more complex for them. A *bustee* is defined in the Calcutta Municipal Act as an 'area of land occupied by any collection of huts on a plot of land not less than ten cottahs' (1/6th acre). The *bustees* of Calcutta, unlike the *jhompris* of Delhi or the *jhopada-pattis* of Bombay, are not squatter settlements but tenancy arrangements wherein the land belongs to one person, the huts to another, and the slum-dweller is only a tenant paying a monthly rent without any claim either to the land or to the hut. The *bustee* is a tenancy settlement with a distinct three-tier arrangement. At one level are the slum dwellers who do not own the huts but who have rented a hut or a portion of it, the monthly rent varying from Rs 14 to Rs 20. At the next level are the *thika* tenants who own the huts on land they have leased. The land-owners constitute the third level. Sometimes, the *thika* tenants are themselves *bustee* dwellers. Most of the *bustees* were set up around ponds which were the main source of water. In most cases, the sites were poorly drained: circulation was more on the village pattern with narrow meandering lanes between closely packed huts. There was no underground drainage or sewer system since the city itself had such a network only for a small portion, but each hut or group of huts was provided service privies.

In 1958-59, the West Bengal State Statistical Bureau (SSB) carried out an extensive survey of the *bustees* in Calcutta. According to this survey, there were 3,093 holdings declared as *bustees* in the Calcutta Corporation's registers. It should be noted that a holding is a unit for property tax and may consist of several huts. The system of registering *bustees* came into vogue as these holdings pay municipal taxes at a lower-rate. The SSB survey revealed that registered *bustee* holdings had about 28,600 huts in which about 1,89,000 families or 6,69,000 persons were living. The average size of a *bustee* holding was about half an acre and contained about eight to ten huts. Each hut had about six to seven families living in them and, on an average, each room had four occupants. The survey also indicated that out of the 1,89,000 families, about 1,50,000 were natural families (comprising husband, wife, children or near relations living together) and about 35,000 were messing families (establishments comprising two to three or more individuals, messing and living together but not related to each other).

With respect to the physical condition of the *bustees*, 60 per cent of the structures were *katcha* with roofs of tile or tin with bamboo rafters. About 67 per cent of the huts were found to be dark and poorly ventilated. About 32 per cent of the huts covered less than 1000 sq. ft. while another 43 per cent occupied between 1,000-2,000 sq. ft. About 78 per cent of the huts were shared by more than six families. About 90 per cent of the families lived in only one room which also implied that kitchen, privy and bathing facilities were shared.

According to the SSB Survey, about 27 per cent of the *bustee* dwellers came from erstwhile East Pakistan, 22 per cent from Bihar, about 39 per cent from West Bengal and the remaining 12 per cent from other States. Calcutta's *bustees* are not just residential settlements but are work places as well. About 40 per cent of the rooms are used for a variety of purposes like petty manufacturing and trade. As for the occupational distribution, about 31 per cent of the workers were engaged either in factory or casual labour, 23 per cent in handicrafts or petty manufacturing (mainly manual) and about 22 per cent in trade and other services. It was estimated that 67 per cent of the workers received less than Rs 300 a month at current prices.

It is important to note that the registered *bustees* of Calcutta city are not the only abode of the urban poor. These account for just about a fifth of the total number of people living in marginal settlements of one kind or another. The residential pattern of the urban poor is shown in Table 2.

At this stage, it will be useful to refer to pavement dwellers or houseless peop, since much has been said or written about this category of people. The 1971 Census registered about 48,000 as shelterless people within Calcutta city. A CMDA survey carried out in 1975 indicates that, unlike

TABLE 2

	No. of Persons
In the registered *bustees* of Calcutta city	7,00,000
In the unregistered *bustees* and refugee colonies in the city	3,00,000
In the *bustees* in other parts of the Metropolitan District	15,00,000
In the refugee colonies outside Calcutta	10,00,000
Total	35,00,000

refugee and *bustee* occupants, pavement dwellers come mainly from the adjoining districts and the migratory flows are seasonal depending mainly on agricultural conditions in these adjoining areas. For example, the 1974 drought swelled the number of pavement dwellers to nearly 1,00,000 in the city, yet 20 per cent of those registered were found to have stayed in the city for more than ten years.

THE DEVELOPMENT PROGRAMME

The period that followed the release of the Basic Development Plan, as noted earlier, was one of economic stagnation and political instability. The State elections of 1967 and 1969 brought two coalitions of leftist parties into power. In each instance, the coalition failed and was followed by a spell of President's Rule. The political instability was reflected in widespread unrest, decline in investment and considerable public disorder. At the beginning of 1970, the chances of a major attack on Calcutta's ills seemed as remote as ever. In the middle of 1970, however, some earnest efforts began at the instance of the Prime Minister, to organise a development programme. During discussions between the Government of India and State officials, a four-year package of schemes to be launched from the fiscal year 1970-71 was identified. Special arrangements were worked out to finance the package that envisaged an outlay of about Rs 150 crores. A tax on goods entering the Metropolitan District was introduced with the proceeds earmarked partly to service bonds to be issued in support of the programme. Special loans and grants to be received from the Government of India were also agreed upon. A Calcutta Metropolitan Development Authority (CMDA) was also set up under a special statute to administer the development fund and the programme.

One of the important components of the Development Programme was the scheme for environmental improvements in the slums. The rationale for slum improvement was enunciated in the Basic Development Plan as follows:

(a) That in the interest of public health and welfare, a massive attack must be undertaken without delay to improve living conditions in the densely populated central areas of the metropolis, particularly to eradicate endemie and epidemic diseases such as cholera;

(b) That total clearance of all the *bustees* in Calcutta and Howrah and the provision of adequate sanitary housing for the 9,12,000 *bustee* dwellers, must be the long-term goal; but this total clearance, with the accompanying enormous rehousing programme, in all likelihood will not be completed for decades. Therefore, a programme of *bustee* improvement must be devised to bring the basic amenities of sanitation and environmental decency to the hundreds of thousands of *bustee* dwellers who must remain in their present *bustees* for many years to come;

(c) That economic as well as urgent health considerations, require the adoption of a basic policy of intensive *bustee* clearance in the central areas for Calcutta and Howrah, and extensive *bustee* improvement in the remaining *bustee* area;

(d) That the per capita cost of improvements (sanitation, water supply, drainage, filling of insanitary tanks, paving of passageways, and street lighting) are comparatively low and that a programme covering several hundred thousand *bustee* inhabitants is financially feasible;

(e) That the legal complications now frustrating effective action in dealing with *bustees* in Calcutta, Howrah and other municipal towns must be removed through a bold and direct approach expressed in new legislation;

(f) That a satisfactory solution of the *bustee* problem would rapidly benefit not only the *bustee* dwellers but every citizen of the Calcutta Metropolitan District.

COST

On the assumption that these proposed improvements would cost an average of about Rs 100 per head, the CMDA decided to commence the programme with an initial coverage of 1 million slum dwellers. Of the required Rs 100 million, the Government of India agreed to provide Rs 80 million as a grant. In the first phase, slums located in the north, south-west and south-east parts of Calcutta city, as also the slums in the industrial zones on the west and east banks of the river were taken up because of their density and pressing need for betterment. Though the SSB survey had provided broad physical and socio-economic data, these were not sufficient to prepare improvement schemes and implement them. The first task was, therefore, to carry out a physical survey of the *bustees*, identify their basic needs and prepare engineering plans and estimates for effecting the desired improvements. For this purpose, the *bustees* were grouped into 'clusters', each cluster comprising several *bustee* holdings with an average population of 5,000 to 6,000 people. The cluster was taken as the basic operational unit, and four or five clusters formed the basic organisational unit under an assistant engineer with supporting staff. Apart from the 500 odd engineers and other technical staff who were recruited for the programme, the CMDA also received the support of some prominent consulting firms in the city which took the initiative in forming several business co-operatives of hitherto unemployed young engineers or technicians to whom the jobs of survey, scheme preparation and implementation were farmed out. It was, therefore, possible to commence work on a fairly large scale.

In the beginning, it was decided to adopt the norms and standards formulated in the Basic Development Plan for the physical improvements. These standards, however, were derived from some sample studies and had not been tested in the field. Besides, the assumption of Rs 100 as the per capita cost had also been made on the prices prevailing a few years earlier. As a result of a special exercise undertaken by officials of the CMDA, the Corporation of Calcutta, the CMPO and the engineering units carrying out the surveys and field work, the per capita ceiling cost was raised to Rs 146.

While the technology adopted in providing these improvements is quite simple, the working conditions are rendered very
difficult because of the acute congestion in the *bustees* and
their scattered location. For instance, the sanitary latrines,
perhaps the most important component from the health point
of view, are simple enough structures, but the location of each
had to be decided in consultation with six or seven families
living in a hut. Quite often, a free space of over $4' \times 4'$ would
not be available and the sanitary latrine had to be put up in
exactly the same place where a service privy stood, after removing all the filth. In the Calcutta programme, community
latrines at the fringe of the slum have not been favoured. That
the latrine for the hutment, though used by several families,
is kept reasonably clean is an evidence of its acceptance by the
bustee dwellers. Water taps have also had to be provided
separately for each hutment quadrangle.

ENVIRONMENTAL IMPROVEMENT

The process of physical improvement has been in progress now
for about six years. The work has been extensive and, so far,
about Rs 15 crores have been spent on the programme. From
the modest start confined to some registered *bustees* in north-
west Calcutta, the programme coverage has been steadily
enlarged to include registered slums as also other marginal
settlements in south and south-east Calcutta, the industrial
slums in Howrah and other parts of the Metropolitan District.
In the 1,500 odd slums in Calcutta city and nearly an equal
number in the Metropolitan District where improvement works
have been completed already, the change is apparent. The
conversion of service latrines to sanitary latrines (about 30,000
have been installed so far) has itself produced a major impact
on the scene. Contrary to earlier apprehensions, the latrines
are being looked after by the residents who are watchful against
misuse. The 12,000 odd water points and bathing platforms are
regarded as a major facility. The pathways paved so for exceed
7,00,000 sq. metres. The 6,00,000 metres of sewer and underground drainage networks have replaced, in most slums, the
unsightly and insanitary mess of open drains. Even a casual
visitor to any of the improved *bustees* cannot only see the

change in the environment but will also notice that the residents welcome the improvements.

Undoubtedly, the *bustee* programme in Calcutta has been one of the largest slum renewal efforts in the world. In pointed contrast to previous attitudes, the Calcutta experience has also prompted increasing acceptance in the country as a whole of slum improvement as a realistic alternative to demolition and clearance. Within two years after the programme started in Calcutta, it was extended to other major cities with Central Government assistance. In the Fifth Plan, slum improvement has been included as a component of the 'Minimum Needs' programme. The lessons of the Calcutta experience, though limited to the physical environment, are, therefore, relevant to urban development.

MAINTENANCE

The maintenance of the improved facilities has been a major and, as yet, unresolved question. The record of maintenance of public utilities in the city has rarely been good and it is fair to say that many development schemes taken up have been necessitated by long accumulated maintenance neglect. The *bustee* scene is not an exception to this general phenomenon. In fact, it is worse, for the line of distinction between capital works and maintenance in a *bustee* is very thin indeed. It has been the Authority's sad experience that the maintenance of improved facilities in the *bustees* has yet to be adequately organised. The Corporation and other Municipal bodies whose responsibility it is to maintain the facilities have invariably cited lack of resources as the main reason. This plea cannot be brushed aside either, because Municipal taxes, low and poorly collected as they are, are practically non-existent in the *bustees*. As mentioned earlier, under the Calcutta Municipal Act, rates in respect of *bustees* are limited by a ceiling of 18 per cent of the annual value compared to 33 per cent in other cases. Very recently, the State Government has passed legislation removing this ceiling in *bustees* where improvements have been carried on.

In many cases, the environment deficiencies are not confined to the bustees but are present beyond their boundaries as well. In south-west Calcutta, for instance, where *bustees* came up in the wake of the Docks a hundred years ago, sewer and drainage networks even in the non-*bustee* areas have been generally over-loaded. Water supply and waste removal have been just as poor. In such cases, physical improvements cannot be confined to the *bustees* but have to cover the area as a whole. But there are serious cost and technical limitations in the process and, quite often, the desired effect of improving the *bustee* environment is not attained.

In many Calcutta slums, cattle and people co-exist. The city's milk supply system has not been adequate and a large number of cattle sheds have been set up over the years in the slums. One estimate places the number at about 2,500. Removal of cattle wastes is a serious problem and it is just not possible to sustain a sewer network that can service cattle as well. In many of the *bustees*, pits have been constructed to contain cattle wastes but this has not been very effective. Recently, the CMDA and the State Government initiated a major scheme to remove about 70,000 cattle from the Calcutta and Howrah urban areas and resettle them in a number of small dairies at the metropolitan fringe.

LAN OWNERSHIP

A major criticism of the programme has been that it leaves the quality of the shelter and the pattern of the slums untouched. Of course, the objective has been to concentrate on the environmental improvement rather than the shelter. Yet, within limits, there is scope to bring about some modest improvements to the shelter and possibly the street pattern. An important limitation in this regard has been the land ownership pattern. The three-tier structure of landlord, *thika* tenant and hutment dweller has been mentioned earlier. Since the *bustee* lands in Calcutta are privately owned, unlike many other cities where slums are usually on public land, a question arose in 1970-71 about the desirability of carrying out improvements on such lands at public expense. The West Bengal Slum Areas (Improvement and Clearance) Act 1971 was enacted to deal with this and other related issues. Under the Act, easement rights have been conferred on the public authority carrying out the improvements. Where clearance, redevelopment and rehousing are envisaged, the Act also

provides for taking over the rights of the landlord and the *thika*
tenant with compensation at twenty-five times and five times the
net annual income respectively. According to one estimate, the
compensation to be paid in respect of all the registered slums in
Calcutta might not exceed Rs 50 crores. But it is not the land
cost but the cost of the dwelling unit itself that forbids large-
scale redevelopment. At current technology, the cheapest *pakka*
dwelling unit in Calcutta costs not less than Rs 7,000 or a
monthly payment of Rs 45-50 which is clearly beyond the means
of the *bustee* dwellers. For a system of house improvement,
adequate legal and administrative arrangements have to be made
first to acquire title to land and structure and thereafter transfer
it to the hut dwellers, jointly or severally, against payment and
in a manner where it can be used as a collateral to finance house
improvement. These complexities have tended to inhibit action,
but unless these are sorted out, mere acquisition of land, it is
feared, would just block capital.

PARTICIPATION

The participation of the *bustee* dwellers in the programme has
been quite significant. While the initial stages like survey and
scheme preparation were viewed with scepticism, there was
much interaction with the public when engineering works com-
menced on the ground. In most *bustees*, local youth clubs or
recreation clubs interacted with the CMDA officials on the location of various facilities and in securing the co-operation of the
hutment dwellers in getting the work done. Any process of public
interaction has its hostile element as well and the *bustees* were
no exception, but, on the whole, the programme was welcomed.
Even in some *bustees* where political extremists had found refuge,
the CMDA staff and the improvement works were not resisted.
In this process of public participation, a major factor was the
youthfulness and idealism of the engineering staff. They were
also assisted by a small group of social workers, recruited by
the CMDA, for contacting local bodies and organisations in
the *bustees* and for selecting suitable locations not only for the
physical improvement but also for facilities like schools and
dispensaries, etc., which were to be set up under other sectors
of the CMDA's programme.

The contribution of physical labour is sometimes regarded as a true measure of public participation. The *bustees* of Calcutta, it is to be noted, are the abode of the urban poor who depend on a variety of jobs for their daily sustenance. Many work as labourers in the Port or the factories and many are self-employed. Those who have skills to offer, like masons and carpenters, did participate in the *bustee* programme, but as paid workers. Neither the type of work nor the scale of operation was conducive to any organised contribution of voluntary labour.

WIDER RELEVANCE

It is too early to assess in qualitative terms the effects of the 'sanitising' programme on the health of *bustee* dwellers and the environment. Currently, an elaborate, metropolitan-wide survey is in progress, initiated by the CMDA and the State Government's Health Department and assisted by the Ford Foundation, to identify present morbidity/mortality characteristics. The survey seeks to establish bench marks which could be reviewed periodically. Preliminary results indicate a slight decline in gastro-intestinal diseases in the improved *bustees*, but we should wait for the survey to conclude. Besides, health and environment in the *bustees* depend on a variety of other factors, such as nutrition, child care, medical facilities, density of living, quality of the air and so on, and efforts are being made in this regard under the CMDA and other programmes in recent years.

The problem of the maintenance of the improved facilities brought about by the CMDA urban development programme remains unresolved. At the current levels of investment, it is estimated that expenditure for operation and maintenance will be about Rs 20 million for 1975-76 and will increase to Rs 40 million in 1980-81. If capital amortisation of only one-third of the investments is added, this will imply an additional Rs 30 million per annum. Current levels of taxation and accounting for civic services are nowhere near meeting this bill. While the present development programme marks the beginning of a major effort to resolve the problems of physical obsolescence, its continuation and success will depend on the organisational framework that will sustain the change in the quality of urban living that has been achieved to some extent.

The problems of urban renewal in Calcutta are similar to those in other cities in India and the less developed countries of Asia. What is of critical importance is the need of an institutional framework capable of dealing with the maintenance of the urban infrastructure and basic services. Since the Calcutta Municipal Corporation evolved historically as the focus of national and provincial politics rather than as a civic institution, it was able to perform some maintenance functions but could not be the instrument of urban development. The CMDA was set up outside the municipal framework so that it could adopt a metropolitan, multi-sectoral approach to the question of the urban development of Calcutta. The CMDA marks the emergence of a new model of urban government and inter-agency co-ordination that is necessary for the emergence of a 'metropolitan' view of the problems and the future development of the city, and to provide a rational framework in which municipal institutions and special purpose government agencies can participate efficiently in the implementation of development plans.

The high cost of urban renewal has been mentioned. In June 1973, IDA credit of $ 35 million was made available for forty-four out of a total of 125 CMDA schemes. This raises the question of whether, in the light of the experience of Calcutta, urban renewal is possible in the less developed countries without international financial assistance. This is a major question and would require careful analysis and considerable thought. As it is, international assistance for urban development—mainly channelled by the World Bank—is limited to planning support and marginally to execution. Any observation on the effectiveness of such international assistance will have to be preceded by a careful study of the various programmes of urban development which are being currently carried on in various less developed countries.

8

Housing for the Urban Poor in Ahmedabad: An Integrated Urban Development Approach

Kirtee Shah

Ahmedabad, the sixth largest city in India, has been associated with Mahatma Gandhi, the textile industry and some internationally renowned institutions. It is also famous for its historical and modern architecture. Two of the world's most celebrated architects, Le Corbusier and Louis Kahn, contributed to the city's architectural glory, not to mention works done by a score of their local disciples, followers and imitators. Unplastered brick walls, exposed concrete, deep recessed French windows and landscaped gardens in the front, have become a new status symbol for the affluent Ahmedabadis.

The Ahmedabad of modern beautiful architecture is one city— largely confined to its relatively new residential areas in the western half across the river Sabarmati, inhabited mainly by the rich and the affluent middle classes. But, there is another, conspicuously less-known city of the poor, where as many as half of its 1.80 million live in about 700 slums and squatter settlements dotted all over the city—predominantly in its eastern half—and 1,140 dilapidated, badly ventilated and poorly serviced *chawls*. The contrast between the life-style of the affluent, manifested only partly through the facade of their buildings and that of the poor with their indigenous, spontaneous, self-help architecture of mud and gunny bag walls, bamboo thatch and tin-sheet roofs, is symptomatic and symbolic of the deeper contradictions inherent in our social, economic and political system.

Gujarat is one of the most highly urbanised States in India. In 1961, for the country as a whole, the percentage of urban population to the total was 18; in Gujarat it was 25.77. In 1971, the urban population of the country increased to 19.87 per cent, while for Gujarat it increased to 28.13 per cent.

Ahmedabad, the largest metropolitan city of Gujarat, has been experiencing a rapid growth. The percentage population growth of Ahmedabad during 1901-1971 period was 841.0 per cent, which was higher than that of Calcutta (653.5 per cent), Greater Bombay (635.2 per cent), Madras (485.7 per cent), Hyderabad (300.8 per cent), Kanpur (531.1 per cent) and Poona (578.6 per cent). Out of the nine largest metropolitan cities of India, Ahmedabad has remained behind only two cities—Delhi, which experienced a phenomenal growth rate of 1604.2 per cent and Bangalore, which was only slightly ahead with 926.76 per cent.[1]

From a mere 1.95 lakh people in 1901, Ahmedabad grew to 788 lakhs in 1951, to 11.50 lakhs in 1961 and 15.85 lakhs in 1971, averaging an annual growth rate of nearly 4 per cent. It is projected that the city will have about 35 lakhs living in the year A.D. 2000.[2] Of this increase in population, as suggested by the available statistics for the period between 1931 to 1951, 24.8 per cent was due to new births, 14.2 per cent due to extension of municipal limits and 61.5 per cent due to migration.[3]

The city has not been able to absorb the continuous and ever-increasing urban growth and has lagged behind in providing infrastructural services, community facilities and residential accommodation. This has resulted in a severe housing shortage and the mushroom growth of slums and squatter settlements. The intensity of the housing problem was highlighted by the

[1]*Census Abstract on Urbanisation*, Town and Country Planning Organisation, Ahmedabad, 1971.

[2]*Revised Development Plan 1975-1985*, Ahmedabad Municipal Corporation, Town Development Department, Ahmedabad, 1975.

[3]See the Administrative Reports of the Ahmedabad Municipal Corporation for the year 1931-51.

"Expert Committee on Methods for Achieving Low Cost, Large-scale Housing Construction in the Major Cities", appointed by the Government of India. According to the findings of the committee, the shortage of *pakka* houses in Ahmedabad, classified according to income groups, as on July 1, 1970, was as follows:

TABLE 1

Monthly income range	Housing shortage (in units)
Rs 0-100	65,300
Rs 101-250	23,600
Rs 251-500	9,300
Rs 501-1,000	4,200
Rs 1,001 and above	2,600

The investigations revealed that 84.5 per cent of the total housing shortage in Ahmedabad was among the families earning less than Rs 250 per month. More importantly, it pointed out that as many as 65,300 families, in need of shelter, earned less than Rs 100 per month.

SLUM CHARACTERISTICS

A Census of Slums carried out by the Ahmedabad Municipal Corporation in May 1976 has thrown light on various aspects of life and conditions in the slums of Ahmedabad. This survey identified 81,255 families with 4,15,103 members, who were residing in about 700 slums and squatter settlements all over the city.

Over 83 per cent of these families had migrated to Ahmedabad from other States and the rural areas of Gujarat; 78.9 per cent of them were occupying private land, whereas those on Municipal and Government plots constituted only 8 per cent and 5.9 per cent respectively. The average family size was 5.1 persons with 40.2 per cent having more than five members in the household. Literacy rate was as low as 10.8 per cent, over 83 per cent of the people were Hindu and 14.78 per cent Muslim. While 28.9 per cent of the households earned less than Rs 200 per month, 54.5 per cent of the households had an average monthly income of Rs 200-400. It was found that 53.2 per cent of these households occupied a ground area of only 100-200 sq. ft., while about 27 per cent were accommodated in plots of 50-100 sq. ft. only. About 28 per cent had built their houses with mud walls, 25.88 per cent with burnt bricks and mud mortar, while 63.18 per cent had tin-sheet roofs.

Only 5 per cent of the households owned the land and their huts, and out of the remaining non-owners, 64.70 per cent were paying rent. Among those who paid rent, 7.69 per cent paid less than Rs 5 per month, 34.48 per cent Rs 5-10, 29.93 per cent Rs 10-15 and 12.20 per cent Rs 15-20; only 15.70 per cent paid a rent of Rs 20 and above. When asked about their ability and willingness to pay for the house, 29.72 per cent wanted to pay below Rs 15 a month, 25.58 per cent Rs 15-20; 21.54 per cent Rs 20-25 and only 11.68 per cent expressed their ability to pay Rs 25-30.[4]

There are 81,255 households in slums, and 59,456 in 1,094 *chawls*. This number refers to only those *chawls*, out of a total of 1,140, on the Municipal records. In these old, dilapidated structures, the living conditions are only slightly better compared to slum huts. Out of 1,094 *chawls*, 899 (81.2 per cent) have no running water. In 124 (11.30 per cent) *chawls*, there is no provision for basic facilities like latrines. In 952 *chawls* (86.93 per cent) there are community latrines but 122 (11.15 per cent) of them have latrines without any drainage.

GOVERNMENT RESPONSE

These statistics of the inadequate housing and appalling living conditions of large segments of the city community look even more depressing when judged from the half-hearted and un-imaginative efforts on the part of the concerned authorities. According to the Perspective Plan of Gujarat, the number of tenements constructed under the Slum Clearance Housing Scheme in Gujarat during the Second Plan (1956-61), Third Plan (1961-66) and the three Annual Plans (1966 to 1969) were

[4]See *Census of Slums*, Ahmedabad Municipal Corporation, Ahmedabad, 1976.

2,400, 2,930 and 2,714 respectively, totalling only 8,044 house units in thirteen years. What was even more surprising was the provision in the Fifth Perspective Plan of the State of Rs 2 crores to build only 3,000 housing units for the slum-dwellers in the whole of Gujarat.[5]

The Ahmedabad Municipal Corporation, until the Slum Clearance Board was formed in 1972, was the prime agency for providing houses to the slum-dwellers in the city. The Corporation built 1,736 tenements under the Slum Clearance Schemes during the Second Plan (1956-61), 3,130 during the Third Plan (1961-66) and 2,090 during the Three Annual Plans (1966 to 1969) totalling 6,959 house units in thirteen years. According to the Revised Development Plan, 1975-1985 of the Ahmedabad Municipal Corporation, no houses were constructed under the Slum Clearance Scheme during the year 1969. In 1970 only twenty-four, in 1971, 240 and in 1972, 768 houses were built. By any reckoning, this must be termed a poor performance in the face of such a massive backlog of housing and increasing demand.

Another public sector agency responsible for the promotion of housing is the State Housing Board. This agency's lack of involvement with the urban poor was evident from the fact that in Ahmedabad, where 84.5 per cent of the housing deficit has been amongst families earning less than Rs 250 per month, its lowest category of housing—the LIG Schemes—were meant for families earning Rs 350-600 per month, which meant that till the schemes for the economically weaker sections (less than Rs 350 per month household income) were introduced in the early seventies, the SHB had no effective programme for the real poor.

INEFFECTIVENESS OF GOVERNMENT PROGRAMMES

The slum clearance efforts, though well-intentioned, fluctuated between two extremes—indiscriminate bulldozing on the one hand, and *pakka*, expensive, multi-storey housing on the other. Their fortunes swung with the change in the political climate and the mood of the local politicians. The sudden uprooting of the slum communities, in the absence of any alternative, caused panic and resulted in severe personal, social and economic

[5]Ahmedabad: *The Perspective Plan of Gujarat*, Vol. I.

dislocations. The continual threat of locational instability, besides encouraging an undesirable system of protection money to the anti-social elements, left the vulnerable poor at the mercy of small-time politicians and made them victims of political manipulation.

On the other end of the spectrum were highly subsidised, uneconomic, and socio-culturally undesirable, slum clearance tenements. They were symbolic as they were too expensive to be built on a scale to make any significant impact. They were ill-conceived and dysfunctional as they ignored the life-styles, interaction patterns, living habits and cultural traditions of the slum communities coping with a transient rural-urban culture. The multi-storey *pakka* houses, ostensibly built for achieving higher densities, were converted into vertical, concrete-box slums replacing horizontal shanty towns because they were designed to meet extraneous requirements and not the people's felt needs. Slum clearance tenements were uneconomic for the occupants as their non-subsidised rents were beyond the paying capacity of the poor. They were expensive and, therefore, beyond the capacity of the State exchequer. The economic artificality caused by the heavy subsidy resulted in a high degree of sub-letting, pushing the real poor back into the slums and thus defeating the real purpose of the undertaking. It must be some measure of the insensitivity of our system and the weight of the *status quo* on our establishment that, despite such glaring limitations, old fashioned slum clearance is still talked about and is vigorously implemented in many places.

NEW APPROACH

The accumulating experience with regard to the futility of multi-storey slum clearance housing, together with the lack of resources and the increasing pressure of funding institutions resulted in a much-needed pragmatism, and more rational and realistic programmes such as *in situ* environmental improvement of existing slums and Site and Services Schemes. Unfortunately, both these programmes received luke-warm treatment at the hands of politicians, administrators, planners and implementors. The *in situ* environmental improvement programme got bogged down in legal squabbles, as a majority of the city slums were on private lands. (In Ahmedabad, for instance, 79 per cent of the slums are on private land, 8 per cent on municipal land and 5 per cent on government land.) Uneven topography and high densities created practical problems in laying services or finding open spaces for additional toilets or class-rooms or health centres. Some work was attempted in the initial phase of the scheme, but it did not progress very far.

The Site and Services idea remained very much on paper, lack of political will contributing largely to its hesitant start. Some attempts here and there are being discussed, but neither the present involvement nor the future plans indicate any serious commitment to this approach. This, in a nutshell, was the scenario in Ahmedabad with regard to the housing problem and the efforts to mitigate the suffering of the slum-dwellers before the Integrated Urban Development Project was conceived.

IUDP: MORE THAN FLOOD RELIEF

The Integrated Urban Development Project (IUDP) at Vasna, Ahmedabad, was set up after the August-September 1973 flood of the river Sabarmati swept away more than 3,000 slum and squatter colonies situated along its banks.

While the Ahmedabad Municipal Corporation was engaged in the task of providing emergency relief and settling a few flood-affected families in transit camps, the Ahmedabad Study Action Group, (ASAG), a voluntary, inter-disciplinary organisation of professionals submitted, after establishing informal contracts with the affected slum community, an exploratory proposal to the municipal authorities, who were already contemplating some action. ASAG's proposal reflected its not-housing-but-development bias and emphasis on participatory action which was based on intensive experience with the urban and rural poor, observations of the effects of the previous and on-going efforts by the Government and other agencies dealing with the problem of slums. Before embarking on the IUD Project, ASAG had worked with twenty rural communities in constructing 2,500 low cost houses and a slum relocation programme for a community of 300 families in Nadiad.

ASAG emphasised the following points in its proposal:

1. The flood had caused a temporary fear psychosis among the river bank slum dwellers. They had recognised the fact that the habitation on the river was no longer safe and relocation was necessary. If a viable alternative that was acceptable and cheap could be provided, they would voluntarily agree to shift. It was pointed out that the earlier efforts had met with resistance as people were simply driven out or offered accommodation they could not afford.

2. For a successful relocation effort, involvement of the flood-affected people at every stage in the process was indispensable. It was argued that previous attempts at relocation had failed as decisions were imposed from the top without consulting the people.

3. 'Slums are people, not places', ASAG emphasised. The slum is more a reflection on attitudes towards life than of physical or environmental conditions. The slum was not simply a housing problem but a complex socio-economic, cultural and political problem. A comprehensive approach incorporating social, economic, educational and motivational inputs, along with housing, would lead to the emergence of an alternative value system and bring about far-reaching attitudinal and behavioural changes. ASAG suggested that not merely a housing programme but a comprehensive developmental effort was needed for integrated urban renewal.

SHARED RESPONSIBILITY

The Ahmedabad Municipal Corporation decided to adopt the broad-based, comprehensive developmental strategy outlined by the ASAG in its proposal. The Government of Gujarat, as a part of its flood rehabilitation policy, consented to allocate a 43 acre site, about seven kilometres from the centre of the city, together with a subsidy of Rs 700 per family. OXFAM, a British international voluntary agency, emphasising the developmental perspective, agreed to provide Rs 400 per family and an additional sum to support the 'social action component'. Though the site was outside its jurisdiction, the Ahmedabad Municipal Corporation, in an unprecedented gesture, decided to provide infrastructural services including piped water, sewerage, street lighting, roads and community facilities such as kindergartens, schools, shops, health and community centres. The Housing and Urban Development Corporation (HUDCO) approved a low interest, easy instalment loan to be repaid over a twenty-year period by the occupants. When a majority of the flood-affected slum dwellers, after weighing the short and long-term implications of relocation, agreed to move, the Integrated Urban Development Project was born.

PROCESS OF DEVELOPMENT

The floods swept Ahmedabad in August-September 1973. The first brick on the site was laid on 15 May 1974. By the end of September 1975, 2,248 houses, along with infrastructural services such as water supply, sewerage, street lighting, were completed in a short period of sixteen months. For the 2,248 houses at the new habitat, 1,879 families had paid their eligibility deposit by mid-March 1976, indicating their willingness to shift voluntarily, and 1,246 families had already moved. At present, some 1,700 families live there. When fully occupied, about 12,000 people will be housed in the new township meant exclusively for former slum dwellers.

The Integrated Urban Development Project's significance is not so much in its final outcome as in the process. The IUDP has attempted a departure from the conventional slum clearance housing. In form and content, it is different from the previous efforts to house the city's poor. Instead of bulldozing the poor without their consent and against their will, a negotiated settlement based on the voluntary choice of the people has been attempted. Instead of being passive recipients of dole, people have been made active partners in the process designed to foster their entry into the mainstream of the city's life from their previous illegal and marginal existence. Instead of providing uneconomic and culturally undesirable multi-storey houses, modest shelters have been built to suit their life-style. Recognising the futility of exclusive housing in bringing about the desired social and economic transition, social, educational, organisational and motivational objectives have been integrated into the housing and environmental improvement schemes. An attempt is being made to enhance their productive capacity and to increase their income to off-set the negative consequences of relocation. Through the IUDP, an opportunity has been created for Governmental agencies and voluntary institutions to work together for the benefit of the people.

VOLUNTARY AGENCY INTERVENTION

Before describing the ways in which this was done, it is necessary to understand the factors and processes which facilitated such an approach. It must be realised that the Integrated Urban Development project was primarily an inter-Governmental effort to rehabilitate the flood victims. To start with, it was a Municipal Corporation project. The major resource inputs came from the local and the State Government. But for the positive intervention of agencies outside the Governmental system, it is conceivable that this project too would have been like any other conventional flood rehabilitation or slum clearance programmes: the contractor would have built houses and the flood victims would have occupied them after they were completed. The story would have begun and ended with houses.

This positive intervention was exercised by a voluntary agency, ASAG. As mentioned elsewhere, ASAG not only brought in a developmental bias, but due to its flexible structure, people orientation, multidisciplinary nature, institutional know-how and rapport with the community, it could provide the credibility, rationale and an organisational base to convince the Municipal Corporation to attempt an unconventional approach. It does not need to be stressed that Government agencies due to their structural limitations, bureaucratic rigidities, target-orientation, impersonal methods, and sectoral view of the task at hand would be hesitant to initiate a participatory approach or accept a multiple involvement. Neither their organisational culture nor their perception of the problem would permit them anything more than the building of houses.

The second important factor which generated a conducive climate for the Integrated Urban Development project, was the decision by the Ahmedabad Municipal Corporation to create a semi-autonomous organisation for decision-making and

implementation. This arrangement not only insulated the project
from political interference but also safeguarded its interest
during the political crisis which brought about the downfall of
the Government at the State as well as at the Municipal level.
The arrangement for institutional co-ordination, through the
mechanism of a semi-autonomous Project Committee, distributed areas of responsibility to the participating agencies according
to their respective strengths. Thus, representatives of the
Government of Gujarat and the Ahmedabad Municipal
Corporation, as members of the Project Committee, helped in
obtaining resources, provided policy guidelines, advised in
administrative, procedural and technical matters: but the entire
sphere of project planning, implementation, community involvement and related matters was assigned to the ASAG. Much of
the project's success may be ascribed to the helping relationship
and restrained but positive role played by the various contributing agencies. Undoubtedly, the relationship of trust between
the Municipal Corporation and the ASAG, while it lasted,
proved the major asset of the project.

The third positive influence and support came from OXFAM,
which helped the ASAG to sell the developmental package to
the Government officials who are usually suspicious of ambitious, long-term and intangible plans. OXFAM's willingness
to support the social action component, through which many
community, organisational, educational, medical, motivational,
training and income supplementary activities have been initiated and maintained, helped the ASAG in building a nucleus of
people who continue providing essentially managerial and
organisational assistance to the community, which hopes to
prepare itself to look after its own affairs.

The Integrated Urban Development project at Vasna,
Ahmedabad comprises two mutually complementary, overlapping – symbiotic, if you like—streams of activities. The first
relates to the provision of the physical infrastructure for living
through the erection of a township on the city outskirts for
about 12,000 people, who lived an unhygienic, deprived and
forgotten existence in the slums of the city. The physical infrastructure for living includes housing, services such as water
supply, drainage, street lighting, roads, transportation, and
community facilities like pre-primary and primary schools, health

centres, shops, community buildings, recreation areas and other amenities. The second stream of activities attempts to build *people*—a cohesive community of self-respecting, self-reliant individuals. This is being done through various activities under the social action component.

The reference frame and the guiding principles, which ultimately determined the house cost, design and site lay-out, were based on inferences drawn from three sources. Largely negative inferences, in terms of what not to do, were based on the performance of earlier slum clearance and other housing efforts by local and State Governments in different parts of the country. The positive inferences were drawn from the feedback data available from ASAG's previous efforts at housing low income families. Periodic observations on the functional adaptability of space arrangements, appropriateness of the materials, impact on the modalities of group behaviour and the indigenous changes made by the users were chosen for testing and modifying the planning hypothesis. However, the most important factors determining the shape, cost and community lay-out were the living habits, economics, felt needs and interaction patterns of this specific community.

FINANCE

Through numerous meetings in the community and discussions with their accepted leaders, alternative housing strategies were unfolded by the trained community workers. There were three possibilities: (i) to build on their own whatever they desired, with the available flood relief subsidy on the Site and Services model; (ii) to add whatever they could from their savings and borrowing and to build individually; or (iii) to obtain collective borrowing depending on their repayment ability and to organise a collective housing effort.

An overwhelming number opted for the third alternative. They wanted to build houses, not serviced plots. Left on their own, without any flood relief subsidy, they had no capacity to invest or to repay the borrowed capital which would be needed to construct good houses. They argued that by adding a little more they could build permanent houses rather than temporary shelters. They believed that this was an opportunity to invest

in their future and they did not want to squander the chance.
Not many had savings. Only 27.40 per cent of the initial 1,475
families surveyed had saved between Rs 150 and Rs 300.
After detailed investigation through personal contacts, interviews and surveys, it was found that a large majority of them
was willing to and capable of spending between Rs 15 and Rs 20
per month per family for housing. A larger number of them
expressed their desire to invest an amount on which they would
not have to pay more than Rs 20 a month.

The Housing and Urban Development Corporation
(HUDCO) provides loans at 6 per cent for the housing of low
income families. This loan is to be repaid in monthly instalments over a period of twenty years. Deducting about
Rs 4-5 for the taxes and maintenance of services from Rs 20
(the people's expressed capacity to pay for the house), it was
worked out that Rs 1,700 to Rs 1,800 could be made available
for the purpose. This, added to the flood relief subsidy of
Rs 700 from the Government of Gujarat and Rs 400 from
OXFAM, made a sum of Rs 2,800-2,900 that could be spent
on the house. The completed house at Vasna cost only Rs. 2,860;
this means that, if the subsidy amount of Rs 1,000 is deducted,
only Rs 1,760 was borrowed from HUDCO. The occupants
are expected to pay Rs 20 a month out of which Rs 14.06 goes
to HUDCO towards the repayment of loan and interest, Rs 4
to the Ahmedabad Municipal Corporation for the maintenance
of infrastructural services and Rs 1.38 goes towards building
a Community Contingency Fund.

PEOPLE'S PARTICIPATION

Attempts were made to involve the community in the design
of the houses and the site lay-out. A few schematic, skeleton,
preliminary design outlines were evolved based on the feedback
studies of the earlier housing efforts, and the expressed needs
of the target community. Large-scale models of various alternative design possibilities were taken to different settlement
clusters by a group of community workers and architects. These
plans were discussed at the family, neighbourhood, cluster and
leadership level. Their reactions, comments and observations
resulted in many important changes in the design of the house.

At one stage in these continuing negotiations, the community's limitation in perceiving a finished house through wooden models was pointed out. In order to help people contribute more meaningfully, a block of eight houses was constructed on the site for demonstration and feedback purposes. A formal foundation stone laying ceremony attracted about 4,000 people to see the houses. The changes suggested by the people were accommodated within the budget limits, determined by people's repayment capacity.

Participation in the construction of the houses was optional and voluntary. Only 19 per cent of the families contacted were able to participate in the construction. Others found it difficult due to lack of construction experience, higher paying jobs elsewhere or simply physical disability for manual labour. Yet, about 130 consenting families were moved to a transit camp near the site. They worked for some time building houses but gradually their number dwindled for several reasons.

In Vasna, instead of multi-storey tenements, single storey, low cost (Rs 11.25 per sq. ft.), low specification houses have been constructed. Every family has been provided a plot of about 300 sq. ft. on which a house with plinth area of about 248 sq. ft. has been built. Each house has a multi-purpose room, a covered verandah, cooking and storing alcoves, a bathroom, a toilet for two families and a common backyard between four families. There is a water tap in each house and a regular sewer for waste disposal. Each house has an asbestos cement roof, 9″ outer walls and 4½″ intermediate walls of brick and cement mortar. Mud and cowdung have been used for wall plaster and flooring.

Outdoor life is an important aspect of their living. In their immediate slum surrounding as well as in the villages, family activities spill over into the open spaces in front of the houses. To provide extension open spaces in front of each house and to facilitate community activities, the houses at Vasna have been built around large, interlinking community courtyards. On an average, a courtyard for eight families measures about 40′ × 52′. These courtyards have become the focus of family and group activities.

ALLOCATION

Much before the first family moved to the new township, the project planners had realised the complexities involved in the allotment of houses. Loss of identity, personal dislocations, lack of co-operation and even hostility, among the neighbours in a newly-built community are often attributed to faulty allotment of houses.

At Vasna, the risks were unusually high. Approximately 44 per cent of the eligible families were Muslims and the remaining Hindus. To decide to segregate them in the new place because of the known history of hostility, tension and conflict would have meant the perpetuation of prejudices and a loss of a great opportunity to achieve social integration. On the other hand, to mix them together indiscriminately would run the risk of generative conflict. The age-old method of drawing lots was not only improper, but in this case, also dangerous.

It was decided to leave the choice to the people. Each family was given the option of choosing its own neighbours. In a complex socio-metric exercise, spanning over nine months, people were asked to make their own decisions in chosing neighbours who would share their toilet, backyard and courtyard. It was a lively and stimulating experience in group behaviour. Through the dialogue that ensued, people learned to weigh their options, use their discretion and make decisions. More importantly, they learned to accept responsibility. No one at Vasna can complain that he has been saddled with an unwanted neighbour. Though it is premature to judge, there are indications that a fairly cohesive neighbourhood pattern based on a helping relationship is emerging.

COMMUNITY

In order to draw a profile of the target community a household survey was made immediately after the floods. The survey revealed that the affected families were living in about twenty independent clusters on the river bank. The average family size was smaller (4.56 persons as against the average city slum family of 5.20). The families of the two predominant religious groups, Hindu and Muslim, were almost equally divided—44.4

per cent of them being Muslim and 53.8 per cent Hindu (the percentage of Muslims and Hindus for the entire city is 14.78 and 83.24 respectively). According to the occupation of the principal earners, over 21 per cent of the households were hawkers, traders and vendors; 18.70 per cent casual labourers; 12.65 office workers; 10.50 per cent transport workers: 10 per cent factory workers; 4.75. per cent domestic workers; 2 per cent construction workers; 1 per cent beggars; 1 per cent entertainers and 7.65 per cent unemployed. Approximately 23 per cent of the households earned Rs 75-150 per month, another 23 per cent earned Rs 150-225 and 20 per cent of them made Rs 225-300 per month.

The housing conditions of these slums were very depressing. Out of 1,475 families who were studied, 4.6 per cent lived in shacks measuring less than 50 sq. ft.; 60 per cent of them occupied 50-150 sq. ft. of land; 17.60 per cent covered 150-250 sq.ft. ground area, and only 1.40 per cent were occupying plots larger than 350 sq. ft. Twenty-three per cent of these houses were made of gunny bags, plastic and canvas, 25.60 per cent of them had mud walls; 6.58 per cent had walls of unbaked bricks; 6.20 per cent had no walls at all and 2.30 per cent were without any protection whatsoever.

SOCIAL ACTION COMPONENT

The most distinguishing—probably unique—characteristic of the Vasna project is its 'social action component', necessitated by the project's participatory nature and its emphasis on a wider concept of human development. The social action component conceived as an integral part of the resettlement process, has been designed with the following objectives in mind:

1. To solicit community participation in decision-making, problem solving, resource raising, etc;
2. To help rectify social and economic dislocations caused by the change in the location of residence and distance from the place of work;
3. To assist in bringing and supplementing primary services like health, education, welfare, etc., to build a base for human development;

4. To help increase the productive abilities and earning potential
    of the people by skill upgrading, training, credit referral,
    job opportunities and managerial and organisation assis-
    tance;
5. To identify, strengthen, upgrade, support and build com-
    munity level indigenous organisations and institutions to
    cultivate a culture of self-reliance and self-respect.

Community Organisation

Trained community workers are the agents of change under
the social action component. Working *with* the people,
and not for them, they are trying to play an enabling or
facilitating role. They are organising the community to feel, to
want, to participate, to invest and to protest. They are trying
to initiate a process of learning through involvement and
action.

   In the early pre-action state, the community workers were
the carriers of information and the channels of communication.
After establishing a rapport with the community, they initiated
an on-going dialogue, explaining the project objectives and
observing the reactions of the people. They prepared the people
to participate meaningfully. Even when the people were in
their make-shift shacks on the river, the community workers
created a climate for intensive involvement through programmes
like enrolment of dropouts in nearby schools, regular health
checks and income-supplementing activities.

   During the planning stage, collective decision-making was
facilitated by the community workers. They organised the
people to seek their views on the selection of site, design
of the house, community layout and other matters. During
the transfer phase, the community workers helped the people
solve their problems of adjustment. In the post-occupation
and maintenance phase, new leaders are being identified
and trained for self-governance; groups and sub-groups are
being formed around issues to form popular opinion to take
action for the resolution of problems identified by the group.
Formal and informal indigenous organisations are being activated and people are being helped in institution building and
to develop management skills. The community workers are

also busy in organising, maintaining, or assisting income-supplementary activities, and on-going impact and need surveys to provide feedback information for altering or modifying the involvement strategy.

The community workers are aware that they are outsiders and their role is only transitional. They know that their function is not to replace the people's initiative by their own. They realise that they are initiators or facilitators and not the doers. One of the criteria in designing activities at Vasna has been the period of withdrawal of external resources, human as well as material, since the dependency factor is crucial in assessing the success or failure of the undertaking.

Income Supplementation

In the earlier stages of the project, it was thought that a change in the place of living would result in some economic hardships. Repayment of housing loan, increased cost of living due to improved services and better access to social amenities, higher transportation costs involved in maintaining the social and economic ties with the previous place of residence, and loss of job opportunities due to increased distance, were considered some of the factors responsible for additional financial burdens on those who moved. To prevent sub-letting and shifting back to the old settlements; to avoid a drastic cut in the essential needs of life like food, nutrition and education; to meet the new obligations and, more importantly, to sustain the process of change and development initiated primarily through outside intervention, it was considered necessary to start income-generating activities as an integral part of the housing programme. The additional monthly financial burden was estimated at Rs 35, which meant approximately Rs 1 million per year for all the 2,250 families. Since it was impossible to generate an additional income of Rs 1 million, a selective approach was adopted and it was decided to work with 300 families, whose income was below Rs 250.

Many activities have been started. At a training and production centre seventy women have been trained and fifty of them earn Rs 3.50 a day. Their products—cushion covers, shoulder bags, bedspreads, wall hangings, etc.—are accepted in the local market and also exported. The expansion plan will involve about eighty to a hundred women. The sewing centre, in addition to upgrading the skills of the workers is trying to obtain work orders on a collective basis. An Amber Charkha unit, which was limping along till recently, has been revived and it is expected that the workers will earn Rs 3 for an eight-hour work day.

Through the intermediary credit referral services provided by the project, about 215 people have been given loans by the banks. Approximately eighty-five of them are small entrepreneurs; others have borrowed money to purchase bicycles to continue their earlier income generating activities in the city. About 200 more applications are being processed.

Health

An attempt is being made to develop a low cost health delivery system through community level para-medical health workers. The three-tier arrangement which emphasises preventive health care and health education intends to move away from the highly trained doctor as the centre of health care. Ten community health workers are being trained by a qualified nurse, who also runs a community health centre.

Education

The community workers, in co-operation with the district panchayat, started a primary school—present enrolment 550 children—immediately after the families began moving to the new township.

Though the inadequacies of formal education—particularly for this community—are recognised, for obvious reasons the project could not accept responsibility for creating an alternative educational system for the entire community. However, through 'Sarjan,' an experimental education programme for the pre-primary and primary school children, opportunities are offered to bring out the creative abilities of children. They are provided simple tools—newspapers, discarded tooth brushes. charcoal, colour, water bowls, etc.—to express themselves creatively in drawing, painting, music and other media. The response on the part of the children and their parents is overwhelming and, what is more important, a qualitative change is apparent in their behaviour and performance. The school teachers maintain that the children involved with the 'Sarjan' programme are far more attentive, display leadership qualities, perform better in the class work, attend school regularly, are more disciplined and comparatively more motivated than others.

Welfare

Another important dimension of the social component is social welfare. A creche, which employs women from the community itself, looks after seventy-five children while their mothers are working. A family planning programme has been integrated into the health care system. Nutrition education, maternal and child care, and a supplementary feeding programme has been set up for 350 children and fifty pregnant women. These programmes have been organised to provide the necessary security and welfare so vital in a development process.

Self-reliance

It must be emphasised here that all these activities, and others being planned, are in the initial stages. For obvious reasons, the project inputs—human as well as material—are substantial, but the process of building peoples' own organisations is going on and efforts are being made to delegate responsibility for their management and maintenance to the people them- selves. Community workers and other support personnel are involved in training local people to assume more and more responsibility. Though it sounds somewhat ambitious, the present plan is to withdraw all project inputs by the end of 1978. The success of the social action component will be measured by only one criterion—its ability in preparing people to manage their own affairs.

PROBLEM AREAS

From what has been reported here, it may appear that the

Integrated Urban Development Project is an immense success story. It is not. There are problems, shortcomings, contradictions, and mistakes. For a balanced judgement, it is necessary to mention them here.

There are in-built difficulties in an ambitious attempt to relocate some 12,000-13,000 people, and these are even more when the target is not only relocation or rehabilitation, but development. Many of these difficulties are transitional in nature. Some of them are related to the sharply rising expectations of the people due to a sudden and dramatic change in their living environment. Some of the problems have roots in inter-group rivalries and local politics, and a few are due to the lack of administrative and organisational arrangements to deal with the new issues that arise. Some problems are there simply because designers have made mistakes and others because the modest shelters at Vasna do not fit into the people's long-cherished dream of a *pakka*, cement-concrete house.

There are complaints, protests, threats and demonstrations. Though not a single family was moved under coercion of any kind, a few, unable to accommodate and adjust, have moved back to the slum on the river. There was some corruption in the allotment of the houses and even though investigations are going on and the guilty are being brought to book, the relationship between the municipality, the community and ASAG has become strained. The municipality has not been able to fulfil its commitment to build a community centre, primary school, health unit and shops. People complain about the inadequacy of water supply, malfunctioning of the drainage system and frequent black-outs due to the failure of the street lights. Even though a few houses have been added, there are persistent complaints about their unavailability and consequent hardships. There is a stalemate in the completion of the remaining work as occupants are refusing to pay the rents and the municipality is insisting on the payment of arrears and the promise of regular payment as a precondition for a dialogue. As the municipality has not been able to control a *nala* that cuts across the site, there were floods in the area during the last monsoon.

There is no end to the complaints that the houses are

inferior and allegations that the project funds have been mis-
appropriated. Inter-group rivalries and bitter competition for
power and leadership prevent people from presenting a united
front and this weakens their bargaining power with the establishment and reduces the effectiveness of the developmental
process. Community workers find people slow to respond
while the experts on community development feel that the over-
enthusiasm of the community workers to show results tends to
make them forget their facilitator's role as they replace the
people's initiative by their own. On the other hand, there are
many who think that efforts through the social action component to alleviate the effects of the dislocation caused by the
shift in residence and to create a base for sustained development, are very inadequate.

Yet, at Vasna, a living community has come into existence.
The people have already made sizeable investments in improving and modifying their houses. Although the municipal shops
are yet to be built, they have, on their own, opened about fifty
shops in the front verandah of their houses or have erected
wooden stalls in public places. Even though the school has
not yet been built, parents are eager to get their children
enrolled in it. The people are organising themselves to redress
their grievances. They make periodic representations to whoever
is in authority about what they feel are their problems. A few
months ago, they staged a *dharna*, stopping all buses on the
road and secured their long-standing demand for a bus stop
within the township. Recently, a group of concerned members
of this community filed a civil suit against the Government of
Gujarat, the Municipal Corporation and the Project Committee
for failing to fulfil the promises made to the people. As one
community worker, who refused to be daunted by anything less
than 4,500 problems (his formula for normalcy is of a minimum
two problems per house) put it:

The IUDP like any other programme of its kind is not
without its weaknesses and failures. Had it been only a
housing effort, the problems would have been fewer; had
the people been treated as faceless masses, subject to the
dictates of the planners and the government, the difficulties
would have been even fewer. But IUDP is not merely a housing

project. It is an attempt to initiate a process of development. It has started by saying that 'slums are people not places!' It has attempted to meet human needs rather than housing needs. It is a learning laboratory, an experiment. And no experiment is a failure if one learns from it.

CONCLUSION

Is the IUDP a successful project? Does it provide a replicable model? These two questions are constantly asked by administrators, planners, social scientists and funding agencies. There is no easy answer.

Seen as only a housing project for slum dwellers and compared to past and present Government efforts to house the poor, the IUDP may seem an impressive and unqualified success. In comparison to the snail's pace at which housing projects generally move, to have completed 2,250 houses and infrastructural services in just sixteen months will certainly appear remarkably efficient. Construction costs remained very economical at Rs 11.25 per sq. ft., and overheads were held at a minimum of about 5-7 per cent, since the project work was not given to contractors, as compared to the 12-16 per cent agency overheads normally charged for mere supervision. All this makes the IUDP unusual, innovative, and successful.

Involvement and Change

But housing was only one of the components of the IUDP. The second goal of the programme was to 'build people'—to stimulate a social and economic transformation in a former slum community, to facilitate a development process that would ultimately become self-initiated and self-managed. In this respect, a judgement may be too premature although some positive signs have begun to manifest themselves in the community. According to a study, which evaluated the people's response to the project, they have become more involved in the Government system, vocalise their demands more forcefully to the local authorities, appreciate the value of education and cleanliness, are in the process of integrating more scientific explanations of reality into their traditional beliefs, are rejecting money-lenders for banks, increasing their savings, and investing in their homes and new business, are buying more consumer durables, aspire to a higher standard of living, and have a more positive outlook towards life.

But, the study also indicated a leadership crisis; a continuing reliance on outside agencies for the maintenance of public spaces; inadequate care given to children and a continuing high rate of malnutrition; a less than impressive participation in the socio-economic programmes of the IUDP; a relatively high incidence of crime; underemployment and unemployment especially among women; less leisure time spent as a family and a community; and a lower level of security due to the separation from relatives and friends in the city.

Methodology

The IUDP may be considered less than successful because the 'take-off' stage has not yet been achieved, even though the IUDP represents a significant break-through because of the developmental processes it has initiated. The IUDP also hoped to serve as a project model, to develop a methodology to deal with the problems of slums. To quote one of the objectives stated in the project blueprint:

> At the city level, it is important to measure the dimensions and implications of change. Without question, an attempt to move 2,250 families from the centre to the outskirts has a great bearing on the fate of the city's ultimate hygiene. The continuing exodus from the rural areas and the unchecked population explosion have posed a serious threat to the well-being of the city structure and a few, sporadic but bold experiments, to redeem the situation, are not only welcome but should be closely watched. The city needs a methodology to deal with its problems. It is an inbuilt responsibility of this project to provide guidelines for future urban actions.

Replication

An important criterion in any evaluation of the project would be the capacity of the IUDP model to be replicated. IUDP would be a failure if it only solved the problems of 2,250 families at Vasna without providing clues as to how it could be applied to solve comparable urban situations. In the course of the IUDP, it was realised that economic viability is just not possible so far as housing for the poor in metropolitan areas is concerned. In Ahmedabad, where 84.5 per cent of the housing shortage is among families earning less than Rs 250 per month, a substantial subsidy will certainly be required for low income housing projects for a long time to come. Although the rate of subsidy was significantly less as compared to other Government projects, and although this subsidy was shared between several Government and voluntary agencies, the IUDP still had a 65 per cent subsidy component. This certainly makes it doubtful, given the unavailability of resources to match the awesome demand, whether the IUDP can be replicated on a sufficiently large scale. This suggests that a project-mix emphasising *in situ* environmental improvement, and Site and Services schemes may be a better alternative. However, in some situations, housing will be required, as in the case of the IUDP where the continual threat of floods made the original location on the riverbank unsafe. Under such circumstances, where the necessary subsidy is available, the IUDP could provide a model.

Housing can become a tool for development and change if resources are available for a social action component. This could be accomplished in any of three ways. First, funding institutions with a strong developmental orientation could be tapped to implement the socio-economic objectives of the development project. However, such funding agencies have a limited capacity and cannot be relied upon exclusively. Second, Government housing projects could adopt the IUDP construction model which has substantially lowered overheads by eliminating the contractor. These savings in construction overheads could then be creatively diverted into a social action component. Third, substantial efforts could be made to integrate existing community development programmes into housing projects to produce a comprehensive development approach. Again, such co-ordinated planning efforts could use the IUDP as a flexible model upon which improvements could be made in stimulating a sustained process of development.

Resources notwithstanding, appropriate institutional and implementation mechanisms are required if the IUDP model is to be replicated. An inter-institutional arrangement in which there is a climate of faith, mutual trust, and co-operative understanding between Governmental agencies and voluntary, people-based, grassroots institutions is absolutely necessary so that development can become people-oriented. This requires Government agencies to be 'open' and include voluntary organisations, as intermediaries and facilitators, in their housing and development programmes. Equally important is the need for voluntary agencies to become truly involved in the development process —to gain experience, develop expertise, to become the people's advocate. Only then can the development model of the IUDP be capable of replication.

Finally, is the concept, ideal and spirit of the IUDP repeatable? It must be. For physical inputs are grossly inadequate to deal with the problems of slums which remain essentially attitudinal, political, behavioural, economic, and social in nature. Housing is only an entry point into the community, but the emphasis is on the process of development. This, if nothing else, is the most important statement that the Integrated Urban Development Project has made.

9

Urban Community Development in Hyderabad

W.J. Cousins

Beginning in 1958 with the Delhi Pilot Project financed by the Ford Foundation, there have been a series of Urban Community Development Projects in India.[1] The Delhi Project was followed in 1962 by the short-lived Ahmedabad Project which was also funded by the Ford Foundation. The third project was sponsored by the American Friends Service Committee in Baroda in 1965 and continues today under the Baroda Citizens Council. These pilot projects, supported by non-Governmental agencies, were followed in late 1966 by a series of fourteen pilot projects throughout the country sponsored originally by the Central Government through the then Ministry of Health, Family Planning and Urban Development. Several of these projects are still functioning today.[2] This paper will discuss the experience of one of these, which may be applicable in other

---

[1]See Marshall B. Clinard, *Slums* and *Community Development*, The Free Press, New York, 1968, for an account of the Delhi Project.

[2]See Subash Chandra and S.P. Punalekar, *Urban Community Development Programme in India*, National Institute of Public Cooperation and Child Development, New Delhi, 1975, for an evaluation of six of these projects : Aurangabad, Delhi, Hyderabad, Kanpur, Ludhiana and Surat.

cities, the Hyderabad Urban Community Development Project.[3]

STAFF

The Project started in 1967 with the standard staffing pattern of eight community organisers and one Project Officer, all of whom came out of the rural community development programme. After one community organiser left, the Project has carried on with the other original seven community organisers plus the Project Officer. This consistency in staff may be part of the secret of the Project's success in addition to their shared commitment to the principle of self-help. With a budget of Rs 50,000, they began work in one project area. It is my conviction that their slender budget may have been a pragmatic reinforcement of their commitment to the principle of self-help. In 1970, they added another project area and in 1974, yet another. By 1976, with three projects, they were covering three areas which included about 60,000 slum people in a total population of 2,25,600; the others being mostly lower middle class. At this time the budget had grown to approximately Rs 2.4 lakhs or Rs 4 per slum dweller covered.

By this time, the staff had added eight social workers plus 'volunteers'. The latter category consisted of local people who were recruited for specific activities and were given small monthly stipends; originally Rs 75 per month and later Rs 100 per month. The volunteers ran *balwadis*, sewing centres etc. Thus the activities of the project could be extended at very little expense despite its small professional staff.

THE PHILOSOPHY

Self-help has been the philosophy of this Project since the beginning. The Project proceeded on the assumption:

> That any neighbourhood, no matter how poor, can do something to improve itself by its own efforts; and that any

[3]A detailed case study of this project, sponsor by UNICEF, is presently under preparation entitled *The Hyderabad Experience* by Catherine Goyder and W.J. Cousins. This paper draws freely on this study.

approach for outside help should be resorted to, only after it has exhausted its own resources fully.[4]

This was not always an easy message to get across to poor people who sometimes felt that the Government should freely meet their needs *because* they were poor. Further, the Project's desire to be thought of as a 'people's Project' may also have posed difficulties because it was, after all, a Government Project. Basically, it was the intention of the Project to encourage people to identify their own felt needs and to be involved fully in meeting them. It was hoped that through a process of community education and community self-help action, people's lives could be enriched and improved.

The success of the Project depended almost entirely upon the work of each individual community organiser who had to stimulate, guide and sustain the whole process by working with individuals and groups and bringing in outside help when needed. The task required a great deal of patience, sensitivity and commitment to the aims of the Project.

THE WORK

The staff soon learned that the most commonly felt needs discussed by the people were physical and economic. People wanted more public water taps, street lighting, dustbins, better drainage, road repairs, the paving of lanes, public latrines. They also indicated the need for some cottage industries for women. The Project would only come forward to help on these problems when local people showed their willingness to help themselves. Gradually, these problems were tackled, either through self-help projects like *Shramdan* or through helping them approach the appropriate municipal authorities, or a combination of both.

Over the past ten years, the Project and the people have been involved in a broad range of activities as can be seen by the following list.

[4]Taken from a pamphlet prepared to publicise the Project. 'Urban Community Development Pilot Project—A People's Programme in Ward No. 22', M.C.H. 1968.

PROJECT ACTIVITIES

1. Environmental sanitation, water and other physical improvement activities.
2. Family welfare activities: (a) Immunisation; (b) Health and first-aid classes; (c) Cooking and home-making demonstrations; (d) Family Welfare meetings; (e) Comprehensive medical check-up schemes; (f) Eye camps; (g) Family Planning work.
3. Suppplementary feeding programme: (a) Special nutrition programme; (b) Mid-day meals programmes.
4. Recreational and cultural activities and youth programmes.
5. Educational activities: (a) *Balwadis* and primary schools; (b) Night schools; (c) Vocational training: (i) Sewing classes; (ii) Other vocational courses—typing and shorthand, auto-rickshaw driving, motor driving, photography, radio repairs, air-conditioning and refrigeration; (d) Non-formal education: (i) Study tours; (ii) Other activities, e.g., community dinners, exhibition and dramas, libraries and reading rooms.
6. Economic activities: (a) Bank loans; (b) Sewing production centres; (c) Co-operatives.
7. Construction of community halls and housing improvement.

SOME CASES

Some brief descriptions of a few specific activities are given here which are illustrative of the work of the Project.

Lijjad Papad Co-operative

It was started with a loan from the Lijjad Papad parent organisation in Bombay, for the purchase of the 'capital equipment' for making the dough for papads. Over time, this loan has been repaid from the profits. Each day, the dough is mixed by some young men hired for this purpose by the Co-operative. Then it is divided into kilo lots and put in plastic bags. The local women who are members come each morning and pick up the dough to be taken home and rolled into papads in their spare time. These papads are of a standard size and thickness.

The next day they bring the papads and pick up more dough. Each day they are paid for the amount of work they have done. This comes to about Rs 3 per day. Each papad is checked to see that it conforms to standards and is then packed in plastic. Those which do not meet the standards are packed and sold as 'seconds' at a cheaper price. It is a very efficient organisation run by the wife of a local school teacher and a paid accountant. Thus, the Project helped to organise it, but now it runs on its own.

Balwadis

A number of these have been started in community centres, rented rooms and sometimes open sheds. They are run by local girls, usually high school graduates, who are trained and given stipends of Rs 100 per month by the Project. In some *balwadis* there is an *ayah* paid by the local *mahila mandal* or the *basti* committee.

Before the Project gives its support, the local people must (i) provide a place; and (ii) make a list of all the eligible children between three and six years whose parents wish to enroll them. Parents contribute 50 paise per month per child. They also contribute towards equipment and the Project then gives a matching grant. So far, thirty-six *balwadis* with 2,200 children have been organised on this basis.

Devnagar Housing

Today, Devnagar consists of nineteen little brick houses on both sides of an L-shaped lane paved with stone blocks. Each house is built on a 400 sq. ft. plot. Some of them have mosaic floors and are plastered and painted on the outside and others have earthen floors and unplastered brick walls. The degree of finishing reflects the financial status of the owner. It is a very neat, tidy and pleasant community with potted plants and shrubs, and a block of community latrines and a public water tap at one end. The first time I visited this community, I was not accompanied by a staff member, so a local resident volunteered to explain the Project and show me around. He was a police constable who was full of community pride and even pulled out his album to show me 'before' and 'after' pictures.

In this community, the UCD Project co-ordinated the assistance of the Rotary Club and the Municipal Corporation with the self-help activities of the people. (And it all sounds so simple, after the fact.)

At the beginning of this Project, the people themselves pulled down the huts and moved to a communal camp until their houses were built. They also raised Rs 9,500 towards the cost of rebuilding their colony by giving concerts. The city engineer designed the layout with uniform plots and straight lanes, but first the Project had to convince the municipal authorities to permit a twelve foot lane since this was not as broad as the regulations require. For each house, the Rotary Club contributed about Rs 1,000 which were used to provide reinforced concrete pillars and concrete slabs for the roofs. This formed the basic shell of the house which was then completed with bricks by the people at their own pace. The Rotary Club also provided ventilators which were installed in the front and back walls of the house for the circulation of air. (The ventilator is a kind of a concrete *jali*.) The Project provided sand and cement and helped the community to get building materials at reduced prices.

At the start of the venture, seventeen loans of Rs 1,000 each were secured from the bank. Each borrower had to nominate a relative who was prepared to guarantee the monthly repayment. The rest of the money came from money-lenders at an interest rate of 12 to 15 per cent. The house costs about Rs 5,000 to build.

EXPENSION OF THE PROJECT

After much discussion and planning over the past year, the Municipal Corporation of Hyderabad, the State Government and the Department of Social Welfare (Government of India) have agreed that the Project should be expanded with UNICEF assistance. Over the next three years, the Project will expand to cover all the slums in the twin cities of Hyderabad and Secunderabad. At present this is estimated at 300 slums with about 3,00,000 people. The Municipal Corporation of

Hyderabad has also given the Urban Community Development Department responsibility for co-ordinating the major programmes in the slums; namely, slum improvement and slum clearance, health and family planning and supplementary nutrition. Thus,the perennial dream of the community developer— programme co-ordination—may actually be realised here.

In addition, once these decisions had been made, the Secretary for Housing, Municipal Administration and Urban Development of the State Government decided to ask the Urban Community Development Department to take the responsibility for the construction of some 13,000 houses for slum dwellers who had been given deeds (*pattas*) for the land on which they are living. The Project has approached this task with the same philosophy of self-help. When I asked the staff if they were not frightened at the enormity of this task, one of them replied, typically, '*We're* not building any houses, the *people* are. There are 13,000 families and each one is building its own house. Why should it be a problem? One family, one house.' And this is actually how it is; like Devanagar multiplied 650 times.

A town planning wing and an engineering wing have been added to the UCD Department. The planners design the new layout of the slum, once the residents indicate their desire to participate. There are both human and technical problems to sort out in realigning lanes, sewer lines and laying out each plot. The engineers design model houses and give technical supervision and assistance throughout the building process.[5]

The Department has also defined and recruited a new staff member to work in areas where housing is being built. He is called a *basti sahayak* or 'slum helper'. He is a high school graduate who is paid Rs 200 per month and expected to live in the slum community where he works. Each *basti sahayak* works with about 100 families. His first tasks are to get to know the families and then act as a facilitator between them and the Project. He notifies the Project when the technical people are needed and facilitates their work in his area;

[5]Each house costs Rs 5,000 which includes a hand flushed water seal latrine of the type introduced into villages. These individual latrines costing approximately Rs 35 will be a great improvement over community latrines.

he lets the Project know when a family has completed a stage of its work and is ready for another loan instalment. He will also help people identify and take action on other community needs. Once the housing project is completed, he will be the first line community development worker because housing is seen as a means rather than an end in the community development process.

The method of financing this project is not new; but the scale is certainly significant, as is the self-help emphasis. Eight commercial banks, with eighty-six branches have agreed to lend up to Rs 4,000 to each family with the *pattas* as security. The family contributes about Rs 1,000 in cash, kind and labour. Most of the unskilled labour goes into digging foundations, carrying bricks, etc. The people are also given credit for the amount which would normally be paid for contractor's charges (7 per cent) and PWD overhead for supervision (8 per cent). This 15 per cent of the total cost comes to Rs 750 and is justified by the fact that the people themselves fulfil these functions.

SIGNIFICANCE OF THE PROJECT

The Hyderabad Project is significant for several reasons:

1. It demonstrates that the classical community development approach to the problems of the urban poor can be effective both in providing improved social services cheaply and also for meeting the basic problems of poverty.
2. It also shows that despite the central problem of poverty, there are enormous potential economic resources in most slum communities which can be actualised with the help of sensitive community workers.
3. It shows that one key to success in community development is the staff and its approach. In fact, the selection and training of staff is probably the most important element in any community development programme.
4. It demonstrates the importance of the effective co-ordination and use of both internal and external resources.
5. It also demonstrates the importance of certain basic linkages in the development process. These include:

(a) The integration of physical improvements within the community development process.
(b) The systematic linking of voluntary organisations with slum communities.
(c) The systematic linking of slum residents with financial institutions in the formal sector of the urban economy.

The exploration of these linkages in more detail will illuminate the other generalisations.

The integration of physical improvements such as drainage, water supply, paved lanes and improved housing within the community development process.

For example, the reconstruction of a slum community according to a planned layout requires the willing co-operation of the residents so that they give up part of their plots or part of their buildings in order that straight lanes may be made, or drainage lines laid. It has not been uncommon in many cities for engineers to come into slum areas selected for political and technical reasons, and arbitrarily install water or drainage systems or construct low-cost housing without much consultation with local residents. One classical result is that the attitude of the people is 'you built it, so you can maintain it'. This is one of the explanations for the maintenance problems which afflict many housing and slum improvement projects. When community workers indicate when and where the people are ready for these improvements and also act as a liaison between the people and the engineers, the changes are more likely to be welcomed, understood and long-lasting.

The systematic linking of voluntary organisations with slum communities.

There are many under-utilised resources in any city besides Governmental ones. Some of these are well-established local branches of international service organisations such as the Lions and Rotary Clubs. Others are national bodies such as the Lijjad Papad. Still others are local groups ranging from University service organisations to neighbourhood sports and cultural groups. One of the goals of the Hyderabad UCD Project is the identification and systematic involvement of such groups in slum development activities. This is a very important resource which is often dissipated by not being used systematically.

The third linkage, which has many implications, is that between slum residents and financial institutions in the so-called 'formal sector' of the urban economy.

The very fact that much of the economic activity of the urban poor takes place in what is termed the 'informal sector' of the economy indicates that existing linkages are insufficient. Some studies have shown that there is inadequate understanding and awareness of the important functions fulfilled by the urban poor in the economy of cities.

In addition to the innumerable 'services' performed by people such as domestic servants, *dhobis, dudhwallas,* fruit and vegetable vendors, *Kabariwallas,* snake charmers, *tamashawallas,* etc., any large city has a host of slum family-based enterprises. These enterprises are usually labour-intensive and feed larger enterprise in the formal sector of the economy. They range from *beedi* making and *agarbatti* making to leather work, basketry, textiles and carpentry to metal work and even light industries. If these service enterprises cease to function, there would be serious lacunae in both urban social life and the urban economy.

BANKS

One of the important contributions of the Hyderabad UCD Project has been to persuade banks to extend loans to selected categories of slum workers. For example, loans to cycle-rickshaw-wallas to enable them to purchase their own rickshaws. This has meant that rickshaw drivers have been able to make loan payments at a rate lower than that of their previous rickshaw rentals. It means further that as owners of their vehicles, they have a different sort of stake in the economy and the possibility of increasing their family incomes. Further, for the first time they have had the experience of dealing with a bank—an experience previously confined to middle class citizens. This immediately decreases their 'marginality' as citizens and draws them more into the formal system. By the same token, it is a new educational role for the banks. The banks probably begin by feeling that it is an opportunity for them to perform an act of charity. But closer analysis will show that it is also good banking business. The experience with small loans seems to indicate that the rate of recovery is very high if the groundwork is done properly.

In addition, a considerable amount of aggregate capital may be involved. For example, in the plan to assist 13,000 slum dwellers to build their own houses over the next two years, 13,000 loans of Rs 4,000 each comes to Rs 5,20,00,000 or more than Rs 5 crores investment from the urban poor. Even if only half of this goal is reached, it is still more than Rs 2½ crores. This makes one wonder what is meant by the 'informal sector' of the economy.

EXPERIENCE OF OTHER PROJECTS WITH LINKAGES

The Ahmedabad Study Action Group (ASAG) has also linked slum people with major financial institutions in the Vasna Project.[6] This Project involves the resettlement of 2,250 families who had previously lived in squatter settlements which were flooded out by the Sabarmati river in 1975. It involves the co-operation of the State Government, which donated the land for the colony, the Municipal Corporation of Ahmedabad, which developed the physical infrastructure, and HUDCO which financed the construction of the housing. ASAG, a non-profit organisation consisting of an inter-disciplinary group of professionals co-ordinated the entire activity and oversaw the design and construction of the houses. OXFAM underwrote the expenses for the social development side of the project. The residents are repaying the loan from HUDCO in instalments over a period of twenty years. In addition to the relationship with HUDCO, the Ahmedabad Study Action Group has also arranged for the residents to get small loans for the purchase of bicycles from

[6]See the paper by Kirtee Shah in this books for a more detailed analysis of this project.

commercial banks since the colony is at some distance from the centre of the city. To date, about 200 families have been loaned approximately Rs 1.5 lakhs by the various banks for small enterprises as well as for cycles.

The Baroda Citizens Council began its activity on the assumption that every city has many underutilised resources. From the beginning, it organised a governing body—Baroda Citizens Council—which included representatives of the Municipal Corporation and the Municipal Council, local industries and labour unions, members of the University community, social workers and so on. This Citizens Council, after the withdrawal of the American Friends Service Committee's financial support, has taken responsibility for continuing the Project. In itself, it has become a firmly established link between the basic formal organisations and institutions in the city and slum communities.

REPLICABILITY

It used to be the fashion to expect that a successful pilot project should be completely replicable elsewhere. Because none were, we tended to criticise them as inadequate or ill-planned in various ways; thus throwing out the baby with the bath-water. I now reject this 'cloning model' as simplistic, unrealistic and unnecessary. I think that we have suffered too much in the past from the 'block pattern' fallacy, i.e., a standard pattern of staffing, programming and budgeting to be offered as the key to all problems and infinitely replicated throughout the land. This has led to inflexibility and unreality.

It seems to me now, that we should not be looking for total replicability but for *elements of replicability*: interesting ideas, approaches, schemes which could be taken and adapted in other projects. It may be an approach to the selection of training, a way of financing a scheme, an organisational innovation or a combination of these. It is too much of a burden on a project to ask it to be perfectly replicable in every city of a certain size in India. I have heard it said of the Baroda project, 'Well it could only be done in Baroda and may be one other city, because of the kind of local pride you find there'. This does not make it less valuable. The first lesson is to build imaginatively upon whatever local strengths or unique qualities one can find. The second lesson, is to isolate elements in the Baroda project which could be tried effectively elsewhere.

And so with ASAG—they came along with some talented staff and experience and ideas, just at a time when the Municipal Corporation wanted to do something after a disaster. They built upon this fortunate combination of variables and developed their 'Integrated Urban development Project' which led to the construction of the Vasna colony. The lesson in over-simplified terms is that disaster can be transformed into development.

Thus, it is true that UNICEF may not come along just after the State Government has given *pattas* to slum residents in other cities; nor will there always be an understanding and supportive Special Officer running the Corporation nor an experienced and dedicated UCD staff. But there are other funding sources, other good officers and staff and we see now how important the *pattas* are in motivating the poor to improve their housing. We also have the precedent of individual bank loans and self-help housing on a large scale as well as the innovation of the *basti-sahayaks*. We see too, that a UCD project can play an important role in co-ordinating services in the slums.

Most important, the twin cities of Hyderabad-Secunderabad, together making up the fifth largest city in India, represent a sizeable universe in themselves. If the UCD project is even modestly successful in improving the lives of most of the slum residents in Hyderabad, it is an outstanding achievement in itself; a kind of replication *in situ*.

It will also have been a useful demonstration to other cities. It is a commitment to link physical improvements with social development and to improve all of the slums in Hyderabad using the principles of self-help and people's participation.

It is true that Hyderabad has some advantages over many other cities; such as proportionately fewer slum-dwellers in its population, more available space than most cities; a political decision to give slum-dwellers the legal right to dwell on their land; *and* a first rate UCD programme. At the same time, it *is* the fifth largest city in India and if such a programme can prove successful here, it can have implications for many cities which are smaller than Hyderabad.

ORGANISING THE POOR

In his M.N. Roy Memorial Lecture this year, Dr. Raj Krishna of Delhi University, citing Myron Weiner's *Politics of Scarcity* has said that one of the most significant changes in India since independence has been the 'organisational revolution'. However, according to Dr. Raj Krishna, almost everyone has become organised except the poor (excluding the five and a half million industrial workers who belong to unions). He went on to suggest that the ideal of a democratic socialist society would never be realised until the poor were organised also.

One consequence of community development programmes which is insufficiently understood is the organisation of the poor *per se*. It is usually couched in terms of organising poor people to undertake self-help activities to improve their lives. Shrewd politicians political recognise and use this organisation for their own ends, or if they are in power they are quick to recognise the potential political threat in such organisations. This threat may lie in the emergence of new leadership from below or in the additional pressure which is to be put on municipal governments as poorpeople demand services which they feel are rightfully theirs. The experience of the disciples of Saul Alinsky in the United States and of the 'war on poverty' are examples of this fact.[7]

This is an important implication of community development projects such as that in Hyderabad. It also involves a paradox. On the one hand, the urban poor become more integrated into the 'formal sector' of the economy and into the accepted main stream of social life. In this sense, they become more part of the *status quo*. On the other hand, as poor people learn to identify and work together to meet their problems and needs, they also begin to call for help which they feel is their right as citizens. The difference is that they begin to see the services which result from this process as their own and not simply those of the Municipal Corporation. The implication is that poor

[7]One explicit attempt to give power to the poor through organisation is Anjali Sen's Project under the Cathedral Relief Service in Calcutta.

people themselves and the municipal authorities, more and more begin to see the urban poor as legitimate citizens fulfilling important functions, *and having power* rather than as merely nuisances or objects of charity.

10

Entrepreneurial Patterns in the Urban Informal Sector: The Case of Tribal Entrepreneurs in Ranchi

M. Van den Bogaert

There is a growing awareness in recent years of the urban informal sector and the important role it plays in the economy of the cities in the developing countries of the Third World.[1] Urban planners are now concerned with programmes of urban development in which the focus is on the informal sector and on ways in which rural migrants to the city may be integrated into the organised or formal sector.

This paper explores the functioning of the informal sector of Ranchi city, a growing industrial centre in the tribal belt of Chotanagpur, Bihar. Within this overall perspective, the focus is on the manner in which the tribals participate in the economic

[1]See Paulo R. Souza and Victor E. Tokman, 'The Informal Urban Sector in Latin America', *International Labour Review*, 114, n. 3, November-December 1976, pp. 355-65; John Weeks, 'Policies for Expanding Employment in the Informal Urban Sector of Developing Economies', *International Labour Review*, 111, n. 1, January, 1975, pp. 1-13; Heather Joshi, Harold Lubell and Jean Mouly, 'Urban Development and Employment in Abidjan', *International Labour Review*, 111, n. 4, April 1975, pp. 286-306; Heather and Vijay Joshi, *Surplus Labour and the City: A Study of Bombay*, Oxford University Press, Bombay, 1976; Jan Breman, "A Dualistic Labour System? A Critique of the 'Informal Sector' Concept", *Economic and Political Weekly*, Bombay, 27 November 1976, pp. 1870-6; December 11, 1939-44.

life of Ranchi as entrepreneurs or self-employed persons. The tribals have been selected not only because Chotanagpur is their original habitat, but also to understand how an underprivileged group, whose culture does not equip them for industry or trade, plays a vital, even if secondary, role in the economy of Ranchi city. The tribals constitute 58.08 per cent of the District's population but only 13.94 per cent of the population of Ranchi city. The presence of large numbers of tribals during the day in the informal sector of the city, points to an urban-rural nexus which is peculiar to Ranchi and distinguishes it from modes of participation in metropolitan cities such as Calcutta, described elsewhere in this book.

The informal urban sector performs more than one role for the tribal population: (i) it acts as a refuge, providing manual employment to many tribals who have been displaced from farms around the city, by the establishment of factories such as the Heavy Engineering Corporation; (ii) it provides seasonal employment to the tribal population living within a radius of twelve to twenty km from the town, during the off-season, or to those family members who have been pushed off the land, or whose land has been alienated through mortgages or law-suits; (iii) it offers a means of livelihood to the 'native' tribal population of Ranchi city itself, i.e., the original inhabitants who still are found in the 'tolas' or tribal *bustees*, off the main streets of the town; (iv) it functions as an educational arena where tribal entrepreneurs get their first experience in setting up and managing small business enterprises before they can qualify for entry into the ranks of the middle class.

An experiment carried out by the Xavier Institute of Social Service suggests that the process of tribal acceptance of entrepreneurship can be speeded up through informal training and the provision of basic infrastructures. Before describing this experiment, there will be a brief discussion of the concept of the informal sector which will be followed by the presentation, in summarised form, of data from the 1971 Census on the size and characteristics of the urban informal sector in Ranchi and also a description of the manner in which the tribals participate in it.

THE URBAN INFORMAL SECTOR: SOME CONCEPTS

A number of studies have been conducted in Africa, South America and Asia by the ILO to study the social and economic characteristics of the unorganised or urban informal sector. Though there is still no complete consensus on the definition of the informal sector and standards of measurement, certain common characteristics emerge which seem to be applicable to the urban informal sector whether in Africa, Latin America or Asia. The informal sector has also been the traditional or unorganised and unenumerated sector. Labour statistics have until now bypassed this sector with the result that figures and estimates of unemployed persons in the Third World may be considerably overestimated.

Concept

S.V. Sethuraman in a recent article in the *International Labour Review* proceeds by elimination to a definition of the informal sector, which is vague, no doubt, but has the advantage of relating the urban informal sector to the masses of the urban poor.

> One of the most convenient ways of identifying the informal sector is to define it in terms of the source of employment of the urban poor. Since a vast majority of the urban labour force, particularly the urban poor, depends on private sources of employment, public sector employment is considered to fall outside the informal sector. Likewise, large industrial and commercial establishments in the private sector, particularly foreign-financed ones, are excluded for the simple reason that only a small fraction of their labour force consists of the urban poor. Thus, the informal sector, defined as a residual included all the remaining private enterprises in the urban economy.
> In this context an enterprise is broadly defined to include any economic unit engaged in the production of goods and services—whether it employs only one person (the proprietor) or more; whether or not it uses fixed capital; whether or not it has a fixed location for conducting business. Thus,

a self-employed construction worker, a self-employed service worker (a shoeshine boy, for example) are all treated as constituting an individual enterprise even though they hire no employees, own little or no capital, have no fixed business location and produce only services. Defined in this way, the universe consisting of informal sector enterprises is indeed a large one compared with that covered by the conventional definition used by statisticians for collecting data on establishments.[2]

Characteristics

Though there is diversity in the characteristics of the informal urban sector, which can be largely attributed to socio-cultural factors, it will be useful to examine the contrasting requirements of the formal and informal sectors.[3]

INFORMAL SECTOR	FORMAL SECTOR
Entry by new enterprises is comparatively easy (Kenya)	Entry by new enterprises is difficult
Enterprises rely on indigenous resources (Kenya)	Enterprises frequently depend on overseas resources
Enterprises are family-owned (Kenya)	Enterprises are corporately-owned
Operate on small scale in unregulated and competitive markets	Operate on large scale and in protected markets
Use labour-intensive and adapted technology (Kenya)	Use capital-intensive and often imported technology
Workers have skills acquired outside the formal school system (Kenya)	Workers have formally acquired skills and are often expatriates
Sharp distinction between the supplier of capital and supplier of labour is absent (Latin America)	Clear distinction between 'owners', 'managers' and 'labour'
Producers are in competitive markets, and not in a position to fix prices or make exceptional profits (Latin America)	Producers are in a sellers' market and can fix prices

[2]S.V. Sethuraman, 'The Urban Informal Sector: Concept, Measurement and Policy', *International Labour Review*, 114, n. 1, July-August 1976, pp. 75-6.

[3]Ibid., p. 71; Souza and Tokman, op. cit., pp. 359 ff.

Higher rate of female employment and also of younger and older workers (Latin America)	Predominance of male, middle-aged workers
Relatively higher rate of heads of families employed in this sector (Latin America)	Proportion of heads of families is lower
High proportion of least educated or illiterate workers	Most workers have had a minimum of formal schooling
Mainly made up of immigrants from impoverished rural areas	Proportion of urban-born workers is larger
No access to credit especially institutionalised credit or if there is access, it is at exorbitant rates and stringent conditions (Latin America)	Institutional finance and credit is more easily available, even with government subsidies

The Formal-Informal Continuum

It is useful to distinguish the two urban sectors to understand better their structure and inter-relationship. Since there is no water-tight division between the formal and informal sectors, one should avoid a dualistic approach.

There are links between the two, and even varying degrees of homogeneity. They share the same urban market, and the degree of structural heterogeneity within the sectors, especially in the formal sector, is in any case such that it precludes the use of a single analytical category for each. The concept of a stratified formal labour market makes it possible in fact, to view the informal sector as merely the bottom layer in the heterogeneity of the urban economy.[4]

The Analytical Criteria

This brings us to the problem of how to decide whether an industry is in the formal or informal sector. We have given several criteria suggested by Sethuraman to identify enterprises of the informal sector. Using these criteria as heuristic tools, it is possible to categorise the 1971 Census data on establishments in Ranchi according to their formal and informal characteristics.

[4]Souza and Tokman op. cit., p. 356.

SUGGESTED CRITERIA FOR IDENTIFYING INFORMAL SECTOR ENTERPRISES[5]

1. Manufacturing

A manufacturing enterprise may be included in the informal sector if it satisfies one or more of the following conditions:

(a) It employs 10 persons or less (including part-time and casual workers).
(b) It operates on an illegal basis, contrary to government regulations.
(c) Members of the household of the head of the enterprise work in it.
(d) It does not observe fixed hours/days of operation.
(e) It operates in semi-permanent or temporary premises, or in a shifting location.
(f) It does not use any electricity in the manufacturing process.
(g) It does not depend on formal financial institutions for its credit needs.
(h) Its output is normally distributed directly to the final consumer.
(i) Almost all those working in it have fewer than six years of formal schooling.

2. Construction

A construction enterprise may be included in the informal sector if it satisfies one or more of the following conditions:

(a) Any of 1(a)-(c) or (i) above.
(b) It does not own power-operated construction machinery and equipment.
(c) It is engaged in the construction of semi-permanent or temporary buildings only.

3. Transport

An enterprise providing services related to transport, storage

[5]Sethuraman, op. cit., p. 31.

and communications may be included in the informal sector if it satisfies one or more of the following conditions:

   (a) Any of 1(a)-(e), (g) or (i) above. Condition 1(e) does
       not apply to transport activity *per se*.
   (b) It does not use any mechanical power.

4. Trade

A trading enterprise may be included in the informal sector if it satisfies one or more of the following conditions:

   (a) Any of 1(a)-(e) above.
   (b) It deals in second-hand goods, or sells prepared foods.

5. Services

A service enterprise may be included in the informal sector if it satisfies one or more of the following conditions:

   Any of 1(a)-(e) above.

Entrepreneurs

The informal sector constitutes the arena of the barefoot entrepreneur who is understood here as a self-employed person engaged in btoh traditional and non-traditional activities. This type of entrepreneur performs the basic functions of organising and maintaining a small business enterprise and, irrespective of the level of capital employed, is responsible for decision-making and financial risk-taking.

The tribal entrepreneurs referred to in the title of this paper belonged to the Scheduled Tribes and the data reported here are from a study conducted by the Xavier Institute of Social Service. There is of course no distinctive 'tribal' way of running a business but the use of this term həlps to identify a modern phenomenon among the tribals. Though traditionally tribals have been agriculturists and food-gatherers, the more educated among them are employed as industrial workers and in the service occupations. Entry into business, however, is a new development and, in the public opinion as well as among tribals themselves, business and trade are activities they are not supposed to be good at. The study of tribal entrepreneurs was conducted with the purpose, among others, of testing the validity of this commonly accepted opinion. The emergence of tribals as entrepreneurs may be considered as important as 'Black Capitalism' was among the Blacks of the ghettos in the USA about twenty years ago.[6]

RANCHI CITY AND ESTIMATION OF ITS URBAN INFORMAL SECTOR

The Ranchi Urban Agglomeration consists of Ranchi Municipality, the Doranda Notified Area, and the new industrial city of Jagannathnagar, more commonly known as Hatia or Dhurwa. It is the fourth largest city in Bihar with a population in 1971 of 2,55,551, after Patna, Jamshedpur and Dhanbad. Originally, the population of Ranchi was practically entirely tribal. In 1971, their percentage had been reduced to 13.94 per cent making Ranchi, however, the second most 'tribal' city in Bihar, after Bokaro (14.38 per cent). The literacy rate was 59.30 per cent, or 67.56 per cent for men and only 49.06 per cent for women. The sex ratio was 860 women to 1000 men.

Ranchi has experienced rapid growth during the past seventy years as is clear from Table 1.

TABLE 1 : RANCHI: POPULATION DECENNIAL AND GROWTH RATES

Census		Total city population	Growth rate (per cent)
1901		25,970	—
1911		32,994	27.04
1921		44,159	33.83
1931		57,238	29.61
1941		62,562	9.30
1951		106,849	70.78
1961	Ranchi Municipality	122,416	14.57
	Doranda	17,837	31.26 (Total)
1971	Ranchi Municipality	175,934 ⎫	43.96
	Doranda	23,954 ⎬ 255,551	82.54 (Total)
	Jagannathnagar	55,663 ⎭	

Source: *Census of India, 1951, 1961 and 1971*, Bihar.

[6]See Theodore Cross, *Black Capitalism, Strategy for Business in the Ghetto*, Atheneum, New York, 1969, pp. XII, 274.

During the Second World War, the growth of Ranchi was phenomenal. It became the headquarters of the Eastern Command. During the 1960s an even faster growth rate was witnessed due to the establishment of the Heavy Engineering Corporation, the headquarters of Hindustan Steel Ltd., and the National Coal Development Corporation (now Central Coalfields Ltd.) and other important enterprises in the private sector. Ranchi also has several important offices of the Government of Bihar and it is a University city. Functionally, it is categorised in the Census as service-cum-trade and commerce-cum-industry, Doranda simply as services and Jagannathnagar as industry.

The total area covered by the Ranchi Urban Agglomeration amounts to 89.98 sq. km. It has a total of 44,077 residential houses inhabited by 48.514 households, or an average of 5.27 persons per household.

The breakdown of the population according to economic activity is given in Table 2 (page 196). The data of the last three Censuses are not strictly comparable because of definitional changes introduced after the 1961 and 1971 Censuses.

When taken together, the asterisked sectors have increased from 84.88 per cent to 92.11 per cent of all economic activities in which the active population is engaged. This is mainly due to the decrease in the importance of cultivation as an economic activity.

Estimation of the Urban Informal Sector

It is possible to come to a closer estimation of the urban informal sector by analysing the types of establishments enumerated in the 1971 Census.

The Census gives information about unregistered workshops, a criterion according to Sethuraman, for placing an establishment in the urban informal sector. From the 1971 Census, it would appear that 90.66 per cent of all enumerated establishments at Ranchi could fall within the informal sector. This impression is further reinforced when the number of persons employed in such establishments is considered.

From Table 4 it will be seen that 1,173 out of the 1.301 stablishments enumerated, or 90.16 per cent had less than ten

TABLE 2: POPULATION OF RANCHI ACCORDING TO ECONOMIC
ACTIVITY (PER CENT)

1951 Census		1961 Census		1971 Census
Population:	106,849	140,253		255,551
Workers: not known		42,585=30.36		68,216=26.69
Non-workers: not known		97,668=69.63		187,33=73.31
Cultivators, Cultivating labourers and dependents	13.82	Cultivators	4.73	2.36
Non-cultivating owners of land and rent receivers	1.29	Agricultural Labourers	1.21	3.04
Production other than cultivation	11.45*	Livestock forestry fishing Punting plant Mining and quarrying	2·70	1.45
		Mining and quarrying		1.01
		Manufacturing:		
		(a) household	3.95*	3.07*
		(b) Other than household	16.44*	29.96*
		Construction	4.71*	2.39*
Commerce	20.57*	Trade and Commerce	13.80*	19.37*
Transport	4.81*	Transport and storage and communications	9.27*	9.70*
Other services and miscellaneous sources	48.05*	Other services	43.19*	27.62*
Total of sectors in which urban Industrial sector can occur	84.88*		91.36*	92.11*

Source: *Census of India 1951, 1961, 1971*, Bihar.

*Indicates economic activities which could fall within the urban informal
sector.

TABLE 3 : ESTABLISHMENTS IN MANUFACTURING, PROCESSING, SERVICING, TRADE AND BUSINESS IN RANCHI CITY, 1971

Type of establishments	Govern-mental/ quasi-govt.	Private	Co-oper-ative	Total
Manufacturing, Processing and Servicing				
Registered factories	4	93	—	97
Unregistered workshops	7	1,197*	—	1,204
Household industries	—	130*	—	130
Trade and business establishments				
Wholesale	1	305	2	308
Retail	23	2,731*	5	2,759
Others	17	399*	2	418
Total	52	4,855	9	4,916
Total of those in which urban informal sector can occur	—	4,457* (90.66%)	—	

Source: *Census of India 1971*, Bihar, Series 4, Part III-B, Establishment Tables.

TABLE 4: REGISTERED AND UNREGISTERED ESTABLISHMENTS IN MANUFACTURING AND REPAIRS ACCORDING TO NUMBER OF PERSONS EMPLOYED

Size of units	Registered units		Unregistered units	
	Number of units	Persons employed	Number of units	Persons employed
Single person units	—	—	314*	314*
2-4 person units	—	—	664*	1,751*
5-9 person units	—	—	195*	1,215*
10-19 person units	64	769	31	365
20-49 person units	21	563	—	—
50-99 person units	8	445	—	—
100-299 person units	3	446	—	—
300-499 person units	1	473	—	—
Total	97	2,696	1,204	3,645
Total of those in which urban informal sector could occur			1,173*	3,280*

Source: *Census of India 1971*, Bihar, Series 4, Part III-B, Establishment Tables.

employees, which would be an additional criterion to classify them under the informal sector. These establishments employed 3,280 persons or 51.72 per cent of those engaged in manufacturing/repairs establishments.

The Census also gives information about the type of energy used. Those establishments which use electricity can be separated and the residual establishments, not using electric power could qualify for inclusion in the informal sector. This has been done in Table 5.

TABLE 5 : DISTRIBUTION OF MANUFACTURING, PROCESSING OR SERVICING ESTABLISHMENTS OTHER THAN HOUSEHOLD INDUSTRIES CLASSIFIED BY FUEL/POWER USED AND SIZE

Size of units	Establishments using electricity		Establishments using other power than electricity		Total	
	Number of units	Persons employed	Number of units	Persons employed	Number of units	Persons employed
Single-person units	71	71	243*	243*	314	314
2-4 person units	157	412	507*	1,339*	664	1,751
5-9 person units	54	344	141*	871*	195	1,215
10-19 person units	49	597	46	537	95	1,134
20-49 person units	9	226	12	337	21	563
50-99 person units	5	256	3	189	8	445
100-299 person units	3	446	—	—	3	446
300-499 person units	1	473	—	—	1	473
Total	349	2,825	925	3,516	1,301	6,341
Total of establishments that could fall in the informal sector			891* (68.48%)	2,453* (69.76%)		

Source : *Census of India 1971*, Bihar, Series 4, Part III-B, Establishment Tables.

A total of 68.48 per cent of all establishments in manufacturing, processing or servicing use sources of energy other than electricity *and* employ less than ten persons. There are two criteria for including them in the informal sector. These

TABLE 6: TRADE AND COMMERCIAL ESTABLISHMENTS, RETAIL
TRADE, 1971

Type of trade (retail)	Total number of establishments		Single unit establishments		2-4 person units		5-9 person units	
	Number	Persons employed	Number	Persons employed	Number	Persons employed	Number	Persons employed
Food, tobacco, beverages	1,589	2,578	1,056	1,056	496	1,170	26	144
Textiles	207	438	94	94	103	229	7	45
Fuel, household utensils	382	764	172	172	190	456	17	97
Others	581	1,347	222	222	312	762	37	230
Restaurants and hotels	379	1,259	99	99	202	528	55	350
Total	3,138	6,386	1,643	1,643	1,303	3,145	142	866
Total of commercial establishments	3,485	7,599	1,702	1,702	1,525	3,747	186	1,120
Percentage of units in the informal sector	90.04	84.03	96.53	96.53	85.44	83.93	76.34	77.32

Source: *Census of India 1971*, Bihar, Series, 4, Part III-B, Establishment
Tables.

establishments employed nearly 70 per cent of all the manpower engaged in the manufacturing sector. As regards the 130
household industries, enumerated earlier, these *ipso facto* could
be classified as falling within the informal sector.

It is also possible to arrive at an estimate of certain trade
and commercial establishments especially those engaging in
retail trade. Of a total of 3,485 trade and commercial establishments, 3,138 were retail shops (90.04 per cent) dealing in wares
that are usually handled by the informal sector. These employed
84.03 per cent of the labour force engaged in that sector. Table
6 further indicates that a very large proportion of these retail
shops employed less than ten persons, which is an additional
reason for classifying them under the informal sector.

The data presented in Tables 3-6 suggest that about 80 per cent of all establishments in manufacturing, servicing and trade could be classified under the informal sector. In these establishments are to be found approximately 75 per cent of the labour force employed in the secondary and tertiary sectors in Ranchi city in 1971. These are the most important sources of employment opportunities for the urban poor. It must also be remembered that the Census leaves several important sectors of the informal sector unenumerated, such as the cycle rickshaw drivers, who belong to the informal transport sector of the city.

TRIBAL PARTICIPATION IN RANCHI'S INFORMAL SECTOR

Tribal entrepreneurship will be better understood if it is studied in the context of the informal urban sector of Ranchi.

Rickshaw Drivers

One of the most 'visible' forms of participation by tribals in Ranchi's informal urban sector is by plying cycle rickshaws. At present there are approximately 6,500 registered cycle rickshaws in Ranchi. A field survey done in 1975 by Xavier Institute showed that 45 per cent of the rickshaw drivers were tribals.[7] This means that approximately 3,000 tribals earned their living in the informal sector, without counting those who ply an unregistered rickshaw or the cases, where two drivers ply one vehicle in two shifts.

Two years ago, the rickshaw drivers became the owners of the vehicles which previously they had to hire from owners who charged Rs 1.50-2 per day. The commercial banks paid compensation to these rickshaw owners, and the drivers were expected to deposit some money every day in the bank towards the repayment of the loan. The rickshaw drivers have become more aware of their dignity. The rates they charge have gone up, and they cannot be ordered about or shouted down, as was the case earlier. Initially, their rate of repayment of bank loans

---

[7]See Utpal Dutta, Kayomours H. Gandhi and Gautam Shee, 'Socio-Economic Conditions of Cycle Rickshaw Drivers in Ranchi Town', *Axis* (Annual of Xavier Institute, 1975), pp. 22-4.

was satisfactory, but slackened over a period of time, and the banks now despair of recovering these loans. In spite of the multiplication of scooter rickshaws and minibuses in the city over the past five years, the cycle rickshaw has withstood the competition commendably, and there is no sign of its being squeezed out by motorised transport. Hardworking rickshaw drivers can earn Rs 15-20 per day, but part of this money has to be saved to meet the costs of repairs and spares. A number of tribal rickshaw drivers spend the night in their vehicle along the main roads, but an even larger number drive them out of town at night to the surrounding villages from which Ranchi recruits its work force.

Daily Labourers

Another area in which tribals from the surrounding villages 'specialise' is daily wage labour. This is especially the case with young tribal women—known locally as *rejas*—who work on construction sites, loading and unloading trucks carrying building materials. These *rejas* have made a reputation for themselves as hardy and good workers. They work in teams of four or five, usually girls of the same village. At times they wear a head cloth of a bright colour, as protection against the dust and to indicate the team or truck to which they belong. The *rejas* are attached to a particular building or transport contractor and work on a construction site till it is completed. Work hours go by the sun and overtime is a word that has never been heard of.

Male and female coolies also hire themselves out on a daily basis. This is a custom restricted to tribal workers. In the morning, considerable numbers of tribal men and women congregate at important road corners, called *chowks*, where they offer themselves for work. Some of them bring along a spade and a basket. They wait till a person comes and hires them for the day, or just for a couple of hours for unskilled jobs such as digging, whitewashing and loading. They are paid at the end of the day or after the work is completed.

Trade in Grass, Firewood and Leaves

There are other forms in which tribals, especially women,

participate in the informal trade of Ranchi city an d keep it supplied with humble but vital inputs. During the rainy season, literally hundreds of tribal women converge on the city each day, carrying big bundles of fresh grass on the head. As they proceed towards the heart of the city, the grass is bought by the milkmen, who keep cows and buffaloes in every nook and corner of the city. The sale of grass tapers off as the dry season sets in. In other parts of the city, a brisk trade in firewood can be observed during the early morning hours. Scores of tribal women arrive from the area on the eastern side of the city, where there are still some forests (Horap Jungle), and sell the firewood directly to the customer.

Still other tribal women keep the hotels of Ranchi regularly supplied with leaf cups and leaf plates, in which sweets are served or sold to customers. Now that minibuses are plying on roads connecting the villages with the city, this trade has become very brisk, and every morning a minibus, known as the 'Kosi Express,' comes from the north bringing huge bundles of these cups and plates into the city. There are also the tribals women, who do the rounds with 'tooth sticks' called *datuns*. A characteristic of these forms of trade is that there does not seem to be any middle-man between the primary producer and the consumer of the product. The primary producer with his or her family members spends one or two days collecting these forest products and another day in selling them in the city.

Workers in Informal Sector Enterprises

A large number of tribals are employed in tiny enterprises falling within the informal urban sector. Tribal workers 'specialise' in the following enterprises: small printing presses, fabrication shops, carpentry and saw mills, photography, watch repairs, cycle, motorcycle, motorcar repairs, truck and bus body building. In these enterprises, it is estimated that tribals constitute nearly 50 per cent of the work force.

A good number of these workers are drop-outs from technical schools, or persons who have worked for a time in the formal sector. They constitute a floating labour force shifting from one employer to another, if the latter offers a slightly higher wage. There are no formal appointments, no regular work hours, no social benefits; but these are standard practices in the informal urban sector everywhere in the Third World.

Tribal workers, especially the women folk, have a good rating among the employers, as being less talkative and more 'sincere' than non-tribal workers. They can do routine tasks for prolonged periods with very little supervision. The only weakness they suffer from is addiction to drink, as a result of which absenteeism after pay days is high, and they are often in debt.

To sum up, the participation of the tribal population from the surrounding villages in the formal urban sector of Ranchi's economy is extensive and varied.

The relationship between the city and the hinterland from where it draws its labour can be compared to rhythmic breathing, wherein the city inhales thousands of tribal workers and tiny entrepreneurs and traders during the morning hours and exhales them again towards the evening. Without the contribution of these little people, the economy of the city would grind to a halt. At certain times of the day and of the week, esepcially on market days, the presence of the urban informal sector and the tribal people involved therein, becomes so overwhelming that the main arteries of the city such as Main Road, Upper Bazar and Ratu Road cannot be used by vehicular transport.

TRIBAL ENTREPRENEURS IN RANCHI'S URBAN INFORMAL SECTOR

Distribution of Tribal Entrepreneurs

The most significant, creative and promising form of tribal participation in the urban sector of Ranchi city are the self-employed entrepreneurs who manage tiny businesses. A careful exploration[8] of the *mohallas* and streets of the city—since no reference list existed—yielded a population according to sector in Table 7.

With the help of precentages given at the bottom of the Table it is possible to compare the population of tribal entrepreneurs

---

[8]The data presented in this section were collected during a research project carried out in Ranchi (1971-72) with the financial assistance of the ICSSR. See M.V.d. Bogaert, E. Toppo and N.C. Das, 'Tribal Entrepreneurs', *ICSSR Research Abstracts Quarterly*, 2, n. 4, pp. 250-64.

TABLE 7: POPULATION OF TRIBAL ENTREPRENEURS IN RANCHI
ACCORDING TO SECTOR, 1971-72

Primary sector	Population	Secondary sector	Population	Tertiary sector	Population
Agriculture		Manufacturing		Trade, retail, food, beverages, tobacco	
Vegetable growing	64	Carpentry	5		
		Flour and rice mill	3	Vegetables	18
Animal husbandry					
Dairying	46	Printing press	2	Tea stalls	37
				Hotels	14
Piggery	2	Repairs		Mess	2
		Cycle repairs	40	Grocery stores	19
		Motorcycle repairs	5	Liquor sales	9
		Automobile repairs	2	Pan shops	48
		Watch repairs	1	Tobacco	1
		Household industries		Trade, non-foods	
		Tailoring	20	Coal	5
		Blacksmithy	2	Trinkets	1
		Book binding	1		
		Embroidery	1	Transport	
		Cane work	1	Bus and taxi services	5
		Building contractors	4	Autorickshaw	2
				Rickshaw hire	2
				Cycle hire	1
				Services	
				Medical service	4
				Commerc. inst.	1
Total	112		87		169

Grand total=368

	Primary	Secondary	Tertiary
Percentage of population	30.43	23.64	45.92
Corresponding per cent Census 1971	17.86	35.42	56.69

with the Census data of 1971 (see also Table 2). There is a considerable concentration of tribal entrepreneurs, 30.43 per cent in the primary sector, as compared to 7.86 per cent in the 1971 Census. This can be explained by the fact that the primary sector is closer to the traditional culture of the tribal people and also that tribals, who constitute the original population of Ranchi city, still own some land in the heart of the city on which they grow vegetables for the market; further, the Chhotanagpur Tenancy Act 1908 imposes severe restrictions on transfer of tribal land to non-tribals. The proportion of tribal entrepreneurs in the secondary and tertiary sectors is somewhat lower than that of the population in general. Even so, participation in the tertiary sector accounts for 45.92 per cent of the tribal entrepreneur population, with a heavy concentration (40.21 per cent) in the retail trade of foods, beverages and tobacco.

MAIN VARIABLES OF PERFORMANCE

Table 8 gives in highly summarised form some of the performance variables of a sample of 181 tribal entrepreneurs. Tribal entrepreneurs begin their business with an average initial capital of Rs 1,376 but amongst vegetable growers it is as low as Rs 240, while amongst building contractors it reaches Rs 16,333. The average number of years in business for the whole sample —not indicated in the Table—is 7.11 years or an annual increase of Rs 447. On a capital of Rs 1,376 this would mean a rate of growth of 32.48 per cent.

The average mean educational level of tribal entrepreneurs amounts to only 2.97 years of formal training, but there is a marked difference from trade to trade, being as high as 10.25 years in 'services' and as low as 1.17 years amongst vegetable growers.

Besides engaging in business, many tribal entrepreneurs also have another source of income. Since they are only part-time entrepreneurs, they minimise the risks of running a business, but they are not able to give the single-minded attention necessary to achieve a real breakthrough in their business. The average monthly income from 'other sources' amounts to Rs 196, while from business it is only Rs 293 (mean annual income divided by 12.)

The total gross labour, that is family labour and non-family labour combined comes to 3.31 units. If related to

TABLE 8: MEANS OF PERFORMANCE VARIABLES OF TRIBAL ENTREPRENEURS

Type of business	Number of observations	Mean initial capital	Mean educt. score	Mean monthly income from other sources	Mean annual income	Mean family labour	Mean non-family labour
Agriculture							
Vegetable	18	240.56	1.17	305.28	1,166.67	4.17	—
Animal husbandry	19	1,775.26	2.95	258.26	2,592.63	3.15	0.59
Primary sector	37	1,028.65	2.08	281.13	1,898.92	3.64	0.29
Manufacturing	9	2,761.11	5.44	148.89	6,813.33	1.89	2.78
Repairs	26	361.85	3.35	171.54	3,900.00	1.52	1.42
Household industries	20	242.35	4.10	146.75	2,679.00	1.67	1.15
Contractors	3	16,333.32	4.67	416.67	8,600.00	1.00	22.33
Secondary sector	58	1,519.05	4.00	172.15	4,174.10	1.69	2.62
Food trades	67	437.28	1.55	148.90	3,068.95	1.78	0.61
Non-food trades	7	671.43	3.43	242.86	2,940.00	2.71	0.43
Transport	8	9,687.50	7.50	320.37	10,125.00	1.59	1.00
Service	4	2,837.50	10.25	222.50	4,470.00	1.00	0.50
Tertiary sector	86	1,428.45	2.66	175.92	3,780.00	1.80	0.63
Grand mean	181	1,375.80	2.97	196.22	3,521.76	2.11	1.20

present capital, which is Rs 4,555, this would imply that an average investment of Rs 1,376 would help a TE to generate one additional job. This indicates the low capital investment ratio needed to increase employment when compared to the investment needed for every additional job in the small-scale industries of the formal sector. According to figures given by the Union Minister for Industries in 1976, these would have been respectively Rs 2,758 and 20,833, or a ratio of 1:2:15. Thus, for one job in large industries, the small-scale entrepreneur generates 7.5 jobs, but the tribal entrepreneur in Ranchi city would generate fifteen jobs.[9] One touches here the heart of the matter, and the reason why organisations like the ILO are turning to the urban informal sector: its capacity to generate employment with very small investment.

CENTRAL FINDING OF THE STUDY

Weak Points

TEs operate on a weak financial basis, having to depend on their own capital to start or expand their business. During the last few years efforts have been made to make institutional credit available, but there are still formidable communication gaps which restrict the flow of needed capital.

TEs show a low capacity to save for future investment. Since they cannot rely on their own resources, credit becomes expensive. Because of this inability to save, TEs are not likely to make a major breakthrough in business or enter the ranks of the middle class in the near future.

On the other hand, they are not aware of or show little interest in the many Government-sponsored opportunities for credit, projects, sites, etc., that are supposedly available for TEs. They lack technical and business skills. TEs cannot pick these up from their own family or caste background, as is the case with *Banias* and other traditional trading communities. TEs are poorly organised. Co-operatives have not succeeded, and other forms of organising them to struggle for common interests

[9]See *The Indian Worker*, New Delhi, INTUC Foundation Day Number, 1976, pp. 55-8.

seem to be totally absent. Everybody is on his own. One does
not notice any vigorous action to expand one's market, or for
product innovation. TEs show little 'aggressiveness' in marketing, even young TEs who have received training in
entrepreneurship.

The position occupied by the TEs in the business world of
Ranchi city is right at the bottom, but some TEs have achieved
some mobility. TEs are marginal as far as the importance and
also location of their business is concerned. Nobody is concerned about them, since they do not offer any serious
competition to enterprises in the formal sector.

Tribals, including the TEs, continue to aspire for employment in the organised or formal sector because of the security
and the status this offers. TEs have not yet succeeded in pro-
jecting themselves as a 'reference group' for tribal youth in
Ranchi.

Strong Points

The fact that TEs exist and survive, and that some of them even
do fairly well, disproves the commonly held opinion that
tribals cannot manage a business entreprise. Most TEs are first-
generation entrepreneurs and, in this sense, show greater
mobility than the traditional trader castes. The majority of
TEs are aware of their shortcomings and show a desire to acquire
better skills through training programmes, consultancy, travel-
ling around, etc. This desire provides a point of entry for an
organisation interested in promoting barefoot entrepreneurship.

There is little or no discrimination on the part of other communities against TEs. As a matter of fact, the climate in a city
like Ranchi is favourable for the promotion of entrepreneurship amongst the under-privileged groups.

Investigation into the factors responsible for the 'success' of
tribal entrepreneurs indicated that controllable factors such as
education, previous experience, motivation, etc., are more
important than the uncontrollable factors such as possession of
ancestral land, tribal affiliation, language, religion or social
status. These findings suggest that through adapted training, the
entry of tribals to the world of entrepreneurship can be
speeded up, and their performance as barefoot managers

improved. We will now describe some of the more important aspects of an entrepreneurial training programme conducted at the Xavier Institute of Social Service.

VI. TRAINING AND PROMOTION OF TRIBAL ENTREPRENEURS

Our experience during the past three years indicates that it is indeed possible to train tribals to become barefoot entrepreneurs and to assist them in launching their enterprises. Experience, as a matter of fact has shown—and a recent scientific evaluation of the programme has further confirmed this[10]—that is is earlier to train such entrepreneurs in a programme under private sponsorship, than to train and help entrepreneurs from the general population, in a programme jointly run with the Government. It must, however, be noted, that the main thrust of these tribal entrepreneur development programmes is oriented towards rural rather than urban areas. We will limit ourselves to some general comments.

Selection of Candidates

This is done on the basis of the candidate's perception of goals, achievement motivation, past experience and moral support from family members rather than on academic degrees or certificates. Those who have completed secondary school or have a certificate or degree tend to look for employment in the formal sector.

Practical Training

For a major part of the four months, the TEs are under training on the shop-floor in establishments of the type they intend to set up themselves after training. Instead of being afraid of competition, most of the small shopkeepers in Ranchi proved to be very helpful, and some have revealed themselves to be excellent barefoot trainers.

[10]Nagendra P. Singh, *Management of Entrepreneurial Development Programme* (A Comparative Analysis of Tribals and Non-Tribals), *Case Study of a Voluntary Organisation*, Small Industry Extension Training Institute, Hyderabad, 1977.

Theoretical Training

This is given in Hindi, and includes sessions on motivation, communication, leadership, principles and practices of management, marketing, shop management, customer service, laws and taxation applicable to small establishments, accounting, financial management, Government schemes to assist small-scale entrepreneurs. These topics are covered by the full-time faculty of the Entrepreneur Development Programme, and a part-time staff of co-operative businessmen, bankers and Government officials.

Market Survey

Towards the end of their four-month training, the trainees go to the field and conduct a market survey on the basis of which they make a project report. This project report, though simple, must contain all the essential information that a banker or other sponsor will need before approving a loan. The trainees are assisted by the faculty and bankers themselves in preparing their reports. The project report must be completed by the time the candidate finishes his training.

Financing

The candidates have to find on their own a part of the initial finance for setting up their business. Arrangements are made with the bank for loans, which are kept within the limit of Rs. 5,000 so that they are eligible for the Differential Interest Rate of 4 per cent instead of the usual rate of 13 per cent or more. Vikas Maitri Kalyan Sanstha stands guarantee for loans issued by the Banks and also helps in the supervision of loan repayment.

Follow-up of Entrepreneurs

To cope with the stress of innovative enterprise, young TEs need emotional support. This aspect is too often overlooked. TEs need to know that somebody is with them, that they are part of a wider network of social and economic relations. A follow-up during the first months after they have started their business is vital for the success of the scheme. The EDP faculty visits the young TEs regularly, checks on how they keep their accounts, and liaises with the local banker. Young TEs also know that they can always approach the EDP faculty for technical and administrative assistance.

A local branch of the National Alliance of Young Entrepreneurs has been organised at Ranchi. This organisation meets every month, and also conducts a monthly guidance cell meeting wherein young entrepreneurs can obtain practical advice from bankers, engineers and Government officials.

Programmes for TEs

Two types of programmes have been organised at Ranchi for tribal entrepreneurs: a *general* Entrepreneurial Development Programme for unemployed engineers, diploma holders, degree holders and ITI trained candidates, under the Half Million Jobs Scheme of the Government of India. There were some tribal candidates amongst the participants of three such programmes conducted so far. This programme is not discussed here. Second, a *tribal* EDP specifically oriented to tribals and other under-privileged groups in the local community. Three such programmes have been conducted so far.

The number of candidates for each trade and the number of those who actually started their business, or are in the process of setting up their business is shown in Table 9. Several of the candidates of the third programme have not yet set up enterprises, and it is too early to say what the rate of success will be.

By local standards, a rate of success beyond 40 per cent can be considered quite good. The other candidates, who have not yet started business, should not be simply written off as drop-outs. Experience shows that it takes, at times, years before the training given in an entrepreneur development programme can be actually used. This depends often on a constellation of circumstances—personal and social—in which the young entrepreneur finds himself.

TABLE 9: NUMBER OF CANDIDATES, AND OF THOSE WHO ACTUALLY
STARTED A BUSINESS, ARRANGED ACCORDING TO
TRADE AND PROGRAMME

Trade	1st Progr. (1974)		2nd Progr. (1975)		3rd Progr. (1977)	
	Cands.	Started business	Cands.	Started business	Cands.	Started business
Flour mill	2	1	—	—	2	—
Photography	3	3	—	—	—	—
Kirana shop	7	2	7	2	6	—
Tailoring	2	2	9	7	10	4
Homeopathy	1	1	—	—	—	—
Vegetable growers	1	—	—	—	—	—
Radio repairs	1	—	—	—	1	—
Cycle repairs	1	—	1	1	4	1
Cloth shop	—	—	2	1	2	—
Carpentry	—	—	1	—	—	—
Watch repairs	—	—	1	1	1	1
Readymade garments	—	—	2	—	5	—
Poultry	—	—	—	—	3	—
Mahuwa trade	—	—	—	—	1	1
Fertiliser and seeds	—	—	—	—	1	—
Pump repairs	—	—	—	—	1	—
Total	18	9	23	12	37	7
Rate of success		50%		52.17%		20.58%

CONCLUSION

The concept of the urban informal sector has brought new
insights into the structure of the urban economy and a better
understanding of the immense contribution which the urban
poor make to the maintenance and development of the economic
life of the city. Because of this, policy-makers who are concerned with urban development must plan for the utilisation of the
productive skills available in the informal sector.

This paper has tried to highlight the distinctive contribution
which the tribal population—partly native population of the
city, partly immigrants from the Chhotanagpur region, and mostly
rural people from the villages surrounding the city—make to
the economic life of Ranchi. So far, Government assistance to
tribal persons has been oriented towards helping them enter
the formal sector of the economy, where jobs are necessarily

scarce and the cost per person trained tends to be high. It would be worthwhile to try a new approach to upgrade the existing skills of tribal people, as is being increasingly attempted by international organisations such as the UNICEF, the FAO and the ILO.[11] The programme for the training of tribal entrepreneurs, described in this chapter, is a modest attempt in this direction. It trains the poor to improve their employment opportunities, income, standard of living, and capacity to generate additional income as well. To do this effectively, barefoot entrepreneurs must be assured greater access to local or regional markets and be given opportunities to acquire the skills to adapt their products to the changing demands of the market.

The competitiveness of the market that is manipulated and controlled by formal sector institutions requires that barefoot entrepreneurs be able to organise themselves in co-operatives to ensure their economic survival. At present, the relations between the formal and informal sectors are those of dominance and dependency in which producers in the informal sector are unable to overcome the barriers raised by the industrial and commercial institutions of the formal sector. It is this exploitative character of the market that makes co-operative action indispensable for the development of small-scale entrepreneurs in the informal sector.

The present industrial policy of the Government acknowledges the existence and importance of the 'tiny sector' as distinguished from the small-scale sector—the cut-off point being Rs 2 lakhs of investment—and the fact that this tiny sector needs special attention.[12] This is a step in the right direction, i.e., towards the recognition of the barefoot entrepreneurs whose investment is usually well below Rs 10,000.

Another vital challenge is the provision of credit to the tiny sector. The nationalised banks are required to make credit available to small-scale and tiny entrepreneurs in the informal sector. However, these focal points of interaction between the

11See Agri Missio, 'Village Education: A Passport to Productivity', *Impact*, 12, n. 8, August 1977, pp. 282-3.

12See George Fernandes, 'Outline of New Industrial Policy', *Laghu Udyog*, August 1977, pp. 2-5.

formal and informal sectors tend to function as structures of exploitation when it is a matter of obtaining bank credit, licences, electrical connections and so on. It is here that the voluntary organisations can play an important role as facilitators in the dialogue between small-scale and barefoot entrepreneurs in the urban informal sector and commercial and Government organisations in the formal sector.

11

Slum Relocation and Urban Planning: Some Social Concerns

K. Raman Unni

The socially oriented planner today, more than ever before, confronts a maze of problems and issues in the relocation of slum-dwellers in Indian cities. An attempt is made here to examine some of the socially significant dimensions worthy to be recognised in these problems and issues and thus to contribute towards illuminating our thinking on future planning for urban development.[1]

A distinction is not made here between slums and squatters (illegal occupants of land). Slums which have become stabilised

[1]Some important studies which will help to understand the social aspects of the urban poor and their housing conditions, and the social dimensions of high density residential settlements of mixed income groups are: *Jhuggi Jhonpri Settlements in Delhi*, Part I, Delhi: Town and Country Planning Organisation, 1973; *Jhuggi Jhonpri Settlements in Delhi*, Part II, *A Sociological Study of Low-Income Migrant Communities*, Delhi: Town and Country Planning Organisation, 1975; Jay A. Weinstein, *Madras: An Analysis of Urban Ecological Structure in India*, London: Sage Publications, 1974, Vol. 2; Govind Gare, *Tribals in an Urban Setting*, Poona: Shubhada Saraswat, 1976; Harish Doshi, *Traditional Neighbourhoods in a Modern City*, New Delhi: Abhinav, 1974; Andrea Menefee Singh, *Neighbourhood and Social Networks in Urban India*, Delhi: Marwah, 1976; T.K. Majumdar, "The Urban Poor and Social Change: A Study of Squatter Settlements in Delhi", *Social Action*, 27, n. 3, July-Sept 1977, pp. 216-240.

for decades in the inner city, owned by the residents and grown as an integral part of the locality, are not dealt with in this paper. Slums of this kind are, to cite a few aspects, characterised by (i) social homogeneity within a pocket in terms of caste/religion/language; (ii) two to four-storeyed development of traditional domestic architecture permitting residential and commercial use; (iii) evidence of frequent structural adaptation of parts of buildings to various uses under expediency for space; (iv) high density living habits which lead to noise, overcrowding and lack of ease in circulation.[2]

Sandwiched in these kinds of localities are tiny pockets of *jhuggis* (hutments of easily perishable material) occupied by the poorest workers serving that area and adding to the speedy deterioration of the little environmental quality which the economically better-off residents try to maintain. Such squatter pockets of *jhuggis* and the larger kind of squatter colonies (spontaneous settlements) distributed in and along peripheral areas of the city and its inner zones, are now challenging city planning expertise for solutions in the field of low cost housing programmes. These *jhuggi* pockets and settlements, some of them having houses of semi-durable construction, which are now the concern of the government and the planner for rehousing, and the debates over possible alternatives in the programme are the theme of this paper.

THE CONTEXT OF RELOCATION

The large-scale relocation programmes carried out in Indian cities, particularly in Delhi, during the last five years have to be understood in the context of perspectives which have evolved regarding urban development. The planning profession, except for rare exceptions concerning individual planners, does not appear to have had a comprehensive awareness of the numerous dimensions of this context and the guidelines for the perspectives. An attempt is made here to enumerate the more important of the dimensions of this context.

(i) Numerous developmental programmes in rural and urban

[2]See the situation described by Rory Fonseca in "The Walled City of Delhi", *Ekistics*, 31, n. 182, January 1971.

areas have led to more economic disparities: the well-placed
are getting better life-chances and the poor are increasing
in numbers. Therefore, all developmental measures, including urban development, have to be with a view to ensuring
growth with social justice.

(ii) The GNP approach (gross national product) to development is being modified by the Gross National Welfare
approach.

(iii) The concept of a static plan is being replaced by the idea
of an evolutionary process in which plans are adapted in
the light of changing conditions. At the empirical level, the
question is how effectively we monitor mistakes and modify
the course once favoured rather than how we should
attempt to see that the plan once prepared is followed necessarily.

(iv) Planning is concerned as much with implementation as with
preparation.

(v) Planning *with* people rather than for people is the ideal to
be sought for conversion into operational guidelines in
future urban development.

(vi) Squatter rehousing is not just resheltering or piecemeal social
welfare effort towards halting the growth of slums or releas-
ing land of high value for public purposes. It is for development of settlements which are a part of the city's socio-
economic structure. It raises numerous socio-economic
issues of critical importance for policies regarding
development at local, State and national levels.

(vii) Squatter relocation programmes should be viewed as efforts
entailing community planning for community development.

(viii) Urban development with massive relocation programmes for
squatters has to be planned with simultaneous emphasis on
rural development. This will reduce subsistence migration
to the city and ensure the long-term success of relocation
programmes.

(ix) Middle class projections of goals and objectives have to be
used very cautiously in dealing with our city planning
problems and issues since the majority of urban households
(over 60 per cent) cannot afford to own a house of minimum
standards except with aid in one form or another.

(x) Planning implies preserving what was loved and preparing for the future. Therefore, social disruption, through the break-up of traditional social groupings which offered various benefits and social values supporting social controls, should be minimised in urban housing programmes, particularly in the relocation of squatter settlements.

(xi) 'Incremental' or 'flexible' housing-planning for the urban poor is the right approach to meet the needs and fit the mood of the people housed. Such designs which make it possible to have a minimum of investment to begin with, with improvements over a period of time (embodied to a commendable extent in the present 'site and services' scheme), are worthy of large-scale implementation.

(xii) Ownership of the plot or a share in the plot which gives the householder sufficient security of tenure, is a basic factor that can provide a thrust towards visible success to any crash programme in a short period. This element of ownership in a housing policy can develop identity of home-life with the habitat and bring about housing satisfaction.

The aspects of the social context enumerated here have posed several challenges to the planning profession. It is important to note that the planning profession in our country has yet to grow up in terms of trained personnel and professional maturity. Constructive thinking to formulate programmes on the basis of the realisation of the context is being nurtured only by a few experts in the profession, and they are few and far between. It is estimated that by 1980, the country needs about 2,100 planners and that the present 700 planners, with an expected addition of about 150 a year, will be far from adequate to meet the need for trained personnel.[3] A 'planning intelligentsia', mature and influential enough to make an impact on policies will, therefore, not appear in the next few years to come, although the planner has by now acquired a basically important place in any comprehensive planning programme in various fields. In many an instance, the planner has to play the role of an adviser to elected or appointed officials. His advice cannot carry much weight unless the planning profession gains

[3]Figures given are according to information available from the office of Institute of Town Planners, Delhi, India, 1977.

more recognition through a realistic approach to the massive problems of urban planning and development in the country. It is at this point that one can appreciate that the contribution of the social scientists can augment substantially the planner's thinking to meet the country's urban needs.

RELEVANCE OF SOCIAL DIMENSIONS

In recent years, a few sociological studies of slums/squatters and studies which highlight various aspects of tradition-oriented urbanism and features of social groupings among the majority of the population of the Indian city have exposed facts which await a judicious use by the planner.[4] These facts, to cite a few, show the importance of caste, kinship, lineage, language, religion, pre-urban rural background in general, voluntary associations influencing the residential enclaves and some social factors shaping the life-chances of the individual. Some of these studies particularly point out the typically Indian character of the dimension of urban ecological development.[5] Also, the importance of the concept of network in appreciating the squatters' choice of location, of shelter and range of spatial mobility has been discussed in a recent study.[6] The role of traditional institutions and values of the social structure in the modernising process has been revealed in the context of the problems of orientation required in the modern management

[4]These studies, to cite a few, are: Sylvia Vatuk, *Kinship and Urbanisation: White Collar Migrants in North India*, University of California Press, London; Andrea Menefee Singh, op.cit.; Owen M. Lynch, 'Rural Cities in India' in Philip Mason (ed.), *India and Ceylon: Unity and Diversity*, Oxford University Press, London, 1967, pp. 142-58; a few contributions on the subject in M.S.A. Rao (ed.), *Urban Sociology in India*, Orient Longmans, New Delhi 1974.

[5]Jay A. Weinstein, op.cit. As he notes (p. 74): 'In Madras, a city of $2\frac{1}{2}$ million people, the adaptation of the ecological structure to the forces of tradition and modernity seems to have produced an organisation of urban villages in a most literal sense. . . . Thus residence patterns in Madras display a high degree of heterogeneity within relatively small areas, because, as with other aspects of urban India, the social structure is only nominally urban in the Western sense.'

[6]Majumdar, op.cit., pp. 229-32.

approach in various fields.[7]

The socially sensitive planner does not belittle the importance of these typically Indian dimensions, variants of which can be seen in most of the developing countries. His concern is how far such features have to be the determinant factors in his planning and design of sites for relocation and his programmes of rehousing. It is precisely at this point that the sociologist has no clear answer, except to offer a readiness to illuminate various aspects of any given rehousing project, and even to venture to suggest, with a futuristic orientation, what might happen if a settlement is planned in a certain specific manner. This means that the planner has to arrive at his choice in the context of a multi-disciplinary decision-making environment.

The planner's problem, we should appreciate, is to reconcile the findings of the sociologist or anthropologist with the need for the kind of socio-technological system of the future for which he wants to plan. He cannot plan settlements for kin or religious groups when universalistic, achievement-oriented, socialistic, secular and democratic ideals are before him. Broadly, the answer lies in two directions: the 'community housing' perspective which should dominate the thinking of the planner and the 'housing management' approach. Each of them will be considered later.

Attempts to accommodate the traditional aspects of the social structure in squatter relocation programmes have now appeared, although they still await popular recognition and full professional acceptance by housing authorities. These attempts — studies,[8] papers and reports by professional training institutions — are likely to influence future thinking in planning and

[7]For instance see M.N. Srinivas, 'Social Environment and Management Responsibilities', *Economic and Political Weekly*, 10, n. 11, 15 March, 1975. As he notes (p. 488), the predominant rurality means that those who inhabit urban areas have a life-style that is only partially urban.

[8]D.V.R. Rao, 'Rehousing Squatters: A Case Study of Delhi', *Urban and Rural Planning Thought*, 15, n. 4, October 1972; D.V.R. Rao, 'Housing of Squatters in Delhi: Search for Solution', *Urban and Rural Planning Thought*, 16, n. 2, April 1973; H.P. Bahri and Neelima Risbud, 'Housing the Urban poor, Strategy for Standards Formulation'. A paper presented at the annual Town and Country Planning Seminar of Institute of Town Planners, India, December 1975.

housing when housing authorities turn more towards feedback from research endeavours of this kind. These studies focus on the main purpose of developing design concepts at the level of the dwelling unit, through the hierarchy of planning levels ending with the settlement as a whole. The objective of such design concepts is not just to rehouse but to lay the foundations for a settlement to develop. Site and services provision and community level self-help programmes are basic principles in these studies.

The decision to relocate has to confront a set of social questions. A large proportion of squatter settlements in the city are small ones with about 100 households. This was the case in the city of Delhi but the reasons for it are mainly those which one can expect to be functioning in most Indian urban areas— an inference which can be gathered from the report on squatters prepared by the Town and Country Planning Organisation, Delhi, and the analysis presented by Majumdar in his study.[9] The question of crucial importance is whether all such statements should be relocated unless they are all constant sources of mounting adverse effects for themselves and the surrounding locality. Studies denouncing relocation efforts are not altogether wanting. John Turner and Byran Roberts in an essay captioned 'Self-help Society' point out, on the basis of studies of relevant situations in developing countries, that 'massive and forced transfers of the poor from inner-city slums and shanty towns to greatly improved dwellings on the urban periphery generally impoverish the poor.' Again: 'When these centralised systems (of Government and administration and housing authorities) are used to house the poor, their scale and the limitations of management rule out the essential variety and flexibility of housing options', which the poor display in their own housing developments evolved over a period.[10] Charles Correa, the architect-planner, well aware of Indian conditions, has pointed out that the poor, given freedom and space, have traditions and the capacity for a judicious choice of houses within their means. Correa notes that '. . . we do not have a problem of *low cost*

[9]Majumdar, op.cit.
[10]John F.C. Turner and Byran Roberts, 'The Self-help Society', in Peter Wilsher and Rosemary Righter, *The Exploding Cities*, Indian Book Company, New Delhi, 1975, pp. 132-3.

housing; what exists is a problem of *land-use planning.* . . .[11] He points to the planner's need to devise solutions, which permit the freedom of the poor to build horizontally without making services, social infrastructure and the transport facilities expensive. It is noteworthy that Correa, in a later paper, suggested valuable ideas to work out solutions to minimise the ill-effects of horizontal occupancy which brings extensive urban land under housing for the poor.[12]

The fact remains that the majority of *jhuggis*, as was the case in Delhi prior to the massive relocation programme, are usually in the areas meant for non-residential land-use under the city's Master Plan. Hence, relocations involve complex issues and, therefore, await multiple solutions.

MULTIPLICITY OF SOLUTIONS

Any suggestions from sources of housing expertise appear to have been single-pronged in terms of the direction of solutions. We need multi-pronged directions in view of our inter-urban and even intra-urban variations in the socio-economic and cultural profiles of the poor. The very history of each city also strengthens the variations. Property rights over the site and the house (or any structure built through aided self-help) tie the poor emotionally to the place and release much of their social and personality resources to focus on prospering in the urban setting. But we have to be sure that for years to come we can supply this resource of space and other resources to migrants for owner occupancy. Else redistributive justice becomes only temporal—confined to a few years until that becomes impossible. There is also the need to house the poor under some kind of rental scheme covered by the innovation known as housing management. This permits them to stay in areas where they have stabilised prospective links with the inner city. This permits residential mobility as well within the city and inter-urban circulation of the low income people.

[11]Cited by Turner and Roberts, ibid., p. 13.

[12]Charles Correa, 'Space as a Resource', a paper of views and suggestions sent to the Department of Science and Technology, Government of India, Delhi, 1976.

A survey of Bombay pavement-dwellers in 1973 showed that two out of every three did not make any attempt to secure alternative accommodation. Further, 11 per cent of the respondents preferred to live where they were located.[13] Commenting on this, a newspaper editorial pointed to the need of a two-pronged solution: one is to clear pavement-dwellers wherever it is possible and relocate them elsewhere; and the other is:

A simpler, as well as a more humanitarian approach, would be to recognise their existence and at least in crowded areas provide night shelters. . . and think of a least expensive approach as well. This is to provide elementary structures —like a raised platform above the level of the pavement —this would both provide a clean area for people to sleep on and also not obstruct the movement of pedestrians.[14]

Though debatable, one could agree with the spirit of this suggestion. This means that we have to be more realistic and provide something where nothing has been done for years, yet resources to meet future needs are still too meagre.

The need for multiple options to the planner to be utilised in one city simultaneously to fit a variety of situations, is advocated in the planning field in developed countries as well. Thinking in the context of the role of social science in planning the city, David Eversely notes that:

there are sociological reasons for advocating horizontally linear cities, vertical cities, garden cities, enlarged villages, super-megalopolises and continuous sea-shore settlements. There are justifications for ultra high densities . . . and apparently equally good ones for not exceeding eight dwellings to the acre net.[15]

In the light of such arguments and of Indian conditions, one can assert that social concerns in Indian planning cannot be

[13]P. Ramachandran, *Pavement Dwellers in Bombay City*, Tata Institute of Social Sciences, Series No. 26, Bombay, 1972.

[14]Ibid.

[15]David Eversely, *The Planner in Society: The Changing Role of a Profession*, Faber and Faber, London, 1973, p. 234.

specifically enumerated but have to be identified for each case/ project in hand. One main reason for such a posture that the sociologist takes is that, in numerous instances, political decisions have much to do with the issues involved and we have a baffling diversity of styles of life within the same big city. Eversely's remark is again very relevant here, although made in the context of British city planning and the options they should seek for the future.

> One set of groups, inspired by sociologists like Ruth Glass and John Rex, would have nothing to do with rehabilitation, with redistribution of population, or with fears of ghettos of colour and income. They would raze all the old buildings to the ground, and build modern dwellings of high density at low rents for those who needed them most. Other groups favour rehabilitation, making houses fit to live in whilst preserving the community spirit. Yet another group wants a mixture of social clauses. . . .[16]

COMMUNITY HOUSING

It is common knowledge today that in our cities neighbourhoods are only physically grouped as though reflecting bonds of community life but, in reality, there is hardly any subjective feeling of community or any overt behavioural patterns revealing a sustained community life among the residents. There is at the same time the awareness that a major source of residential satisfaction, from a sociological perspective, lies in the subjective community feeling which can be fostered in a neighbourhood setting. The social and physical concerns and issues entailed in this approach are encompassed by the comprehensive phrase 'Housing and Community Planning'.[17]

Community planning is in large measure for the development of the community. It implies a process by which the planner creates a 'receptacle' for actual and potential resources. The concept of community development has to be distinguished

[16]Ibid., p. 190.

[17]For an elaborate presentation of this perspective, see K.R. Unni, 'Social Concerns in Housing and Community Planning', *Urban and Rural Planning Thought*, 17, n. 1, January 1974.

from that of community planning. The former involves the integration of households through common interests and also through efforts made to achieve them. In this distinction, the concept of integration relies heavily on local initiative and self-determinism, and usually involves voluntary groups, whereas 'planning' conveys the idea of imposition and manipulation, and more often involves governmental and other formal 'outside' groups. We need both when we want to carry out programmes of housing and community planning.

The subjective community feeling can be seen in the awareness of people in the old sectors of the Indian city's residential areas. In fact, in India we have a long tradition of living in habitation patterns which permitted, at a micro-level, substantial community feeling, especially in villages and small towns. In the Indian city, it has not disappeared completely yet.

The planner, as pointed out earlier, usually feels that natural social groupings such as caste, kin group and the extended family cannot be fostered in the urban setting, and the basis for transplanting the rural pre-industrial kinds of groupings of houses is non-existent; nor is it desirable in a secular, democratic, socialistic society. In this kind of thinking, the tendency is to ignore any aspect of social and cultural life and view the individual household detached from all its traditional styles of life, and further, to expect that planning can determine what is desirable in the housing environment. This issue needs more consideration than can be given here but, briefly, it may be noted that architect-planners of standing reject this kind of architectural determinism. Design determinism as well, has been shown to have serious limitations. The idea that we have to plan not only for the people but *with* people, especially in the case of the low income categories, has now entered into the planning ideology.

A review of literature on this and allied issues shows that in urban housing we cannot achieve community feeling as fully as in the rural setting. But, then, what can be achieved is a 'community of limited liability'. This means that some of the principles of sociologically guided community planning, such as the principle of common use and the principle of visibility, can be used to maximise latent, if not manifest, awareness of neighbourliness among residents so that they feel themselves bound by some strands of harmonious human relations. This is true at the level of middle income residents as well.

From the stage of site planning, dwelling units can be so grouped as to permit selective (optional) use of space by children, adolescents, men, women and the aged. The grouping can also permit withdrawal and privacy if one household does not feel inclined at a particular time to participate in neighbourly life-activities. Depending on income levels, the number of houses to be clustered together to effect such benefits can be considered. At a low level of income, and even below the poverty line, living extends into and across at times, the front-yard (and back-yard too if they have had the tradition of back-yards). In the *cul-de-sac* form of this type in the Indian village or town, a cluster has to be the smallest unit in a community—five to fifteen dwelling units using one front-yard as a semi-private open space. (The principle in a variant scale should be used for higher income groups.)

Our tradition has not been interpreted in a manner pertinent and intelligible to the housing expert. Perhaps sociologists and anthropologists have described the phenomenon of family-household space in their own 'idiom' which has created a certain misunderstanding of the reality. The distinction between joint family and nuclear (or elementary) family is not very relevant in this context. Most of the low castes had only elementary family (husband, wife and unmarried children) households. But the important point is that they resided in a compact residential setting, sharing several contiguous spaces among married brothers who separated and set up separate hearths as independent units of earning and consumption. They continued to share several things in common, never spatially moving out from the residential complex of their parental and grand-parental households (if any). Social controls (mainly moral and sexual-supervisory) functioned in that kind of setting.[18] In towns, even when households are not comprised of close kin, such controls function among low income groups.

[18]For a detailed account of this interpretation of the residential setting, see K. Raman Unni, 'Rural Families in their Residential Setting', in S. Devadas Pillai (ed.), *Aspects of Changing India*, Popular Prakashan Bombay, 1976, pp. 304-14.

The numerous benefits and functional needs of community housing, understood in this perspective, suggest that it is not only social comfort, amusement and the pleasure of social mixing which point to the need of community housing.

Today, the meaning of the term environment has to be understood in a comprehensive manner. An environment becomes meaningful and identified by the occupants as their own if it offers functionally significant meanings to them. Thus schools, transportation, services, play spaces, spaces for community relations (with flexibility for multi-purpose use), job opportunities not far from the immediate environment, are important concerns in community housing. Not only that, there is also the social aspect of the problem of environmental security. Freedom from fear of robbery, pilferage, assault, rape and such threats can be minimised by community housing if it is also concerned with the issue of environmental security. How the design of a housing complex can minimise this kind of insecurity is a matter for research; and it is a dimension most neglected by housing experts in our country.

Community housing, at any income level, does not mean that everything required is delivered ready-made in one package at a time. Depending on their income levels, there are three general areas in which occupants may become involved: (i) improvements concerned with use of community space, needed services and facilities such as schools, etc.; (ii) jobless households or problem families; and (iii) self-improvement through education, recreation, etc., through the best use of modern mass media. Community housing as a social process starts when the houses are occupied and life and living begins to function there. Community housing as a planning and building activity precedes this stage.

SOCIAL INDICATORS AND QUALITY OF LIFE

Monitoring of relocated settlements to assess success provides feedback to identify the real coverage of social needs achieved through a relocation project. Planners and social scientists are now aware of the need for social indicators and indices of quality of life. The notion of quality of life that is linked to the social indicators movement in other countries, needs a multidisciplinary approach suitable to our context. The definition of a set of social indicators relevant to the assessment of the quality of life is itself a matter of values. However, broadly speaking, it should be noted that social indicators should cover the field of health, safety and security, and family life-support, work productivity and school performance, access to employment, services and recreation, participation in the planning, construction and management of housing, and neighbourly satisfaction. These areas need to be elaborated and a series of indicators developed for each of them.

HOUSING MANAGEMENT

The management approach in the development and maintenance of housing environment to achieve the goals and objectives of various housing programmes, including the relocation of squatters, has yet to develop and gain acceptance in our country. It is a unified effort covering all categories of interests of the community and the State/nation to foster development with maximum social satisfaction. At least on an academic level, its role in India has won recognition, but it awaits acceptance by the government and the housing authorities.[19] United Nations directives on the roles of this profession including its place in the pre-occupancy phase in the relocation process also recognise its importance.[20]

Urban community development programmes can be an integral part of the housing management but not a substitute for it. Among other aspects, this approach is oriented mainly to the improvement of the quality of the environment with the participation of the residents. In the context of housing the urban poor, its roles include responding to the individual household's choice regarding locational preferences, co-ordinating

[19]For an understanding of the scope of this profession in India in the light of the experience in other countries and the conditions in this country, see *Urban and Rural Planning Thought*, Special Number on Housing Management, School of Planning and Architecture, Delhi, January-June, 1970.

[20]*Social Aspects and Management of Housing Projects*, United Nations, New York, 1970; *Introduction to Basics of Housing Management*, United Nations, 1969.

the work of all agencies including voluntary ones to function in a unified manner, guidance and control regarding use
of all levels of community spaces and provision for recreation,
team activities for supplementary income, attending to needs
in terms of priorities felt by the people relocated. Transfers
and exchanges between occupants in the same relocated site
and between different settlements are a provision which housing
management judiciously employs to promote neighbourly satisfaction and to deal with cases of problem families. Management makes an effort to attain the social betterment of residents through education, human relations techniques and the
stimulation of tenants' participation in programmes. Management not only deals with efficiency and economy, but equally
with questions of ethics and humanism. A major role of
management is the feedback it can give in the light of experience to planners to design future settlements and houses so as
to make community planning more relevant to the needs of
the people.

Whether rehousing is in high rise buildings or under rental
programmes, the role of housing management, in the light of the
experience of developing countries, is of unquestionable benefit.

Management can also help to foster tendencies which can
contribute to national integration. Metropolitan housing needs
to be planned to accommodate the housing needs of people
coming from different parts and communities of India. What
is not possible in this matter by design/planning can be achieved
by housing management. A phenomenon similar to ethnicity
in the urban area of the USA and the upsurge of the ethnic
community, is incipient in Indian cities. The idea that, in the
USA, the city is a 'melting pot' for divergent immigrant groups
has now been rejected since experience does not at all support
it. Community planning in our country has to anticipate the
national needs of a certain mix of income groups and people
of diverse linguistic and regional loyalties, at various spatial
levels in the development of habitats for the urban poor.

In the next two decades, we have also to consolidate what
we have done, in the sense that misuse of public open spaces,
vandalism of public property and similar issues need to influence
thinking on design for better living. Could not planning reduce
these drawbacks? For instance, open spaces meant for parks

may never be maintained for that purpose: they may remain as bald patches amidst houses, or look like mini-deserts in the summer. Looked at from another perspective, these open spaces are really overutilised for active recreation and, therefore, the absence of grass can be taken as evidence of maximum use by the inhabitants. Rather than finding fault with the residents, it might be better to plant a few trees in such places on the border so that the ground can be used and the benefits of trees in such settings can be gained.

This means that preferred future solutions do not necessarily imply additional expensive inputs but, alteration in aims, consolidation of what has been built with a view to maximising use, innovation to minimise drawbacks repeatedly noted and to maximise gratifications from the housing environment. Thus, mending our mistakes is an important dimension in future planning and futuristic thinking.

It appears that we need more sensitively collected micro-level information to interpret meaningfully the voluminous macro-data which is available today. For example, in surveys, travel to work is usually recorded only with reference to the main male or female earning member. A poor man is prepared to cycle miles to his place of work provided his wife and daughter have work within a short walking distance from their hut. Further, often travel to the work place is not the same as the time taken to return home because, by evening, certain routes are impassable under heavy traffic and hence a poor man has to cycle an extra mile. This is often so among those who own a car or a scooter as well. Therefore, the time taken for travel to work from any one housing area is a better indicator of the time practically spent on the road away from home.[21] Assessing employment opportunities is another case in point. Women in the informal sector prefer to take up such work for which they can move about in a group. As domestic

---

[21]The reasons for longer time for the return journey are several: lack of shopping facilities at one's local level, poor quality of consumables available nearer home or higher prices make the worker to visit various points outside the shortest route to his home. Also 'travel to work' gives the impression of placing more interest in the gains of the employer, the establishment, rather than in the worker in relation to his family life.

workers, they usually come in groups of two or more, often as a mother daughter/daughter-in-law unit, to do domestic work in higher income households. Freedom to move about as an individual, unaccompanied, is looked down upon by others of her social level and given an unfavourable sexual interpretation. This means that the opportunity structure of employment may not always match some aspects of the social structure and norms of discipline. This is a dimension about which we have little information.[22]

Thus, it is time we realised that depth studies with social sensitivity can contribute a good deal to plan slum relocation in a more meaningful way so as to win popular acceptance from the people.

[22]For an understanding of how this dimension operates at the rural level in farm labour, see K. Raman Unni, 'Sources of Farm Labour in Kerala: Some Social Perspectives', in B.N. Nair (ed.), *Culture and Society*, Thompson Press, Delhi, 1975. One easily gets the impression that the urban labour market for unskilled workers in particular, especially in the informal sector, offers limited socially acceptable alternatives for women and, to a lesser extent, to the first-generation migrant males.

Select Bibliography

Alam, S. Manzoor and Pokshishevsky, V.V. (eds.), *Urbanisation in Developing Countries*, Osmania University, Hyderabad, 1976.

Ambannavar, Jaipal P., *Second India Studies: Population*, Macmillan, New Delhi, 1975.

Bairoc, Paul, *Urban Unemployment in Developing Countries*, International Labour Office, Geneva, 1973.

Banerjee, Nirmala, 'What Course for Urbanisation in India?', *Economic and Political Weekly*, 4, July 1969, pp. 1173-84.

Bogue, Donald and Zachariah, K.C., 'Urbanisation and Migration in India', in Roy Turner (ed.), *India's Urban Future*, pp. 27-56.

Bose, Ashish, 'Urban Development with Social Justice', *Economic and Political Weekly*, 5, July 1970, pp. 1247-50.

———*Studies in India's Urbanisation 1901-1971*, Tata-McGraw Hill, Bombay, 1973.

Bose, N.K., *Calcutta: A Social Survey*, Lalvani, Bombay, 1968.

Breese, Gerald, *Urbanisation in Newly Developing Countries*, Prentice-Hall of India, New Delhi, 1967.

Breman, Jan, "A Dualistic Labour System? A Critique of the 'Informal Sector' Concept", *Economic and Political Weekly*,

27 November 1976, pp. 1870-6; 5 December 1976, pp. 1905-8; 11 December 1976, pp. 1939-44.

Bulsara, J.F., *Problems of Rapid Urbanisation in India*, Popular Prakashan, Bombay, 1964.

Caplan, Lionel, 'Social Mobility in Metropolitan Centres: Christians in Madras City', *Contributions to Indian Sociology*, 11, n. 1, January-June 1977, pp. 193-218.

Chandra, Subhash, 'Urban Community Development: Experiments in Participation', *Social Action*, 23, April-June 1973, pp. 181-94.

———*Social Participation in Urban Neighbourhoods*, National, New Delhi, 1977.

Chatterjee, Atreyi, 'Some Implications of the Future Trend of Urbanisation', in Ashish Bose *et al* , (eds.), *Population in India's Development 1947-2000*, pp. 269-80.

Chaudhuri, Kalyan, 'The Human Fall-out', *Economic and Political Weekly*, 11, 21 February 1976, pp. 313-14.

Clinard, Marshall B. and Chatterjee, B., 'Urban Community Development in India: The Delhi Pilot Project', in Roy Turner (ed.), *India's Urban Future*, pp. 71-93.

Correa, Charles, 'No Cost Housing: Space as a Resource', *Indian Journal of Social Work*, 36, October 1975-January 1976, pp. 371-75.

Dandekar, V.M. and Rath, N., *Poverty in India*, Indian School of Political Economy, Bombay, 1971.

Desai, A.R. and Pillai, S. Devadas, *Slums and Urbanisation*, Popular Prakashan, Bombay, 1970.

———*A Profile of an Indian Slum*, University of Bombay, Bombay, 1972.

Doshi, Harish, *Traditional Neighbourhood in a Modern City*, Abhinav, New Delhi, 1974.

D'Souza, Victor S., *Social Structure of a Planned City*, Orient Longman, New Delhi, 1968.

———'Problems of Housing in Chandigarh', *Urban and Rural Planning Thought*, 16, October 1973, pp. 254-66.

———'Urban Development in India: Demographic, Functional and Socio-Cultural Perspectives', *Indian Journal of Social Work*, 36, October 1975-January 1976, pp. 285-91.

———'Does Urbanism Desegregate Scheduled Castes? Evidence

from a District in Punjab', *Contributions to Indian Sociology*, 11, n. 1, January-June 1977, pp. 219-39.

Dwyer, D.J., *The City in the Third World*, Macmillan, London, 1974.

Ellefsen, Richard A., 'City-Hinterland Relationships in India with Special Reference to the Hinterlands of Bombay, Delhi, Madras, Hyderabad and Baroda', in Roy Turner (ed.), *India's Urban Future*, pp. 94-116.

Fox, Richard G., *Realm and Region in Traditional India*, Vikas, New Delhi, 1977.

———*Urban India: Society, Space and Image*, Duke University Monograph Series, Durham, N.C., 1976.

Gillian, Kenneth, *Ahmedabad: A Study in Indian Urban History*, University of California Press, Berkeley and Los Angeles, 1968.

Gore, M.S., *Immigrants and Neighbourhood: Two Aspects of Life in a Metropolitan City*, Tata Institute of Social Sciences, Bombay, 1970.

———'Urban Planning and Some Questions of Social Policy', *Economic and Political Weekly*, 6, Special Number, June 1971, pp. 1619-25.

———'Social Development and a Strategy for Urbanisation: Absence of a Positive Approach to Urbanisation', *Economic and Political Weekly*, 12, 25 January 1975, pp. 110-19.

Gould, Harold A., 'Lucknow Rickshawawallas: The Social Organisation of an Occupational Category', in M.S.A. Rao (ed.), *Urban Sociology in India*, Orient Longman, New Delhi, 1974, pp. 289-308.

Government of India, Ministry of Works and Housing, *Jhuggi Jhonpri Settlements in Delhi*, Town and Country Planning Organisation, New Delhi, Vol. I, 1973 (mimeo).

———*Jhuggi Jhonpri Settlements in Delhi: A Sociological Study of Low Income Migrant Communities*, Town and Country Planning Organisation, New Delhi, Vol. II, 1975 (mimeo).

Hall, Peter, *The World Cities*, Weidenfeld and Nicolson, London, 1968.

Horan, P., 'Urban Demographic Patterns: A Survey of a Delhi Colony', *Social Action*, 22, October-December 1972, pp. 319-326.

Hoselitz, Bert F., "Indian Cities: The Surveys of Calcutta, Kanpur and Jamshedpur', *Economic Weekly*, 13, July 1961, pp. 1071-8.

Jagmohan, *Rebuilding Shahajahanabad: The Walled City of Delhi*, Vikas, New Delhi, 1975.

Joshi, Heather and Vijay, *Surplus Labour and the City: A Study of Bombay*, Oxford University Press, Bombay, 1976.

Kapadia, K.M. and Pillai, S. Devadas, *Industrialisation and Rural Society: A Study of Atul-Bulsar Region*, Popular Prakashan, Bombay, 1972.

Katzenstein, Mary F., 'Politics of Population Movements: The Case of Bombay', *Economic and Political Weekly*, 10, 20 December, 1975 pp. 1955-9.

Kulkarni, M.G., 'Slums in Aurangabad City: An Ecological Approach', in S. Devadas Pillai (ed.), *Aspects of Changing India*, Popular Prakashan, Bombay, 1976.

Kurien, C.T. and Joseph, James, 'Urbanisation and Economic Change', *Economic and Political Weekly*, 10, 22 February 1975, pp. 359-70.

Lubell, Harold, *Urban Development and Employment: The Prospects for Calcutta*, International Labour Office, Geneva, 1974.

Lynch, Owen M., 'Rural Cities in India: Continuities and Discontinuities', in Philip Mason (ed.), *India and Ceylon: Unity and Diversity*, Oxford University Press, London, 1967.

————'Political Mobilisation and Ethnicity among Adi-Dravidas in a Bombay Slum', *Economic and Political Weekly*, 9, n. 39, 28 September 1974, pp. 1657-68.

Mayur, Rashmi, 'The Coming Third World Crisis: Runaway Growth of Large Cities', *The Futurist*, 9, August 1975, pp. 168-175.

Mehta, B.C., 'Urbanisation in Rajasthan: A Study of Differential Rates of Urban Growth', *Social Action*, 26, January-March 1976, pp. 52-65.

Misra, R.P. (ed.), *Million Cities of India*, Vikas Publishing House, New Delhi, 1978.

————and B.S. Bhooshan, 'Rurbanisation', *Seminar*, 215, July 1977, pp. 22-8.

Mitra, Asok, 'Housing the Urban Poor: The Case of Calcutta', *Economic and Political Weekly*, 6, July 1971, pp. 1927-34.

Moorhouse, Geoffrey, *Calcutta*, Penguin Books, Middlesex, 1974.

Muttagi, P.K., (ed.), *Urban Development: A Perspective*, Tata Institute of Social Sciences, Bombay, 1976.

Nair, K.S. *Ethnicity and Urbanisation*, Ajanta Publications, Delhi, 1978.

Narain, Vatsala, 'Demographic Aspects of Urbanisation', *Indian Journal of Social Work*, 36, October 1975-January 1976, pp. 233-58.

National Council of Applied Economic Research, *Techno-Economic Survey of Delhi*, NCAER, New Delhi, 1973.

Patel, Shirish B., 'Future of Bombay: An Alternative Approach', in Ashish Bose *et al.*, (eds.), *Population in India's Development 1947-2000*, pp. 306-16.

Ram, Vinay Bharat, 'Prospects of Urban Employment in 2000 A.D.', *Indian Journal of Industrial Relations*, 13, n. 1 July 1977, pp. 15-26.

Ramachandra, P., *Housing Situation in Greater Bombay*, Somaiya Publications, Bombay, 1977.

Rao, M.S.A., 'Fringe Society and Folk-Urban Continuum', *Sociological Bulletin*, 111, September 1959, pp. 13-18.

———'The Migrant to the City', *Yojana*, 28, n. 20, 15 November 1974, pp. 7-13.

———*Urbanisation and Social Change*, Orient Longman, New Delhi, 1970.

———*Urban Sociology in India*, Orient Longman, New Delhi, 1974.

Rao, V.K.R.V. and Desai, P.B., *Greater Delhi: A Study in Urbanisation 1940-51*, Asia Publishing House, Bombay, 1965.

Rosenthal, Donald B., *The City in Indian Politics*, Thompson Press, New Delhi, 1976.

Saberwal, Satish, *Mobile Men: Limits to Social Change in Urban Punjab*, Vikas, New Delhi, 1976.

Sen, Jai, *The Unintended City: An Essay on the City of the Poor*, Cathedral Social and Relief Services, Calcutta, n.d.

Sen, S.N., *The City of Calcutta: A Socio-Economic Survey, 1954-55 to 1957-58*, Bookland Pvt. Ltd., Calcutta, 1961.

Sethuraman, S.V., 'The Urban Informal Sector: Concept,

Measurement and Policy', *International Labour Review*, 114, July-August 1976, pp. 69-81.

Singh, Andrea Menefee, *Neighbourhood and Social Networks in Urban India*, Marwah, New Delhi, 1976.

Sinha, G.P. and Ranade, S.N., *Women Construction Workers: Reports of Two Surveys*, Indian Council of Social Science Research, New Delhi, 1975.

Sivaramakrishnan, K.C., 'Calcutta 2001: Triumph by Survival', in Ashish Bose, *et al.*, (eds.), *Population in India's Development, 1947-2000*.

————'Metro Cities and New Towns', S.C., Dube (ed.), *India Since Independence*, Vikas, New Delhi, 1977.

Sovani, N.V., *Urbanisation and Urban India*, Asia Publishing House, Bombay, 1966.

Sundaram, K.V., *Urban and Regional Planning in India*, Vikas Publishing House, New Delhi, 1977.

Tangri, Shanti, 'Urban Growth, Housing and Economic Development', *Asian Survey*, 8, July 1968, pp. 519-38.

Todaro, M.P., 'Urban Job Expansion, Induced Migration and Rising Unemployment: A Formulation and Simplified Empirical Test for LDCs', *Journal of Development Economics*, 3, September 1976, pp. 271-76.

Trivedi, Harshad R., *Urbanisation and Macro Social Change*, Chugh Publications, Allahabad, 1973.

Turner, John F.C., *Housing by People: Towards Autonomy in Building Environments*, Pantheon Books, New York, 1977.

Turner, Roy (ed.), *India's Urban Future*, University of California Press, Berkeley and Los Angeles, 1962.

Unni, K.R., 'Social Concerns in Housing and Community Planning', *Urban and Rural Planning Thought*, 17, January 1974, pp. 46-55.

Weinstein, Jay, *Madras: An Analysis of Urban Ecological Structure in India*, Sage Publications, London, 1974.

Wiebe, Paul D., *Social Life in an Indian Slum*, Vikas, New Delhi, 1975.

Wilsher, Peter and Righter, Rosemary, *The Exploding Cities*, Indian Book Company, New Delhi, 1975.

Zacharia, K.C., *Migration in Greater Bombay*, Asia Publishing House, Bombay, 1968.

Index

242

127, 128, 130, 146; see Housing,
Slums
Poverty, culture of, 26, organising
the urban poor, 184-185; rural,
95, 96; structural explanations
of, 27, 28; urban, 2, 4, 14, 18,
26, 97, 218; see Slums

Ramachandran, P., 223
Ranade, S.N., 86
Ranchi, 187, 188, 203, 208, 211, 212;
credit needs of tribal entrepreneurs, 207, 210, 213; informal
urban sector of Ranchi, 194-
200; mobility of, 208; performance of, 205-207; skill needs
of, 207; training of, 209-210,
211; tribal entrepreneurs, 188,
193, 200, 201-203; types of,
203-205; see Employment,
Industry, Slums
Rao, D.V.R,, 220
Rao, M.S.A., 219
Rostow, W., 26
Rowe, William L., 71

Saberwal, Satish, 87
Sen, S.N , 114, 115, 116
Sethuraman, S.V., 3, 20, 189, 190,
192
Sharma, O.P., 89
Singer, Milton, 18
Singh, Andrea Menefee, 62, 80, 81
215, 219
Singh, Nagendra, P., 209
Sinha, G.P., 86
Sivaramakrishnan, K.C., 127
Slums, adjustment mechanisms, 42,
52, 57; associations, 21, 22, 37,
47-48, 49, 52, 65, 66, 89; caste,
21, 23, 24, 31, 33, 44, 47, 50,
51, 52, 53, 54, 58, 62, 65, 66,
69, 71, 89, 90; changing values,
55-57, 59-60, clearance of, 25,
26, 52, 139, 149, 150, 153, 154,
156, 177; contribution to urban
economy, 20, 26, 45; cost of
slum improvement, 47-48, 52,

59, 137, 138, 140, 141, 142,
143; definition of, 133, 216;
"Devendrapur", 63, 64; education, 25, 27, 31, 32, 33, 43, 45,
53, 54, 147, 163, 174; employment patterns, 18, 19, 20, 26,
31, 32, 39-41, 53, 54, 65, 66,
160; family, 41, 42, 57-58, 66,
67, 71, 86, 87; "Hassanpur",
63, 65, 66, 67; health, 43, 67,
85-86, 90, 136, 138, 142, 163,
174; housing, 23, 35-37, 63, 68,
91, 93, 131, 149; income, 19,
30, 32, 41, 42, 53, 54, 147, 148,
157, 160, 162; indebtedness, 19,
42; "Kaharpur", 63, 65; land
settlement, 5, 13, 21, 29, 33-34;
length of residence, 43; life-
styles, 58-59; living conditions
in, 18, 65, 66, 68, 82, 134,
140, 148, 155, 165; maintenance
of services, 139, 143; nutrition,
42, 43, 82-84; occupational
choice, 55, 118; occupational
mobility, 43-46; occupational
specialisation, 45, 116, 118;
"Pallanpur", 63-64; participative process, 37-39, 141-142,
152, 153, 154, 157-158, 159, 160,
161, 173, 175, 178, 179, 183;
policy of government to 5, 36,
148-149; political relations, 20,
21, 22, 38, 53, 54, 64; population of, 25, 63, 64, 65, 66, 145,
147, 148, 150, 172, 176;
provision of services, 27, 36,
64, 66, 67, 133, 138, 151, 153,
155, 158, 173, 177, 178;
religion, 24, 33, 52, 53, 147,
159; relocation of, 5, 63, 151,
152, 154, 160, 215, 216, 217,
222, 231; security of land
tenure, 33, 34, 35, 36, 37, 52,
140-141, 148, 150, 151, 158,
177, 183, 218; sex ratio, 33;
size of, 34; slum improvement,
47-48, 52, 59, 137, 138, 140,
141, 142, 143; social mobilisa-